Political Terrorism and Energy

Political Terrorism and Energy

The Threat and Response

Edited by
Yonah Alexander and
Charles K. Ebinger

Published in cooperation with
the Center for Strategic and International Studies,
Georgetown University.

PRAEGER SPECIAL STUDIES • PRAEGER SCIENTIFIC

Library of Congress Cataloging in Publication Data
    Main entry under title?

Political terrorism and energy.

    "Published in cooperation with the Center for
Strategic and International Studies, Georgetown
University."
    Includes bibliographical references.
    Contents: Definitional aspects / John M.
Collins — The mindsets of high-technology terror-
ists / David Ronfeldt and William Sater — Inter-
national network of terrorism / Yonah Alexander —
Supply security of coal and uranium / James Cobbe
— (etc.)
    1. Terrorism—Addresses, essays, lectures.
2.   Energy industry—Defense measures—Addresses,
essays, lectures. 3.   Terrorism—Prevention—
Government policy—Addresses, essays, lectures.
I. Alexander, Yonah.   II. Ebinger, Charles K.
III. Georgetown University. Center for Strategic
and International Studies.
HV6431.P623   303.6'2   81-15695
ISBN 0-03-059344-1   AACR2

**Published and Distributed by the
Praeger Publishers Division
(ISBN Prefix 0-275)
of Greenwood Press, Inc.,
Westport, Connecticut**

Published in 1982 by Praeger Publishers
CBS Educational and Professional Publishing
a Division of CBS Inc.
521 Fifth Avenue, New York, New York 10175 U.S.A.

© 1982 by Praeger Publishers

23456789   124   987654321

Printed in the United States of America

Table of Contents

Introduction:
Energy and Terrorism

Charles K. Ebinger

The 1980s promise to be replete with political violence, the frequency and magnitude of which is already increasing substantially.

Though relatively few episodes of intense civil strife and even fewer incidents of terrorism have plagued U.S. history, it is time that the United States government recognize not only the potential for such violence but also that certain components of the nation's basic industrial infrastructures are extremely vulnerable to sabotage.

Nowhere is this more true than in the case of the energy industry. As the contributors to this book demonstrate, oil, gas, hydroelectric, coal, and nuclear power operations, comprising production, distribution, upgrading, and storage facilities, are prime targets for any disaffected group possessing knowledge of a particular system and the motivation and will to act. Skill and weaponry are to an extent less important elements in the equation once the saboteurs understand the system's pressure and access points. To a degree unappreciated by most of the U.S. public, a relatively untrained band of terrorists using sophisticated means could, with appropriate structural knowledge of a given system, cripple it in a manner that would significantly affect the domestic economy.

To date, the U.S. government has been singularly reticent to release sensitive information regarding past and current terrorist activities. As a result of the lack of forceful government policies, many energy executives have paid far too little attention to the degree of vulnerability of their energy operations. While there is clearly a danger that confidential information could be made public during oversight hearings analyzing the possibilities for terrorist attacks, energy officials in government and in industry are beginning to realize that the lack of analysis and the postponement of effective contingency planning may be potentially more dangerous than calling attention to the nature and magnitude of the problem.

As John Collins notes in Chapter 1, one of the central problems plaguing effective countermeasures to terrorism is determining the nature, motivation, and degree of threat posed by each terrorist incident. Collins examines the types of threats that an advanced industrial society can expect to encounter and admonishes that counterterrorist strategies will be effective only to the degree that they are appropriate to each individual terrorist threat.

The complexity of terrorist motivations, combined with David Ronfeldt and William Sater's examination of the fascination of nineteenth-century anarchists with dynamite and nitroglycerine, offers a chilling proscription of the magnitude of threats that may be posed to advanced industrial societies in the twentieth century. As they note in Chapter 2, the degree of vulnerability of advanced industrial societies to biological and chemical warfare poses such monumental challenges to democratic institutions and values that it is almost impossible to foresee how we would respond to such unprecedented terrorist challenges. While none of the authors directly raise the issue, one need only contemplate the impact that the release of a relatively small amount of dioxin on the major oilfields of the Persian Gulf could have on global stability. The "crash of '29" could easily become the crash of 1983 or 1986.

However, it is not the use of chemical or bacteriological compounds that seems to worry most of the contributors to this book but rather the degree of vulnerability of energy systems and industrial civilization to attacks using highly sophisticated conventional technology and/or the threatened use of the ultimate weapon: nuclear terrorism.

In Chapter 6, Lisa Maechling not only examines the degree of the threat posed to the conventional oil and gas logistics system but also lists attacks that have already occurred against oil and gas operations around the globe. The bombing of the Commonwealth Oil Refinery in Puerto Rico, the destruction of a giant coal liquefaction plant in South Africa, the disappearance and grounding of supertankers, attacks by Basque terrorists against Spanish nuclear power installations, the sabotage of key pipelines in the Middle East, and the dramatic kidnapping of the OPEC oil ministers are some of the most recent incidents delineated.

Perhaps Maechling's most interesting insights, as well as those of Richard Kessler in Chapter 5, are related to a detailed discussion of those components of the oil logistics systems that are most vulnerable to terrorist attack. Of special note are their observations regarding the extreme vulnerability of the oil loading terminals in the Middle East, especially in Kuwait. Maechling's detailed delineation of the oil loading terminals in the Persian Gulf and the Mediterranean breaks new ground in the field. She observes that these facilities represent the Achilles' heel of the international oil logistical system and recommends that top priority be given to the placement of anti-aircraft weaponry in or around these facilities.

While several of the authors note the threat that would be posed to the global oil logistics system by a closure of the Straits of Hormuz, the destruction of the major oil-pumping stations of Saudi Arabia or of the gas-oil separators could have a longer and more momentous impact on the availability of world oil supplies. It is not realized that many of these pieces of equipment are one of a kind items and that to replace them could take a minimum of from 18 to 24 months. Likewise, Collins is quoted by Maechling as being extremely dubious about how a rapid deployment force would be able to protect the oil facilities of the Gulf if it had to contend with cratered airfield runways, ruined port facilities, and the lack of highly skilled civilian energy workers knowledgeable about the oil and gas operations.

When Collins' concerns are viewed in conjunction with M. C. Peck's Chapter 8 analysis of the myriad of security threats posed to each of the oil producing nations and with Yonah Alexander's Chapter 6 observation that, on a percentage basis, attacks against business targets have been on the rise since 1976, one is left bewildered over how the industrialized world can begin to meet these threats.

There is almost no segment of the energy industry that has not been the victim of terrorist attacks. Between 1970 and mid-1980, the Argonne National Laboratory calculates that 240 attacks occurred against energy-related activities in the United States and 204 outside the United States. Since 1970, there have been more than 100 attacks against electrical utilities. Considerable damage has been inflicted upon various targets, including an electric power substation in Sparta, Wisconsin, powerline poles of Pacific Gas and Electric in San Francisco, the State Electric Board in France, the Valencia Electric Company in Spain, the Cabora-Bassa Hydroelectric Complex in Mozambique, a powerline tower in Medellin, Columbia, and a power plant in Rome. One particularly dramatic incident was the action of the Moro Liberation Front in the Philippines on September 10, 1979, which blacked out almost half of Mindanao as a result of attacks on 10 government power facilities.

As Kessler notes, the U.S. pipeline system, which transports almost three-quarters of the crude oil delivered to refineries and one-third of the refined products sold to consumers, is an extremely soft target. For example, in 1978, the Trans-Alaska pipeline was bombed, spilling about 15,000 barrels of oil. The pipeline was closed for 21 hours (12 for repair, nine for Federal approval to restart). While the damage was easily repaired, the cost was high. If such a bombing were to occur in concert with an oil shortfall in the Middle East, the impact on consumer behavior in the spot market could send the price of oil soaring. Other oil pipelines have been sabotaged in Colombia, Venezuela, Scotland, Japan, Turkey, Lebanon, and Iran.

Still other terrorist activities against the oil industry have targetted the corporate offices of leading oil companies or their oil drilling equipment, refineries, oil depots, or storage tanks. As James Cobbe notes in Chapter 4, similar attacks and disruptions have occurred in the coal and nuclear industries.

Despite the serious nature of these attacks, it is to the prospect of nuclear terrorism that this book gives most attention. Although the public generally is unaware, the authors state that there have already been several hundred nuclear-related incidents, which have serious implications for the future. Some unclassified examples in the United States include the theft in 1973 of "extremely harmful" capsules of iodine-131 from a hospital in Arcadia, California; the "loss" in 1969 of a container of highly enriched uranium hexafluoride, which was shipped from Ohio to Missouri; the 1972 threatened crash of a hijacked airliner into the Oil Ridge National Laboratory in Tennessee; the arson at the Indian Point no. 2 plant near Buchanan, New York, in 1974; the intrusion attempt in 1977 of the Vermont Yankee Nuclear Power Corporation; the 1976 bomb threat at the B&W Naval Nuclear Fuel facility at Lynchburg, Virginia; the bomb detonation next to the visitors' center at the Trojan Nuclear Power Plant in Oregon in 1977; the October 1979 sabotage "in the name of the antinuclear movement" of $30 million of atomic fuel supplies at the Surrey plant in Virginia; and the 1979 Puerto Rican terrorist threat to blow up the Indian Point nuclear power station near Peekskill, New York.

Moreover, thousands of pounds of low-enriched uranium and plutonium have disappeared during the past several years. According to a recent report, more than 50 tons of fissionable material is unaccounted for by some 34 facilities operated by the Energy Research and Development Administration. Furthermore, since 1970, there have been more than a dozen terrorist attacks against nuclear facilities in Argentina, Spain, France, Germany, and so on. Finally, in 1981, Israeli Air Force jets launched what was said to be a pre-emptive strike against Iraqi nuclear facilities, which Israeli intelligence officials said were engaged in the clandestine manufacture of nuclear weapons.

While the record to date provides no evidence that mass casualties or widespread disruptions of the energy industry have resulted from a single terrorist attack, there are no guarantees that self-imposed constraints of terrorist groups will persist indefinitely and that future incidents will not be more costly in terms of personnel, facilities, and/or operations. Although there is no evidence that the Three Mile Island incident occurred as a result of sabotage, the fear of nuclear disasters generated among U.S. citizens in its wake could be played upon by terrorist groups. Even the mere threat of a terrorist incident involving the release of quantities of radioactive materials could, in certain circumstances, invoke mass panic.

N. Livingstone (Chapter 7) and J. F. Pilat (Chapter 9) chronicle in great detail the critical public policy questions that could be precipitated by the outbreak of nuclear terrorism. While both may be criticized somewhat for not paying more attention to the difficulties nuclear terrorists would face in obtaining and utilizing highly radioactive materials, their observations concerning the impact that nuclear terrorism might have on civil liberties in a democratic society are indeed sobering.

Livingstone's statement that 8,000 pounds of fissionable material in the United States has been unaccounted for since World War II, combined with his revelations concerning Israeli covert actions to acquire a nuclear weapons capability, raises the critical question of how many other nations or subnational actors may have been involved in similar activities. Livingstone likewise breaks new ground in his brief analysis regarding the inadequate safety and security mechanisms guarding nuclear weapons.

Finally, Livingstone's remarks concerning the possibility of terrorists stealing nuclear radioactive materials and threatening to poison a city if their demands were not met raise profound questions concerning the implementation of adequate contingency measures to meet such a threat. Chapter 9 serves as a useful compilation of antinuclear activities in the industrialized Western nations and raises the question of how effective measures could be implemented to thwart incidents of nuclear terrorism if perpetrated by surrogate actors rather than directly by the antinuclear actors themselves.

In this regard, Alexander, in Chapter 3 on the international network of terrorism, raises serious issues for U.S. contingency planning. If, as Alexander and Pilat demonstrate, terrorist links are increasingly transnational, effective measures to deal with nuclear terrorism must also be transnational in scope. In such a situation, the known theft or diversion of fissionable materials anywhere must be cause for concern by the entire global community.

Brooks McClure, in Chapter 10 on corporate vulnerability to terrorism and how to assess it, provides a useful framework of analysis for any corporation wishing to reduce its odds of terrorist attack. While most of his analysis focuses on measures to improve a corporation's image in the local community, both he and Livingstone recommend ways to upgrade facilities to at least reduce terrorist damage to corporate facilities.

In Chapter 11, Ernest Evans draws some sobering conclusions about the current state of U.S. policy on terrorism and makes some detailed recommendations for its improvement. Specifically, Evans addresses the necessity for the United States to address how it will handle civil liberties versus national security when confronted by a real case of nuclear terrorism, the urgent necessity for changes in security procedures affecting the guarding of U.S. nuclear weapons technology, the inadequacies of international legal institutions and international law to deal with problems of global terrorism, and the lack of effective U.S. government crisis management policies to deal with terrorist incidents. Evans' criticism of the U.S. government institutional mechanism and of qualified personnel to deal with a crisis should form a central agenda item of any discussion concerning the enactment of a comprehensive U.S. government policy on terrorism.

While the conclusions of all the authors are sobering, each, to a greater or lesser degree, believes that the vulnerability of energy-related industries can be lessened by conscious and immediate action.

More remote siting for nuclear and liquid natural gas plants, as well as more deliberate security strategies for communications networks, truck routes, and railroad yards are a few examples of preventive measures in areas warranting expanded protection. However, a cost/ benefit analysis of the security provided relative to the perceived threat should form a central cornerstone of any security policy.

In a complex industrial environment, no security measure, however sophisticated, can ensure the absolute security of any energy logistics system. However, there is much that can be done, and this book is a thoughtful attempt to inform the U.S. public of the critical issues raised by the expanding nature of global terrorism.

1
Definitional Aspects

John M. Collins

Transnational political terrorism attracts the most attention when experts strive to define the term "terrorism." This chapter separates transnational political terrorism from all other categories of terrorism.

ESSENTIAL ELEMENTS

All terrorism features violence or threats of violence, but not all violence constitutes terrorism, even though terrorist tools and tactics may be employed. Terrorist incidents intentionally seek to frighten prospective victims not present at the scene. Terrorist acts that take place in private have public implications, and repetitive acts predominate.

Terrorism, for example, was not a factor when John W. Hinckley, Jr., fired six fast shots at President Ronald Reagan to impress actress Jody Foster in March of 1981. It would have been a factor, however, had the assassination attempt been part of a "hit list" that put many Republican leaders in peril. No shock waves ensued when parties unknown "put the snatch" on Teamster boss Jimmy Hoffa since that crime seemed personal, but rival gangs "got the word" soon after Al Capone's goons took a few seconds to gun down seven members of "Bugs" Moran's mob in the Saint Valentine's Day Massacre of 1929. The serial disappearance and death of 32 boys later found buried under John Wayne Gacy's cottage failed to scare Chicago citizens because those killings were secret until the culprit was in custody. Atlanta, however, began to tremble when the body count of young blacks passed 15, 20, 25, and kept climbing in banner headlines and news broadcasts.

TYPICAL TRAITS

Five types of terrorism compete for attention: pathological, hedonistic, larcenous, official, and radical. All can occur in hot-war, cold-war, or peacetime situations. Within all categories individuals or small terrorist groups try to exercise inordinate power, violating U.S. moral standards and internationally accepted laws in the process. Distinctions among the types, however, are not always sharp. Overlaps and crossovers from one type to another often take place. Madmen and mercenaries, for example, may infiltrate revolutionary terrorist ranks. Table 1.1 displays customary similarities and differences among the five categories.

Pathological Terrorism

Pathological terrorism is a tragic nuisance whose security implications are normally limited to one community. Solo psychotics and social dropouts, sometimes deranged by drink or drugs, explode in bursts of passion. Son of Sam and Jack the Ripper, for example, petrified females (especially prostitutes) in the Bronx and London. Many maniacs, whose killings cause widespread cold sweats, call or write police stations to take credit and taunt, "Catch me if you can."

Hedonistic Terrorism

Sadistic personalities, typified by bullies tattooed with the slogan "Born to Raise Hell," repeatedly employ terrorist tools and techniques for the fun of it. They occasionally operate independently but, as a general rule, belong to small, loosely structured groups that erupt on the spur of the moment. Incorrigible motorcycle gangs and ruffians who terrorize subway riders are representative.

TABLE 1.1
Types of Terrorism — Similarities and Differences

	Pathological	Hedonistic	Larcenous	Official	Radical* Reactionary	Radical* Revolutionary
War/Peace Context						
Hot War	X	X	X	X	X	X
Cold War	X	X	X	X	X	X
Peace	X	X	X	X	X	X
Geographical Location						
Intranational	X	X	X	X	X	X
Extranational			X	X	X	X
International			X	X	X	X
Primary Participants						
Category						
Psychotics	X					
Insensibles	X					
Sadists		X				
Common Criminals			X			
Police/Military				X		
Security Forces				X		
Reactionaries					X	
Revolutionaries						X

(continued)

Table 1.1, continued

					Radical*	
	Pathological	Hedonistic	Larcenous	Official	Reactionary	Revolutionary
Quantity						
Individuals	X	O	X			
Groups		X	X	X	X	X
Formal Organization						
Complex		X	X	X	O	X
Simple			X		X	O
Nonexistent	X	O	X			
Clandestine						
Yes		X	X		X	X
No				X		
Primary Goals						
Scope						
Strategic			X	X	X	X
Tactical			X	X	X	X
Neither	X	X				
Life Span						
Short Range	X	X	X	O	O	O
Long Range			O	X	X	X

4

Focus						
Rational	X	X	X	X	X	X
Irrational/None	X	X	X	X	X	X
Offensive						
Defensive			X		X	
Desired Gain						
Political, Economic, and/or Social Change						
Regression				X	X	
"Progression"						⊠
Status Quo		X	X	X	X	
Financial					O	O
Military		O	O	O	O	O
Discipline	X	X	O	X	X	
Pleasure						
Inane/None	X					
Operations						
Thoughtfully Planned						
Yes	X	X	X	X	X	X
Sometimes						
Fear as Fulcrum						
Deliberate Use	X	X	X	X	X	
By-product	X	X	X		X	⊠
Violent Threats/Acts	X			X		
Official Status						
Authorized						
Unauthorized	X	X	X	X	X	X

(continued)

Table 1.1, continued

	Pathological	Hedonistic	Larcenous	Official	Reactionary (Radical*)	Revolutionary (Radical*)
Relationships						
Isolated	X	X	X			
Connected			O	X	X	X
Primary Impact						
Physical	X	X	X	X	X	
Psychological			X	X	X	⊠
Targets Related to Goals						
Directly	X	X	X	O	O	O
Indirectly				X	X	⊠
Seek Publicity						
Yes						⊠
Occasionally	X	X	X	X	X	
No						
Military Applications						
Reinforce Armed Forces				X	X	X
Replace Armed Forces				X	X	⊠
Violate Laws						
International Law	X	X	X	X	X	X

Local Laws						
Always	X	X	X	X	X	X
Usually				X	X	
Popular Support						
Commonly Claimed	X	X	X			⊗
Uncommon				X	X	
Never	X	X	X			
Foreign Support						
Occurrence						
Common						
Uncommon			X	X	X	X
Never	X	X	X			
Significance						
Sometimes Critical			X	X	X	⊗
Rarely Critical						
Typical Contacts						
Public				O	O	O
Private			X	X	X	X
Type of Assistance						
Moral Support				X	X	⊗
Theory				X	X	⊗
Advice				X	X	X
Training				X	X	⊗
Intelligence			X	X	X	⊗
Arms/Equipment			X	X	X	⊗
Money						X

(continued)

7

Table 1.1, continued

| | Pathological | Hedonistic | Larcenous | Official | Reactionary | Revolutionary |
					Radical*	
Security Implications						
Local	X	X	X	X	X	X
National			O	X	X	⊠
International			O	O	O	⊠

Note: X = Primary Characteristics; O = Secondary or Occasional Characteristics; ⊠ = Critical Concerns for Counterterrorists. This table features dominant characteristics, but there are exceptions to every rule. Overlaps and crossovers occur. Official terrorism, for example, is frequently reactionary, some sadists fit in all categories, revolutionaries may revert to common crime, and so on.

*So-called Political Terrorism.

Source: Compiled by author.

Larcenous Terrorism

Common criminals, functioning alone, with a few associates, or in syndicates, may terrorize victims and innocent bystanders during carefully planned, recurrent ventures. Fear in most instances is a by-product rather than a primary implement. Little or no damage is done even indirectly to disinterested parties, whether offenses feature blackmail, abduction, robbery, breaking and entering, or some other means of stealing money.

Prominent exceptions to that rule include loan sharks and "enforcers" for "protection" rackets. They find that a few badly beaten backsliders, whose homes or places of business may be bombed, encourage other customers to keep payments coming on time. Strict organizations also use terror deliberately to help maintain discipline among gang members.

Three characteristics sharply separate larcenous terrorism from radical terrorism. Financial gain is a personal end, not an impersonal means. Public support for conventional crime is close to nonexistent, except by a few countercultures and mislead minorities. Law enforcement problems and solutions consequently are straightforward, even when operations circle the globe.[1]

Official Terrorism

There is nothing insane or incidental about state-sponsored terrorism. It is a cold, calculating instrument. Three variations are visible, plus assorted subdivisions.

Repressive Purposes

Governments that truly respect human rights may succumb to temptation under pressure by employing terrorist tactics to counter terrorism.

Repressive terrorism, however, is most common among totalitarian and authoritarian regimes. Police, armed forces, and special security services are the main machines. The Soviet Committee for State Security (KGB) and Ministry of Internal Affairs (MVD), for example, apply terror or threats of terror to enforce conformity and quash all kinds of domestic dissent.[2] Counterparts include such unsavory societies as the Shah of Iran's SAVAK and the Tontons Macoutes, who propped up Papa Doc Duvalier's dictatorship in Haiti.

Terrorism authorized, encouraged, or controlled by governments may also be used to try to crush resistance in occupied territories. Repression by the Gestapo and Waffen SS was rampant after Nazi troops overran Europe. East Asia in the 1930s and 1940s feared Japanese force far more after countries had fallen than before.

Operations against foreigners and home folks, including those abroad, are tactically offensive, but their purpose is strategic defense in support of the status quo. An all-pervasive security octopus puts the fear of God in people.[3] Its tentacles permeate to block level, where informers function freely. Ends allegedly justify means. Legal systems are amended, interpreted leniently, or ignored to allow abridgement of liberties, as local and national leaders require. "House calls" around the clock, search and seizure on the slightest suspicion, whimsical assassinations, abductions, torture, and summary executions are standard practice. Foreign sympathizers may furnish surreptitious support in the form of training, money, and material. Open assistance is rare.

Supplements to Military Conflict

Terroristic activities above and beyond the fear fostered by armed conflict may supplement traditional military concepts and operations.

"A balance of terror" that purposely puts Soviet civilians in peril has been the basic option of U.S. nuclear deterrent strategy for nearly two decades.[4] Terrorist attacks actually took place during World War II, when belligerents blasted noncombatants in cold blood, trying to break their opponents' national will. Thousands died when mushroom clouds blossomed over Hiroshima and Nagasaki. "Buzz bombs" and V-1 rockets fell on Britain with abandon. Firestorms reduced Dresden to rubble, and so on.

Official terrorism sometimes plays important parts in erasing subversive infrastructures cell by cell, while military troops go after guerrillas and insurgent main force units. Operation Phoenix, which helped wreck the revolutionary infrastructure in South Vietnam, frequently looked like a latter day Inquisition. The same could be said of techniques recently used to root out radical undergrounds in many Latin American countries.

Finally, terrorist tactics may demoralize soldiers who barely blink when explosives blow friends to bits. Goums serving the

French during World War I, for example, used to filter into German trenches at night, find sleeping soldiers, and slit the throats of a few, leaving survivors to wonder how long their luck would last.

Substitutes for Military Conflict

Terrorism is cheap to activate and costly to counter. Unfeeling government leaders may carry the fight to foes without fear of reprisal if surrogates conceal true responsibility.[5] Risks of escalation may be reduced, and, consequently, ninth-rate nations could put great pressure on a superpower, such as the United States, by using terrorist tactics.

Radical Terrorism

Radical terrorism does not break cleanly into left and right wings. Some on each side press for positive change, while others fight for the status quo. Categories of "reactionaries" and "revolutionaries" are more realistic.

Reactionaries

Reactionaries are revolutionaries turned inside out. Target types, dynamics, and terrorist incidents sometimes seem identical. Both press for political, economic, and/or social change. Reactionaries, however, want to restore former situations, while revolutionaries want "progressive" replacements.

Reactionaries, called counterrevolutionaries in some circumstances, embrace cabals such as the Ku Klux Klan and Neo Nazis. They also include vigilantes, who tend to take laws into their own hands if official security forces for any reason fail to function effectively. "What they have brought most times to the scene is another political crap game, to become entangled with the one already in progress." Rival factions, if uncontained, can move a country "toward civil war; and the spreading chaos invites a coup d'etat . . . or a takeover by some force from the outside."[6]

Most reactionary factions currently are small. They attract little popular support for aims that try to turn back the clock. Some have national implications, but few ever affect the international scene.[7]

Revolutionaries

Revolution is a form of total war from the standpoint of there being perpetrators without scruples about benevolence, righteousness, or morality.

Revolutionaries generally hope to replace existing styles of government and associated structures with systems they select, although anarchists, who offer no clear alternative, also count in this class. Such leftists as Puerto Rico's Armed Forces of National Liberation (FALN) and fascists are both represented. Hitler, for example, was a full-fledged revolutionary before he came to power, using bully boys from Munich beer halls to introduce an innovative political, economic, and social order.

Small groups with little power seek to manipulate the masses. Impersonal, often impartial, terrorism is a permanent mainstay for some. It assumes a secondary role for others when they gain enough strength to compete militarily with incumbent regimes.

Many factors favor success. Terrorists, for example, can trigger violent threats or acts at sites and times of their choosing. Defending forces must cover all bets, because terrorists feel no need to announce whether they will allow noncombatants or which inanimate targets, if any, will remain off limits. All incidents are interrelated. The intent is to start a chain reaction that will not stop until revolutionary ends are attained.

The whole process epitomizes the indirect approach. Publicity is indispensible. Without it, revolutionary terrorists could not expeditiously expand their spheres of influence. With it, psychological repercussions spread far beyond the point of physical impact. Targets, frequently more symbolic than substantive, are selected mainly as a medium to transmit messages that shape public attitudes and behavior. Blowing up a busload of school children makes sense in that context. It spotlights impotent security forces that, by implication, are powerless to protect any people.

Outside support is not essential, since nothing sophisticated is needed to execute most terrorist plans. Foreign or domestic patronage, however, in the form of theory, training, intelligence, arms, equipment, and money, can telescope the time it takes terrorists to become proficient. It also affords great flexibility in terms of targets and tactics for those already in business.

Loosely linked groups often reinforce and feed on each other internationally. Japan's Red Army (Sekigun), for example, littered

Lod Airport with dead bodies in May 1972, reportedly to pay off the Popular Front for the Liberation of Palestine (PFLP), which helped train its members. The Baader-Meinhoff Gang, based in West Germany, collaborated with many foreign compatriots, including Al Fatah's Black September and Italy's Red Brigades.[8]

Security problems could expand exponentially if any benefactor bestowed chemical, biological, or nuclear weapons on possible proxies and/or provided any band the expertise to employ them.

SIGNIFICANCE OF DISSIMILARITIES

Many distinctions among the several types of terrorists are almost academic, but a few characteristics of revolutionary radicals are critical. Counterterror strategies that work well in other instances will not start to touch this group.

NOTES

1. Revolutionary radical theoreticians clearly separate themselves from "outlaws," "bandit bands," and other criminals whose motives revolve around personal, rather than political profit. See Carlos Marighella, *Urban Guerrilla Minimanual* (Vancouver: Pulp Press, 1974), p. 4; and Che Guevara, *On Guerrilla Warfare* (New York: Praeger, 1962), pp. 6-7.

2. The Soviets accuse everyone of state-sponsored terrorism except themselves and their associates. Representative comments are contained in L. K. Dadiani and S. A. Eferov, "Modern 'Leftist' Terrorism: Myth and Reality," *U.S.S.R. Report, Political and Sociological Affairs* (Arlington: Joint Publication Research Service no. 1103, February 20, 1981), pp. 3-4.

3. Louis de Saint-Just, a Jacobin who lopped off many heads before being led to the guillotine himself in 1794, left a slogan that some see as valid today: "Violence in itself is neither rational nor lawful, but there's no better way of making people respect reason and law." Saint-Just, *Oeuvres Choisies* (Paris: Avantpropos de Dionys Mascolo, 1968), p. 327.

4. Albert Wohlstetter first described "The Delicate Balance of Terror," in *Foreign Affairs* no. 37 (January 1959): 211-34. For the original rationale behind U.S. Assured Destruction Strategy, see Robert S. McNamara, *Statement Before the Senate Armed Services Committee on the Fiscal Year 1969-73 Defense Program and 1969 Defense Budget* (Washington, D.C.: Office of the Secretary of Defense, January 22, 1968), pp. 41-76.

5. Possible Soviet sponsorship of terrorist activities in noncommunist countries is a current issue in the Executive Branch and on Capitol Hill, where

Senator Jeremiah Denton's Subcommittee on Security and Terrorism of the Foreign Relations Committee has held hearings. Secretary of State Alexander Haig charges that "Moscow continues to support terrorism and war by proxy." William E. Colby, a former director of Central Intelligence, says the Soviets "provide the instruments," but neither they nor any other state "is directing the orchestra." John M. Goshko, "Hard Line Toward Soviet Unchanged, Haig Insists," Washington *Post*, April 25, 1981, p. A2; and George Lardner, Jr., "Amid Echos of Past, Hearings Begin on 'New Threat' of Terrorism," Washington *Post*, April 25, 1981, p. A7. For details, see Claire Sterling, *The Terror Network* (New York: Reader's Digest Press/Holt, Rinehart & Winston, 1981), p. 357.

6. Francis M. Watson, *Political Terrorism: The Threat and the Response* (New York: Robert B. Luce, 1976), p. 170.

7. The Organisation Armée Secrète (OAS) was a clandestine force of military personnel and civilian expatriates, led by disaffected French officers, who refused official plans to free Algeria from French colonial rule. Terrorist cells (terrorist group structures) were expert with plastique, a French demolition weapon. Thirty-one serious plots to assassinate President Charles de Gaulle were foiled in the late 1950s and early 1960s. One scheme inspired a work of fiction, later recorded on film, called *The Day of the Jackal* by Frederick Forsythe (New York: Viking Press, 1971). Success surely would have produced worldwide reverberations. OAS exploits are expounded upon in Geoffrey Bocca, *The Secret Army* (Englewood Cliffs: Prentice-Hall, 1968), p. 268; and Paul Henissart, *Wolves in the City: The Death of French Algeria* (New York: Simon & Schuster, 1970), p. 508.

8. Robert Kupperman and Darrell Trent, *Terrorism* (Stanford: Hoover Institution Press, 1979), pp. 22-34.

2

The Mindsets of High-Technology Terrorists: Future Implication from an Historical Analog

David Ronfeldt
William Sater

NINETEENTH-CENTURY DYNAMITE ANARCHISTS: ANALOGS FOR TWENTIETH-CENTURY NUCLEAR TERRORISTS?

> Terror will be terror in the true sense of the word only if it represents the revolutionary implementation of the most advanced technical sciences at any given moment.
>
> > A proponent of dynamite terrorism speaking at the Fifth Conference of Social Revolutionaries in 1909.

This chapter contributes to Rand research on the possible intentions and motivations of individuals or groups who might threaten to use nuclear terrorism in the future. A recent Rand report concluded that "we are liable to see coercive actions in the nuclear domain intended to cause widespread alarm and increase the leverage of a terrorist group making demands on government." The report further hypothesized that nuclear terrorism "would be more likely among the most fanatical and violent terrorist groups, those with more millenial aims as opposed to a concrete political program."[1]

Published with the permission of the Rand Corporation. © 1980 by the Rand Corporation.

To develop such speculative formulations, we have relied largely on an analog methodology that draws inferences from past and present cases of nonnuclear terrorism as well as from other crimes that have attributes likely to be associated with possible future nuclear terrorism. We have sought to penetrate the psychological mindsets of terrorist adversaries by examining the communiques and manifestos of terrorist groups, the biographies and autobiographies of terrorists, and the various theories of terrorist behavior. We have begun looking for patterns among the factors that turn individuals into terrorists, the ways in which terrorists view the world and themselves in it, the motivations that lead them to do what they do, and the reasons for preferring the tactics and targets that characterize their behavior.[2]

The Analog

In searching for potential historical analogs that may provide insights into possible future nuclear terrorism, we noticed that during the late nineteenth century an earlier generation of "high-technology terrorists" specialized in using dynamite, which was the premier scientific explosive of their time. These individuals saw dynamite as possessing special, even mystical, powers in addition to its real physical properties. Some dynamite-prone terrorists created philosophical doctrines that urged revolutionaries to unify around that vanguard technology. They claimed that the use of this technology would guarantee the leveling of the old order, thereby ushering in the creation of a secular millenium. The dynamite-prone terrorists appeared amidst a broader wave of revolutionary anarchism and international terrorism — the first great wave to afflict Europe and America in modern times.

A strict comparison of the physical properties of dynamite and nuclear explosives might make the analogy between nineteenth-century dynamite terrorism and twentieth-century nuclear terrorism seem implausible. Although both are the high-technology, premier explosives of their times, providing a quantum jump in destructive capability over what was previously possible, dynamite (and its volatile cousin, nitroglycerine) never provided a capability to devastate cities or create an apocalyptic holocaust. Dynamite was rapidly and widely introduced for peaceful engineering and industrial uses, thus becoming quite easily accessible for other purposes. The production of dynamite involved a comparatively simple chemical process and required no extraordinary ingredients. Bombs made of dynamite were easily portable and safe to use, and their effects were controllable. Dynamite also could be deployed selectively – for example, for the assassination of a precise individual or the partial demolition of a building. Thus, the rationale for the analogy is limited by the physical properties and capabilities inherent to each kind of device.

What make the analogy meaningful, and potentially instructive, however, are the psychopolitical attributes. The dynamite-prone terrorists believed that dynamite endowed them with extraordinary power to accomplish grandiose purposes – much as we suspect might be the case with nuclear terrorists. Years, even decades, passed before it became entirely clear to terrorists, and to security officials, that dynamite would not in fact enable a few determined radicals to inflict unlimited damage, topple governments, or wreck entire societies. Meanwhile, the motivations, intentions, and mindsets of those dynamite-prone terrorists seem to have had special attributes that we should consider in speculating about future terrorists who might be attracted to high-technology ultra-explosives. The possibility that improvised nuclear devices may become available in the future makes the analogy seem even more pertinent.

Methodology and Limitations

Our methodology relies heavily on readily accessible data on individuals who advocated or practiced "dynamite terrorism." Such information, unfortunately, is scarce and incomplete. We found some information in selected anarchist publications,[3] and some was obtained from secondary anarchist writings. Often we were unable to determine whether quotations were made by armchair propagandists or by genuine activists. We do not know whether individuals we have grouped together as "dynamite terrorists" should be further distinguished as anarchists, syndicalists, socialists, communists, nihilists, millenialists, or something else that may have important consequences for their intentions and motivations. We have included material on dynamite terrorism in the United States and a variety of European countries, although clearly the contextual or environmental factors differed widely among countries. While the data are insufficient to provide an authoritative, scholarly study of dynamite terrorism, we believe that they can serve as a reasonable basis for an exploratory and speculative discussion of why terrorists sometimes become attracted to high-technology explosives. The information, particularly that revealed in quotations, seems to indicate some central themes that have occurred, and that might recur, in the mindsets of such terrorists.

DYNAMITE TERRORISM IN THOUGHT AND ACTION

The past year has been remarkable for the number and grave character of the outrages which have been accomplished or attempted abroad, in furtherance of political, social, industrial, or personal objects. At no former period of our experience have there been so many desperate attempts – some of them only too fatally successful – to destroy life and property by means of dynamite and similar explosives. There is only one gratifying consideration in connexion with the long and dreary list of these outrages, and that is, that the frequency and cosmopolitan character of crimes of this sort probably bring us so much nearer to the time when an international agreement will be arrived at whereby criminals of this class will, like pirates, be treated as enemies of the human race, and persued with relentless vigour from country to country, and debarred from shelter or sympathy in any part of the civilised world, and this without reference to whether the actuating motive was political, industrial or other. Indeed, it is difficult to understand how any motive can be deemed to sanctify or palliate so horrible and dastardly a form of offence, one of the most deplorable features of which, as we have before remarked, is the callous indifference to whether the consequences fall on persons wholly innocent of any participation in, and unconnected with, the particular matter or cause against which the crime is directed.

Col. V. D. Majendie, C.B., His/ Her Majesty's (HM) Inspector of Explosives, 1892

Human capacity for destruction made a quantum jump following the invention of nitroglycerine in Italy in 1846. At first, nitroglycerine suffered from one major defect: its chemical instability made it hazardous for the user. However, after Alfred Nobel tamed the powerful compound in 1867 by mixing it with wood pulp and sodium nitrate, the resulting invention, dynamite, could be employed with little risk. Knowledge of the required chemistry remained restricted to professional circles for a while, but it soon became as readily available as the ingredients for fabrication. As dynamite became relatively cheap and easy to make or acquire, its applications spread from science to industry to politics, and it became the premier explosive of its time.

Dynamite Terrorism in Practice

The proliferation of dynamite coincided with the first great wave of terrorism in the late nineteenth century. In Europe, three terrorist groups who used dynamite proved unusually violent for their times: the Russian People's Will, the transnational Anarchists, and the Irish Fenians. The Russian People's Will fought to destroy authoritarian government and create socialism in Russia. The Anarchists wished to eradicate all institutions of state and property and to spread violence against democratic as well as dictatorial governments. The Fenians were ethnonationalists who sought liberation from British colonial rule. Many of the leaders and members of such groups were from relatively urbane, educated, middle-class backgrounds.

Conventional tactics of shooting and stabbing selected government leaders and bureaucrats had become a favorite way of implementing the idea of "direct action." The Anarchists even formed an international network of assassins intent upon using murder to destroy the capitalist economic system and the states that fostered and protected it. Soon victims began to fall throughout the Western world: an Italian king, a Spanish prime minister, an Austrian empress, the presidents of France and the United States — even an Argentine police chief.

For bigger and more dramatic actions, the anarchists and terrorists turned to the dynamite bomb, which they hoped would shatter the governments and ruling classes. French anarchists had a song praising its destructive qualities, and one secret society published a journal called *Le Dynamite.*[4] August Reinsdorf tried to blow up the kaiser, the crown prince, and various dignitaries at the unveiling of a monument. Stephan Khalturin tried to kill the tsar in 1880 by smuggling into the Winter Palace 100 pounds of dynamite; the ensuing detonation killed 11 and injured 56, but the emperor escaped. Boris Savinkov and other Social Revolutionaries went to enormous lengths to kill tsarist officials with dynamite when more conventional weapons would have sufficed.[5] In France, August Vaillant threw a bomb into a session of the National Assembly, proclaiming that he wished to punish those who were responsible for social misery. Another assassin, Emile Henry, willing to kill the faceless as well as the famous, hurled a bomb at a cafe in order to murder the bourgeoisie whose mere existence offended him.[6] In Britain, the Fenians launched dynamite attacks against the Tower of London and the House of Lords.[7] Elsewhere, Indian nationalists who wanted to oust British colonialists became so entranced with the new explosive that they sent agents to Europe to learn how to make bombs.[8] By comparison, dynamite politics did not seem as popular in the United States – although someone did explode a bomb at Haymarket Square in Chicago, and dynamite played a part in some labor strife.[9]

Some terrorists merely had to threaten the use of dynamite or create hoaxes to spread fear and alarm among the authorities. In 1885, anarchists who were furious at a proposal to change Swiss refugee policy threatened to blow up the Federal Assembly in Bern. German customs officials, when informed of an assassination plot to kill Wilhelm II, began to search frantically for a woman who was supposedly traveling from New York to Bremen transporting four trunks filled with dynamite. Both threats proved to be groundless. Similar hoaxes occurred elsewhere. The German emperor and his nobility as well as the bourgeoisie lived in fear of bomb threats.[10] The British consul in Leghorn once reported to London that some Italian technicians had prepared dynamite bombs, disguised as coal, that were to be placed in the holds of English merchant vessels. While this did not occur, the British police did apprehend various individuals smuggling dynamite into English ports for use by Fenian terrorists.[11] Paris was convulsed by fear of bombs following retalia- tory dynamite attacks launched to avenge the capture of the terrorist Ravachol, who had screamed, "Long live anarchism! Long live dynamite!" when he was captured. It was said that "the smallest sardine-tin flung on a pile of rubbish was mistaken for an explosive device and sent to the municipal laboratory with a thousand precau- tions."[12] Similar hysteria gripped London during the Fenian dynamite raids of 1883-85. Even the United States did not escape the dynamite hoaxes: it was rumored in a radical journal that a Vanderbilt dress ball might become the object of a bomb attack intended as a rebuke to the wealthy.[13]

In the early years of dynamite terrorism, before the limitations of the explosive were clear, perpetrators and defenders alike attributed extraordinary capabilities to dynamite and posed fearful scenarios for its use. It was claimed that dynamite politics could literally destroy cities and make armies useless. For example, Irish terrorists threatened to use dynamite to level London and blow up every English ship. While the threat proved illusory, Fenians used dynamite to attack London's subway system as well as such symbolic targets as the Tower of London, Scotland Yard, Nelson's Column, and the House of Commons.[14] In the United States, General Philip Sheridan reportedly warned that the commerce of entire cities could be destroyed by infuriated people who could easily make the explosives and safely carry them in the pockets of their clothing. And concern spread that a new generation of dynamite weapons, including an "international dynamite rifle," could place even more power in the hands of proletarian revolutionaries and terrorists.[15]

Various governments sought to curb the weapon. The Reichstag passed the "Dynamitgesetz" to punish those who used or owned dynamite and imprisoned for five years anyone who encouraged the use of the explosive or glorified any such act. In just 24 hours, the British parliament rushed through a measure that punished with life imprisonment anyone who exploded a dynamite bomb. Mere illegal possession would bring a sentence of 14 years of penal servitude. France apparently passed similar legislation.[16]

Unrestrained by such penalties, various anarchists who wanted dynamite to become the laborer's weapon of self-defense disseminated information on how to fabricate, purchase, or simply steal the explosive. In the United States, Professor Mezzerof, who might be dubbed the Johnny Appleseed of dynamite, considered it his duty to educate people in how to make and use the explosive. He claimed he would not rest until every American and European commoner knew "how to use explosives against autocratic government and its grasping monopolistic lies."[17] Of particular notoriety in Europe, Johann Most published a German-language anarchist journal, *Freiheit*, which praised dynamite as a force to amplify the people's will. His booklet on anarchist tactics provided the model for a modern version, *The Anarchist Cookbook*, which circulated among student radicals in the 1960s.[18] Convinced that dynamite could be used to change world history, Most went to work in an explosives factory in New Jersey to learn how to produce the weapon. Then he published his report on how workers and revolutionaries could make dynamite with lay knowledge, without squandering money on expensive and complex systems. Furthering his effort to popularize the home fabrication of dynamite, other radical papers either reprinted Most's article or published their own original research. However, Most and many of his colleagues eventually concluded that it was easier, safer, and cheaper to purchase or steal the dynamite than to manufacture it themselves.[19]

The Endowed Powers of Dynamite

Dynamite possessed certain innate attributes, while others were endowed or ascribed to it. The innate attributes included its explosive power, its portability, and the ease and safety of its use. It can be planted, then detonated at a later time by timing devices, and its effects can be controlled and made precise. Soon after its invention, it became publicly accessible, through purchase, fabrication, or theft, so that terrorists acting as single individuals or in small groups could wield unprecedented destructive power, and government officials saw little hope of defending against skilled and determined attackers. The novelty of dynamite, combined with the lack of experience with its terrorist applications, heightened the sense that dynamite was a potent destructive weapon against which the state would be unable to defend itself.

Terrorists and anarchists who were attracted to dynamite because of its innate properties endowed it with special powers as well – political, scientific, moral, humane, and/or magical. Statements about these endowed powers reflect the intentions, motivations, and mindsets of these terrorists.

Power for the People

Many proponents of dynamite terrorism argued that dynamite could endow the ordinarily powerless person with enormous political strength, magnifying the power of individuals and small groups and forcing recognition by the masses as well as by the authorities.

Workers allegedly now had access to a tool that could enable the individual who sought change (that is, good) to overcome the power of the conservative state (that is, evil). It was even possible to eradicate property as the basis of the state. Dynamite could end the state's "monopoly of violence," and henceforth neither the aristocracy nor the bourgeois state could compel the poor to cower.[20] According to Albert Parsons, convicted for participation in the Haymarket Riot,

> Today dynamite comes as the emancipator of man from the domination and enslavement of his fellow man . . . it is democratic; it makes everybody equal . . . it emancipates the world from the domineering of the few over the many. . . . Force is the law of the universe; it is the law of nature, and this newly discovered force makes all men equal and therefore free. . . . Science has now given every human being that power.[21]

Dynamite's ability to strengthen the people was thought to be a natural consequence of historical processes. Dynamite advocates regarded the tools of violence as central to the history of social change: The crossbow had unseated the horse-mounted nobility, and gunpowder had demolished castle walls. Indeed, gunpowder seemed responsible for the destruction of feudalism and the subsequent spread of new movements to free the masses. Now dynamite would enable the industrial working classes to destroy the new bourgeois state. Thus, one exponent of dynamite praised the

> . . . invention of gun powder, cannon, and firearms, making a single man often more formidable than a phalanx of ancient swordsmen. Every increase in the destructiveness of weapons of war has brought increased respect and importance for the individual war maker. Thus, today the poorest Nihilist with his dynamite is an object of more consideration from the Czar and his nobles than would be forty thousand serfs of olden times armed simply with staves and forks.[22]

According to an American anarchist,

> The reign of the bourgeoisie rests, as we have said, on gun powder. It cannot survive the use by the proletariat of a weapon requiring no capital, and against which gun powder would be as impotent as armor and castles against gun powder. Such a weapon is dynamite.[23]

According to a leading theoretician of dynamite terrorism, Johann Most, "It is obvious that these explosives are the decisive factor in the next chapter of human history."[24]

Scientific Power

A good part of dynamite's appeal came from the fact that it was then the ultimate scientific weapon. The terrorists justified dynamite violence by claiming that it could be the scientific instrument for imposing Marxist concepts of scientific socialism. They said it was logical for science, history, and progress to enable the individual to turn science against the state. Thus, one radical declared, "Dynamite! Of all the good stuff, this is the stuff. . . . In giving dynamite to the downtrodden millions of the globe, science has done its best work."[25] The Irish Fenians reportedly believed that dynamite was a "gift of science."[26]

Some extremists believed that dynamite would elevate terrorism to the status of a vanguard scientific movement. Many revolutionaries and terrorists of the time were in fact scientists by education if not by occupation — a background that may have motivated their interests in using "science" as the critical instrument for radical change. An extreme development of this idea emerged at the Fifth Conference of Social Revolutionaries in 1909 when a speaker argued, "Terror will be terror in the true sense of the word only if it represents the revolutionary implementation of the achievements of the most advanced technical sciences at any given moment."[27] This extraordinary view reflects a belief that scientific ends and scientific means justify each other, that using vanguard technology for terror could move the revolutionary struggle into a new, advanced, and more scientific stage. It also seems to imply that "science" rather than "the people" should be the key agent of terrorist violence.

Moral Power

For some terrorists, dynamite represented a moral weapon for political education whose use would enable them to elevate assassination above ordinary murder. Common criminals used the blade or the bullet; revolutionary terrorists should use dynamite. Because conventional weapons for assassination aroused common prejudices, they obscured the morality of revolutionary violence. Resort to the latest scientific weapons — particularly dynamite — would allow the message to transcend banal prejudices. Thus, the choice of weapon had major implications for the morality, clarity, and impact of the message to be conveyed.

In keeping with this rationale, some terrorists became obsessed with assassinating authorities by dynamite. A Russian terrorist of the People's Will, Stephan Khalturin, who worked in the czar's Winter Palace and who had even been alone with the czar, chose to kill him by smuggling 100 pounds of dynamite into the building. The detonation, on February 5, 1908, killed 11 and injured 56 — but the emperor escaped harm. More conventional weapons might have been more effective, but the People's Will rejected such banal alternatives because otherwise "this assassination would not have created the same impression. It would have been interpreted as an ordinary murder, and would not have expressed a new stage in the revolutionary movement."[28]

Humane Power

Many viewed dynamite not only as a moral weapon but also as a humane weapon for destroying the rulers and their states, liberating the poor and working classes, and speeding violent revolution toward its humanitarian ends. This typically reduced to a doctrine of exterminating the few for the benefit of the many. According to an article in *Truth*, "At first the dynamite bomb seems an implement of fiends, but a closer view discovers in it a potent minister of good."[29] To counter objections to the use of such extreme weaponry, another writer declared, "Those who will do so forget that the real humanity will be found in carrying a war as energetically as possible, in order to gain the end proposed as effectually and speedily as may be."[30] In the same vein, another anarchist periodical, *Alarm*, stated the maxim:

> It is clearly more humane to blow ten men into eternity than to make ten men starve to death. When ten men unite to starve one man to death, then it is humane and just to blow up the whole ten men. . . . This is our doctrine and our justification of the application of force.[31]

Mystical, Magical Power

Most of these terrorists treated dynamite power in secular and scientific terms, in keeping with their contemporary socialist, anarchist, and nihilist doctrines. However, some proponents of dynamite politics endowed dynamite with mythical, mystical, or magical qualities. According to one enthusiast, "Jupiter with his lightnings was scarcely more a master of the ancient world than is the mob with the bomb of dynamite the avenging Fate of modern monarchies."[32] August Spies, while denouncing slavery, starvation, and death during his turn in the Haymarket Trials, claimed that "science had penetrated the mystery of nature – such that from Jove's head had once more sprung a Minerva – dynamite."[33] An Easterner, Indian nationalist Tilak Bal Gangadahr, regarded dynamite as "more a magical charge than a visible object manufactured in a factory . . . a kind of witchcraft, a charm, an amulet."[34] Visualizing dynamite in this way, not only as a product of science but also as an expression of mystical and supernatural forces, may have been part of the apocalyptic and millenialist views of future revolution.

The Dynamiters' Objectives

Dynamite was not only considered to provide many kinds of power; the purposes and objectives for which dynamite power might be used were also equally varied. Some appear limited; others were grandiose. The range included attracting attention to demands, avenging past wrongs, defending workers' rights, forcing the government to reform, and destroying the system for the sake of revolution or the millenium. While these themes were often intermingled in the statements of one writer, they are nonetheless distinct. Each has somewhat different implications for tactics; for example, the objective might reflect whether dynamite was perceived primarily as a defensive or offensive weapon and whether it was the appropriate agent for individual assassinations or for large-scale destruction.

Drawing Attention to Demands

Dynamite was said to place such destructive power in the hands of individuals and small groups that the authorities and the masses would have to heed their demands. Thus, dynamite could be used to educate the authorities as well as to compel them to make changes. According to one writer,

> . . . whoever says that the assassination of tyrants does not put intelligence into anybody's head is sadly mistaken. Dynamite in its infant

career has already set more thought and intelligence in motion than the plain, naked wrongs of labor would have brought out in a century.[35]

Another writer voiced similar sentiments:

Thus, it will be found, when the first mad outburst of murder and destruction has cleared away, that there will follow throughout the world a more ready disposition on the part of governments to listen to the petitions of the humblest classes of the community, and to see that no burden of unjust laws are maddening them to revolt.[36]

And Johann Most declared that

. . . lead and dynamite, poison and knives are the weapons with which our brothers will open the skirmish. . . . With these the people will be able to argue more strongly and loudly; with these our goals will be attained more surely and quickly.[37]

While attracting attention to demands was usually subordinate to other objectives, it was a critical starting point for many terrorists.

Vengeance and Punishment

Some terrorists stressed the use of dynamite for avenging past injustices by engaging in reprisals to punish the wrongdoers. French anarchist August Vaillant tossed a dynamite bomb into the French legislature to punish those he believed to be responsible for social misery. French terrorist Ravachol held that "Dynamite is the arm of the weak who avenge themselves or avenge others for the humiliating oppression of the strong and their unconscious accomplices."[38] In a similar vein, an essay in *Truth* once warned that just going around killing leaders would not alter the social situation; destructive violence should not be used promiscuously or indiscriminately, but only in retaliation for some specific wrong.[39]

Self-Defense and Protection

Some proponents of dynamite politics emphasized dynamite's utility for defending and preserving the rights and liberties of the laborer. Since the powerful and privileged classes used force to impose their will, workers must likewise resort to force to protect themselves. Thus, an article on how to make and use dynamite was dedicated ". . . for those who will sooner or later be forced to employ its destructive qualities in defense of their rights as men and a sense of preservation. . . ."[40] When the discussion at a U.S. labor meeting turned to dynamite, various members vowed that using force to protect oneself and one's family was legitimate and that the method of defense was not so important. Dynamite could, they believed, be used to hold off military troops during labor strife.[41]

This theme is prominent in American radical labor politics, with an emphasis on defending the rights of the workers who fought to make the system responsive to their demands. The theme is less noticeable in the writings of European anarchists, largely concerned about taking the offense to create revolutions.

A Last Resort for Reform and Revolution

Many proponents of dynamite politics emphasized its importance as an instrument of last resort, after all other legal means had been exhausted, for compelling the system to reform (although for some, the idea of reform seemed to verge on revolution): since the rulers used force to preserve the status quo, the workers were justified in using violence to introduce reforms; attempting to persuade the rulers to change was pointless.

Whether dynamite had become necessary as the instrument of final resort depended on broad assessments of how the political system was functioning. The ballot was regarded as the primary alternative to the bomb. According to one writer,

> We have a common fallacy that all improvements can be introduced by voting . . . but the first instance has yet to be born where the ballot has introduced a new principle.
> Produce a new principle and the ballot can and frequently does bring out and develop all its parts, and this is the sole business of the ballot . . . (but) a reform must be introduced by a minority or never introduced. When by the use of dynamite, one man can stand off a hundred persecutors, we may expect an age of reformers and reforms. Until then reform must be tediously slow.[42]

The bombs-or-ballots debate became quite heated among the devotees of dynamite. European anarchists, typically convinced that the ballot was meaningless and the system unreformable, viewed bombing as the paramount option. A few Americans who believed the United States was similarly beyond reform welcomed dynamite as the antidote to electoral fraud and corruption. A handbill distributed in Indianapolis declared that "one pound of dynamite is better than a bushel of ballots."[43] However, contrary to the prevailing preference for bombs over ballots among European devotees of dynamite, many American radicals demurred.

While they approved of dynamite politics for fighting monarchy and autocracy in Europe, these Americans apparently opposed similar tactics for the United States until established democratic processes offered no hope. Thus, articles in *Truth*, commenting on the prevalence of dynamite anarchism in Europe, observed:

> The times are not quite ripe for such things over here, but there is no reason to conclude that they never will be ripe for them. Let corporate and money power turn the screws once or twice more upon the thumbs of the people and the times may ripen very quickly.[44]

> The time is coming when journals like *Truth* will be forcibly suppressed, when meetings of honest citizens will be dispersed at the point of the bayonet, when the producers will be shot down like dogs in the street. When that day does dawn, the hour for using DYNAMITE will have struck. See to it, then, that every free man knows how to make and use it.[45]

Even Professor Mezzerof, who worked diligently to spread information on how to make and use dynamite, urged Americans not to deploy his inventions "till the government becomes autocratic and you cannot obtain your rights at the polls."[46]

In contrasting the conditions of Europe and America, the dynamite activists noted not only the higher degree of suppression and exploitation evident in Europe but also the higher degree of political consciousness. One writer, commenting on the reliance on dynamite in Europe, doubted that the same situation would occur in the United States because the people were not "instructed as to the natural rights of man and in their ignorance they imagine their troubles to be a part of the nature of things — something unavoidable."[47] European terrorists seemed more prone to absolutist, black-and-white ideological assessments than their American counterparts.

Anarchic Destruction and Millenial Redemption

Dynamite appealed to some anarchists and terrorists as a means to annihilate the very foundations of the ruling system, namely, state and property. For them, reform was impossible; revolution was essential. For the dynamite-prone anarchist, revolution meant little more than destruction — by destroying the past and the present, the future would take care of itself. An article in *Alarm* made the point:

> Simply by making ourselves master of the use of dynamite, and then declaring we will make no further claims to ownership in anything, and deny every . . . person's right to be owner of anything, and administer instead death, by any and all means, to any and every person who attempts to claim personal ownership of anything. This method, and this alone, can relieve the world of this infernal monster, the "right of property."[48]

Sometimes this prospect introduced an apocalyptic or millenialist aspiration. Franklin Kyrlach urged, "Away with it (property): tear it limb from limb, come down upon it like a hurricane, and sweep it from the face of the earth. Blow it into splinters with dynamite."[49]

The ultimate vision was that of simultaneous explosions all over the earth. Albert Parsons enthusiastically predicted, "A social revolution! One dynamite bomb! Pshaw. When the revolution comes there will be millions of dynamite bombs and they will flash and crash all over the civilized world simultaneously. That's what will happen."[50] And John Kelley claimed, "The effect of a bomb may be slight, but certainly a few tons of dynamite exploded in a heap would make a revolution. Gunpowder clears the air."[51]

The language of some dynamite advocates conveyed an Old Testament quality, as though dynamite could be used to usher in a proletarian Judgment Day.

> The savage blinding light of explosions begins to light up its dreams. Property trembles and cracks under the deafening blows of dynamite, the palaces of stone, where are accumulated the riches stolen from the workers, crack open providing a breach through which will pour the waves of poor and starving.[52]

The notion that dynamite could open a "breach" places the thinker more within the traditions of millenarianism than of anarchism.

These visions reflect little or no concern for using dynamite as an instrument for drawing attention to demands or for compelling the system to adopt reforms. They view dynamite as a weapon for absolute destruction and annihilation. Some terrorists and anarchists seemed to have revered dynamite precisely because, unlike any other weapon then available, it seemed to provide that capability against any victim or target. No number of knives, guns, poisons, or other conventional instruments of terror and assassination could offer this; dynamite alone exposed the very foundations of the state to total extinction. Such wishes for total destruction and millenial redemption appear to have been more widespread in Europe than in the United States, where anarchists tended to advocate dynamite for limited purposes and specific targets.

IMPLICATIONS FOR POSSIBLE FUTURE
NUCLEAR MILLENIALISM

We have sought to identify elements of the mindsets of nineteenth-century dynamite terrorists on the assumption that this may lend some insight into the mindsets of possible future nuclear terrorists. Today, dynamite seems puny and precise compared with nuclear explosive devices. But this difference in physical capabilties does not invalidate the analogy. To nineteenth-century terrorists, dynamite was an extraordinarily powerful high-technology explosive, eminently suitable for arousing terrible fear and alarm among the elite. Some nihilists apparently even believed dynamite could level cities and usher in a political apocalypse. As the premier explosive of its time, dynamite was used to assassinate individuals, murder large numbers of people who represented a particular class or group, attack institutions, and perpetrate hoaxes designed to unnerve the authorities. And indeed, government authorities and security agents feared that dynamite-wielding fanatics might literally destroy the foundations of political and economic order.

The Nature of Super-explosive Power

Dynamite's physical properties are insufficient to account for the power that made it appealing to some nineteenth-century terrorists. It was important, and perhaps politically and psychologically necessary, for them to endow dynamite's power with broader theoretical and philosophical meanings. The following implied powers played a role in the past and may be relevant for future terrorism.

- Superexplosives were interpreted to represent "power to the people," for use against the state: the state used raw power and violence against the people, so they should do likewise in return. Historical human progress, some terrorists argued, was based ultimately on the people's resort to the latest instruments of violence.

- Superexplosives represented scientific power. To some terrorists, it seemed proper for science to enable people to unleash the forces of nature against the state. They believed that the highest form of revolutionary terror should utilize the most advanced science and technology of the time.

- Superexplosive terrorism represented a moral form of power because it elevated violence above the level of common criminality. Dynamite terrorists could express their messages more clearly and carry their struggles to a new, more advanced stage. Conventional weapons might be easier to use, but they aroused conventional prejudices and lacked grandeur.

- Superexplosives were claimed to constitute a humane form of power. Since the state was the real source of inhumanity and immorality, according to some terrorists, the quicker it was destroyed, the better for humanity – even though some people were killed or harmed in the process.

- Superexplosives were seen to impart a mystical, magical kind of power – useful at least to charm the audience and perhaps to create an apocalyptical breakthrough to a new millenium.

Some of these notions might be appealing for a present-day terrorist who wants to justify using nuclear power. We cannot estimate what different combinations of objectives and motivations might occur or how these might influence terrorist actions because our data base does not enable us to identify attribute combinations, even for the dynamiters. But our tentative speculation would be that the most dangerous combination would mix all the themes.

It may seem unlikely that future terrorists would interpret the use of nuclear threats as a way to wield power on behalf of the people. Yet, just as political philosophers have traditionally treated coercive power as the ultimate basis of the state, terrorists have rationalized high-technology violence as the best way to counter and combat that coercive power, claiming that they were promoting "power to the people." The evidence for this tendency in the history of dynamite terrorism suggests that some future extremists, perhaps motivated by political radicalism or ethnic nationalism, might endeavor to create respect and legitimacy for their cause by threatening nuclear violence. The possible future availability of small nuclear weapons could facilitate the adoption of such rationalizations.

Many terrorists, particularly those who were scientists by education or occupation, revered dynamite because it represented the latest achievement of science and technology. To them, dynamite symbolized an aspiration to comprise an ultramodern vanguard that could rely more on "science" than on the "people" for achieving radical change. Since nuclear power represents an even more advanced technology than did dynamite, it could appeal to terrorists (some of whom might emerge from within scientific communities) interested more in wielding "scientific power" than in promoting "power to the people."

There is also a very different possibility. Secular and scientific ideas dominated revolutionary and terrorist thought in Western countries in the late nineteenth century; mystical and millenialist notions were less prevalent. However, the late twentieth century may be marked by a decline in secular and scientific ideas and by a new attraction to mystical and millenialist views. This possibility is indicated by several trends, including the increased influence of Eastern philosophies in the Western world, the continued questioning of scientific rationalism, the spreading belief that the world is irrational, and the growth of religious and mystical cults. Should such trends continue, future terrorists may become more inclined to endow themselves with mystical powers through the threat of nuclear apocalypse. Science and mysticism, far from being contradictory, may blend quite readily in some mindsets.

The Uses of Super-explosive Power

The objectives of dynamite terrorism were as varied as were the interpretations of its power. The following themes recurred among the early advocates of super-explosive terrorism:

- Superexplosives were useful for attracting attention to demands, while simultaneously publicizing the identity and ideals of the perpetrators. The threat of superexplosives served to "educate" the people as well as to compel authorities to acquiesce.

- Superexplosives were deployed to avenge unjust acts. Some terrorists saw the guilty – whether an individual, class, institution, or the "system" – as deserving the worst possible punishment for evil behavior. To them, this kind of violence should not be indiscriminate; it should retaliate for specific wrongdoing.

- The use of superexplosives was justified as an instrument for self-defense, whereby the weak (the people, an ethnic minority, the workers) could prevent further exploitation and oppression by the state.

- Superexplosives were sometimes regarded as offensive weapons for introducing sweeping reforms in a "system." The inability of the system to reform through conventional means justified the resort to super-explosive terrorism.

- Superexplosives held special attraction for some terrorists whose grandiose aim was to eradicate the existing social order – a goal that might require the leveling of all institutions of state and property – or to create an apocalyptic breakthrough to a new millenial redemption.

These themes occurred in various combinations. For example, some who used super-explosive terrorism to attract attention also wished to radically reform the existing political institutions. However, the themes of radical reformism and anarchic or millenial destruction were mutually exclusive. The most dangerous thematic combination may have mixed vengeful punishment with millenial destruction.

Historical analogy suggests that we should expect similar patterns and variations to accompany the possible emergence of nuclear terrorism – especially if miniaturized nuclear devices ever become available. Nuclear power may appeal to terrorists who crave attention to their demands or who wish to wreak vengeful punishment against specific targets. It is difficult to imagine nuclear devices being advocated for defending the interests of the workers — although their place might conceivably be taken by ethnic nationalists, religious cultists, or even environmental extremists in this analogy. It is also difficult to suppose that future terrorists would adopt nuclear force to compel major social reforms as a more effective alternative to the ballot. But the threat of nuclear terrorism might be exploited to create political disruption while leveling radical demands at the authorities. A future nuclear terrorist might conceivably demand that a presidential election be halted or that a specific candidate be withdrawn from contention.

At a minimum, dynamite threats secured immediate attention from the authorities, if not from the public at large. However, the most dangerous dynamite terrorists craved more than mere publicity. Some terrorists and anarchists simply saw dynamite as a scientific weapon for destruction — an explosive that offered the capability to literally eradicate or annihilate the enemy. The fact that some anarchists of the late nineteenth century viewed dynamite as the instrument for annihilating the established order reinforces a contemporary concern: that future terrorists will see the nuclear bomb as the instrument for blasting through to a revolutionary new millenium.

Diverse Tactics

Dynamite terrorism encompassed diverse tactics, as might nuclear terrorism. Dynamite was used for individual or group assassinations, in labor and industrial strife, for symbolic bombings, for institutional bombings, for extortion, and for hoaxes. These could have been accomplished by more conventional means, but dynamite held special appeal because of the kinds of powers previously discussed.

Some terrorists threatened to use dynamite to level cities — although these threats never materialized. We found no mention of incidents in which dynamite terrorists explicitly threatened random mass murder, but there were instances (for example, a cafe bombing) in which representatives of a particular sector were targetted en masse. And some of the more grandiose and millenialist scenarios for destruction implied some random deaths.

For nuclear terrorist threats to follow a similar pattern would require the availability of small weapons that could be deployed selectively against small targets. Otherwise, hoaxes, extortions, and millenialist threats would seem most likely — although a terrorist attempt to annihilate a limited area (for example, Wall Street) should not be discarded from the realm of speculation. Whereas the threat potential and the tactical applications of dynamite were often greatly exaggerated by both the terrorists and the defenders, nuclear terrorism could indeed have disastrous, even apocalyptic, results.

How a Nuclear Terrorist Group Might Be Formed: Two Models

We have not delved deeply enough into the history of dynamite anarchism to understand how groups dedicated to extreme violence come into being; thus we cannot suggest from historical analogs how nuclear terrorist groups might take form. Nonetheless, two models seem possible.

In the first, a nuclear terrorist group emerges from a conventional terrorist group. The decline and failure of a conventional terrorist group might lead to such desperation and divisiveness among its members that a nuclear-prone minority could coalesce to form a new group or capture control of the old organization. In this model, the nuclear-prone minority could favor nuclear terrorism — whether for extortionist, apocalyptic, or other purposes — on the grounds that the failure of the original group was due to insufficient militance and violence against an increasingly oppressive state. The larger the original group, the more possibilities exist for this model to apply — the decline of conventional terrorist groups under police and public pressure could lead to a few small and extremely violent splinter factions. In a metaphysical depiction, the model implies a nuclear Phoenix rising from the ashes of the original conventional terrorist group.

The second model is of a nuclear terrorist group forming from fresh recruits. The group would be entirely new, although some of its members might come from such groups as religious cults, ideological movements, or ethnonationalist sects. The terrorism would be nuclear from the beginning — whether for extortionist, apocalyptic, or other purposes. The metaphor to characterize this model could be that of a nuclear Prometheus bringing fire from heaven to an unholy world.

In either model, the most dangerous outcome would be for the new group to have an apocalyptic or millenarian cast. In the first model, conversion to nuclear millenarianism could occur in response to the disaster perceived to have befallen the original group. In the second model, nuclear millenarianism could dominate if the charismatic leader or the membership came from religious cults that were already infused with millenialist thinking.

NOTES

1. Gail Bass, Brian Jenkins, Konrad Kellen, Joseph Krofcheck, Geraldine Petty, Robert Reinstedt, and David Ronfeldt, *Motivations and Possible Actions of Potential Criminal Adversaries of U.S. Nuclear Programs* (Santa Monica: Rand Corporation, R-2554-SL, February 1980), p. 78.

2. See Konrad Kellen, *Terrorists — What Are They Like? How Some Terrorists Describe Their World and Actions* (Santa Monica: Rand Corporation, N-1300-SL, November 1979).

3. In particular, we relied on two American anarchist periodicals, *Truth* and *Alarm*.

4. Irving L. Horowitz, *Radicalism and the Revolt Against Reason* (Atlantic Highlands, N.J.: Humanities Press, 1961), p. 29; Andrew Carlson, *Anarchism in Germany* (Metuchen, N.J.: Scarecrow Press, 1972), vol. I, p. 254.

5. Franco Venturi, *Roots of Revolution* (New York: Knopf, 1960), p. 686; Boris Savinkov, *Memories of a Terrorist* (New York: Albert and Charles Boni, 1931), pp. 26-37, 76; A. Yarmolinsky, *Road to Revolution* (New York: Macmillan, 1959), pp. 258-59.

6. Max Nomad, *Dreamers, Dynamiters and Demagogues* (New York: Walden Press, 1964), p. 48; John J. C. Longoni, *Four Patients of Dr. Deibler* (London: Lawrence and Wishart, 1970), pp. 30-31, 166.

7. K. R. M. Short, *The Dynamite War* (Atlantic Highlands, N.J.: Humanities Press, 1979), pp. 143, 240.

8. Ram Gopal, *How India Struggled for Freedom* (Bombay: Book Centre, 1967), p. 185.

9. R. Jeffrey-Jones, *Violence and Reform in American History* (New York: New Viewpoints, 1978), p. 71.

10. Carlson, *Anarchism*, pp. 261, 270, 274-75.

11. Short, *The Dynamite War*, pp. 68-69.

12. Longoni, *Four Patients*, p. 31.

13. *Truth*, April 14, 1883; Joseph P. O'Grady, *Irish Americans and Anglo American Relations, 1880-1888* (New York: Arno Press, 1976), p. 200.

14. *Truth*, May 5, 1883.

15. O'Grady, *Irish Americans*, pp. 195-200; *Alarm*, December 6, 1884.

16. Carlson, *Anarchism*, p. 293; Short, *The Dynamite War*, pp. 143, 240; Longoni, *Four Patients*, p. 71; O'Grady, *Irish Americans*, p. 185.

17. *Truth*, May 26, 1883.

18. *Die Freiheit*, New York and London, March 8, 1884, June 27, 1885.

19. Johann Most, *Revolutionare Kriegswissenschaft* (Munich: Internationaler Zeitungs-Verein, 1885).

20. *Alarm*, June 30, 1888.

21. Lucy Parsons, *Mass Violence in America* (New York: Arno Press, 1969), p. 82.

22. *Truth*, June 9, 1883.

23. C. L. James, "Tract for Time," in *Anarchism: Its Philosophy and Scientific Basis*, ed. A. Parsons (Westport, Conn.: Greenwood Press, 1970), p. 162.

24. Most, *Revolutionare Kriegswissenschaft*.

25. From a letter by T. Lizius, in *Alarm*, February 24, 1885.

26. *The Economist*, March 24, 1883.

27. Cited in Ze'ev Iviansky's, "Individual Terror Concept and Typology," *Journal of Contemporary History* 12 (1977): 49.

28. Mikhail Frolenko, "Nachalo Narodnichestra," cited in Iviansky, p. 47.

29. *Truth*, June 9, 1883.

30. *Truth*, November 3, 1883.

31. *Alarm*, January 13, 1885.

32. *Truth*, June 9, 1883.

33. Parsons, *Mass Violence*, p. 15.

34. Gopal, *How India Struggled*, p. 192.

35. *Truth*, July 23, 1883.

36. *Truth*, June 9, 1883.

37. Quoted in Carlson, *Anarchism*, p. 254.

38. Prolo, "Les Anarchistes," Paris, 1912, cited in Robert Hunter, *Violence and the Labour Movement* (New York: Arno Press, 1919), pp. 81 82.

39. *Truth*, April 14, 1883.

40. *Alarm*, June 27, 1885.

41. *Truth*, May 19, 1883.

42. *Alarm*, June 27, 1885.

43. *Alarm*, April 24, 1886.

44. *Truth*, April 14, 1883.

45. *Truth*, June 30, 1883.

46. *Truth*, May 26, 1883.

47. *Truth*, June 23, 1883.

48. Quoted in Henry David, *The Haymarket Affair* (New York: Russell, 1963), p. 112.

49. *Alarm*, March 6, 1886.

50. *Alarm*, November 19, 1887.

51. *Alarm*, July 14, 1888.

52. Longoni, *Four Patients*, p. 149.

3

International Network of Terrorism

Yonah Alexander

Terrorism, the threatened and actual resort to ideological and political violence for the purpose of achieving limited and broad, imaginary or realistic goals, has become a permanent fixture of contemporary life.[1] Recognizing such dangers of terrorism as the safety of individuals, the pace of economic development, the acceptance of the role of law, the expansion of democracy, and the stability of the state system, nations have pursued various approaches in opposition to terrorism.[2] Non-Communist countries spend billions of dollars annually in order to improve security. Increased protection is provided for ordinary citizens and civilian facilities. Special defensive measures have been developed to protect ambassadors and government officials. More than a dozen nations have set up special commando units to fight terrorists and rescue hostages. Multinational corporation executives receive instructions in protecting themselves and their families, and the private sector has spent millions of dollars to safeguard its domestic and overseas investments.[3]

But despite national and international efforts to control terrorism, the level of nonstate violence remains high. The reasons are diverse and include at least ten factors: disagreement about who is a terrorist, lack of understanding of the causes of terrorism, the role of the media, the politicization of religion, double standards of morality, loss of resolve by governments, weak punishment of terrorists, flouting of world law, the support of terrorism by some states, and the existence of an international network of terrorism.[4]

While all these factors deserve serious consideration, this chapter will focus only on the last two because of their relevance to the risk perceptions of the business community.

It is evident that while the resort to ideological and political violence is centuries old, there has been a marked rise in terrorism across national lines in the past decade.[5] This expression of international "extralegal" violence has been undertaken primarily by two types of substate groups: ideologically motivated movements in Third World countries and their imitators in the Western industrialized societies and ethnically based or separatist groups in both developed and developing countries.[6]

The coincidence of time and the formation of these types of terrorist bodies suggest the possibility of common origins, common influences, and common contributing factors. For instance, unique political circumstances existed in the turbulent 1960s: the failure of rural guerrilla movements in Latin America and the resort to urban guerrilla warfare and terrorism, the defeat of the Arabs in the June 1967 war and the subsequent rise of Palestinian terrorism, the Vietnam war and the widespread demonstrations against it, and the Paris students' revolt of 1968.[7]

The importance of technological factors in promoting international terrorism should also be recognized. Indeed, modern technology, particularly increasingly inexpensive and convenient air travel and the development of modern communications, has given terrorist groups a condition that did not exist in the past: intensified interconnection across national boundaries. Collaboration among ideologically linked bodies and even among those without a common philosophy or political interest has increased rapidly and substantially.[8] Significantly, the strategy of terrorism does not prescribe instant victories over established regimes or adversaries. On the contrary, the struggle for fundamental political, economic, and social change is seen as complicated and protracted. Terrorist groups, by their very nature, are too small and too weak to achieve the upper hand in an open struggle for sheer power.

Because of this realization, many subnational movements have developed a "comradeship" disposition in their struggles against "imperialism," "capitalism," and "international Zionism" and for the "liberation" of a people to independence. It is this shared ideology and commitment to revolutionary comradeship that often expresses itself in the exchange of aid and comfort among different terrorist groups. As Ulrike Meinhoff's "Manifesto" clearly rationalized, "We must learn from the revolutionary movements of the world – the Vietcong, the Palestine Liberation Front, the Tupamaros, the Black Panthers."[9] Thus, most terrorist groups did not evolve directly from their own national antecedents, but rather adopted organization models and adopted terrorist tactics from foreign sources, which did not always fit local circumstances. Although these models were foreign transplants, various terrorist movements accepted them for practical purposes. For instance, many of the nationalist or separatist groups adopted Marxist ideologies as a "flag of convenience." They rationalized that Marxism provided a model for revolution against the state, denied the legal authority of the government, established a successful historical example of a revolution, granted some sort of respectable international status, afforded a sense of affinity with other revolutionary movements, and provided some assurance of direct and indirect support by like-minded groups and socialist states. With the adoption of Marxist ideology, however, some of these terrorist movements fell victim to internal ideological debate, division, and conflict emanating from different interpretations of ideology.[10]

Notwithstanding terrorists' disconnectedness with their own historical revolutionary struggles and their reliance on foreign models of ideology, organizational structure, and modus operandi, international linkages among various terrorist groups are profound both regionally and globally.[11]

Interconnections among Castroite, Trotskyite, Peronist, and other opposition forces in Latin America have existed over the years. The rationale behind these relationships was explained by a Montenero leader,[12] "We must unite at the continental level to free ourselves from the yoke of Yankee imperialism and the native oligarchies."[13]

This rhetoric has been translated into action. Thus, operations by one terrorist group in support of another in a foreign country have been common. For instance, in May 1970, a Tupamaro[14] was arrested in Santiago with 880 gold coins stolen from a Uruguayan business manager. These coins apparently were intended for the Chilean Movement of the Revolutionary Left (MIR).[15] Moreover, the MIR, the Argentinian People's Revolutionary Army (ERP),[16] the National Liberation Army of Bolivia,[17] and the Tupamaro guerrillas of Uruguay are cooperating to the extent of being prepared to do combat under a joint command. A declaration by the four groups in 1974 pledged to overthrow "imperialist-capitalist reaction, to annihilate counter revolutionary armies, expel Yankee and European imperialism from Latin American soil, country by country, and initiate the construction of socialism in each of our countries." Also, the Argentinian, Bolivian, Uruguayan, and Chilean terrorist groups set up a "Revolutionary Coordination Board" to finance "a new stage of military development," to establish rural guerrilla movements to mobilize and organize the masses, and to complement the operations of the existing guerrilla units.[18]

Regional collaboration in the western hemisphere exists in Central America.[19] Apparently, terrorist groups in El Salvador, Guatemala, and Nicaragua that have conducted kidnappings, bank robberies, and other profitable activities in the name of "higher" ideological and political principles have also tended to cooperate logistically and operationally.[20]

There are also instances of interconnectedness among U.S. terrorist groups and their counterparts in Latin America. For example, it is clear that Che Guevara's *Guerilla Warfare* and Carlos MaRighella's *Minimanual of the Urban Guerrilla* have had an impact on the thinking of American terrorists. The Symbionese Liberation Army (SLA)[21] patterned its violence according to these revolutionary models. And many political extremists have traveled to Cuba for indoctrination and training. Others have bombed Latin American diplomatic missions in the United States for the sake of the "oppressed" continent.

Interestingly, foreign terrorists located in the United States as well as their U.S. recruits have collaborated with Latin American comrades. A case in point is the Command of United Revolutionary Organizations (CORU), an anti-Castro umbrella structure comprised of the Cuban Action, the Cuban National Liberation Front, the Bay of Pigs Veteran's Association, the April 17th Movement, and the National Cuban Movement.[22] These exile groups are based in Miami, the Dominican Republic, Nicaragua, and Venezuela. CORU is allegedly responsible for the murder of 73 people who died in the October 6, 1976, explosion of a Cuban passenger jet following take-off from the island of Barbados.[23] According to intelligence sources, some Cuban groups "use Dade County as a base for international terrorism against allied governments of Cuba, Cuban shipping, Communists, purported Communists and individuals who take a stand against their terrorist-type tactics."[24] Targets also include "capitalist" firms. For instance, on May 25, 1977, an anti-Castro group claimed credit for a bomb explosion at the Mackey International Airlines offices in Fort Lauderdale. The Miami-based company subsequently canceled its plans to operate regular flights to Cuba.[25]

Also, a recent report related that the 23rd of September Communist League in Mexico[26] has plans to enlist radical Mexican-Americans with military experience. These recruits would assist the league in overthrowing the existing Mexican government and in annexing much of the southwestern United States.[27] Although this alleged scheme is rather unrealistic, the fact remains that crossnational terrorist activities continue to be considered.

Regional contacts for moral, logistic, and operational support also exist in Europe. The Irish Republican Army (IRA),[28] for example, has cooperated in arms deals with the Spanish "Freedom for the Basque Homeland" (ETA)[29] via East Germany. There are parallels in the modus operandi of the two groups. Both maintain links with France's Front for the Liberation of Britanny (FLB).[30] The IRA also developed relations with the Free Welsh Army[31] and German and Italian extremists.

The ETA, for its part, has connections with several French anarchist groups, especially the Group of International Revolutionary Action (GARI).[32] They have collaborated in arms smuggling, attacks against business targets (including the shooting of the Paris manager of the Spanish Bank of Bilbao and the Iberia Airlines office in Brussels), and abortive attempts to blow up trains running between France and Spain in 1973 and 1974.

Some contacts have developed among Swiss anarchist groups and German and Italian terrorists. For instance, on March 20, 1975, members of a Swiss group that included a number of German nationals were apprehended in Zurich. They were responsible for thefts from depots of the Swiss Army, and some of the stolen explosives were found in terrorist "safe houses" in Germany and Italy.[33]

Finally, a report alleges that "a kidnapping plan has been devised by a group of international extremists composed of Portuguese, Spanish, and Italian nationals who are preparing to start a series of violent actions in Portugal."[34]

While these examples of regional cooperation among various terrorist groups in the Americas and Europe suggest the existence of some sort of crossnational "comradeship," it has become increasingly clear that the major global network of terrorism consists of some 30 terrorist movements in the Middle East, Asia, Africa, Europe, and North and South America. It includes the Fatah, the Popular Front for the Liberation of Palestine (PFLP), the Popular Front for the Liberation of Palestine-General Command (PFLP-GP), the Saika, the Democratic Front for the Liberation of Palestine (DFLP), the Arab Liberation Front (ALF), the Palestine Liberation Front (PLF), the Black June, Chad's Frolinat, the Eritrean Liberation Front, the South African People's Organization (SWAPO), the Oman and Persian Gulf Liberation Front, the Popular Army of Turkey, the Iranian National Front, the Japanese Red Army (JRA), the Baader-Meinhoff Group, the Italian Red Brigades, the IRA, the British Revolutionary Party, the Dutch Red Help, ETA, Swiss revolutionaries, Scandinavian extremists, and various Latin American movements.[35]

The Palestinian movement,[36] particularly the PFLP,[37] through a framework known as the Organization of the Arab Armed Struggle (headed by Wadi Haddad),[38] became the catalyst and communications link for other revolutionary forces throughout the world, bringing them together into a collaboration and operational network of violence. One expression of this cooperation is through bilateral relationships. For example, in 1971, Yasser Arafat held meetings with a representative of the Central Command of the Eritrean National Front. More recently, in July 1978, Abu Hatim, Fatah's official in charge of foreign relations, met with a delegation from the Higher Command of the Eritrean revolutionary movements.[39] The clandestine "Voice of Palestine," reporting on this meeting, asserted that the Palestinian and Eritrean "revolutions fight in the same trench and are strategic allies against imperialism, Zionism, reaction and backwardness."[40]

During the same year, other bilateral links were established between Palestinian and Latin American groups. A transnational terrorist agreement was signed between the Democratic Front for the Liberation of Palestine (DFLP)[41] and Nicaragua's Sandinist National Liberation Front (FSLN).[42] These movements joined in a "common cause" to fight Israel, "United States imperialism," and other anti-Communist governments in Latin America.[43] The PLO and FSLN also signed a joint communique in Mexico City in which they stressed the bonds of solidarity between them.[44] Finally, a delegation representing the Argentine Monteneros[45] met with Fatah commanders in Damascus to review their joint cooperation efforts. Moreover, the visitors were given a tour of military installations and training camps in Lebanon.[46]

Aside from bilateral relationships between terrorist groups located in different regions of the world, multilateral meetings have been held over the years as well. For example, in the spring of 1970, representatives of a dozen groups met at a refugee camp in Lebanon in a PFLP-organized conference to explore the possibilities of collaboration across national lines. Since that initial meeting, several other gatherings have either occurred or have been planned. For example, in July 1974, the IRA sponsored an "Anti-Imperialist Festival" in Dublin and Belfast. Among the participants were Palestinians, separatist movements, and Europe Trotskyites. More recently, a Danish "League Against Imperialism" planned a "solidarity" conference with participation by a number of terrorist organizations, including the Fatah and the PFLP. Also invited to this meeting were the Southeast Asia Committee from Sweden, the Palestine Front and the Communist Workers Association from Norway, the Palestinian Workers Union, the Left Socialists (Arhus Middle East group), and the Socialists' League and the Communist League from Denmark.[47]

It is clear that these and other multilateral and bilateral meetings among various terrorist groups and their supporters have strengthened informal and formal linkages that facilitate an accessible machinery for violence on the national, regional, and global planes. This network maintains a service industry in Europe that supplies terrorist needs from clandestine centers in Algeria, Iraq, Lebanon, Libya, South Yemen, and Syria. There are essentially seven levels of collaboration among them: financial support, training, supply of combat materials, organizational support, attacks by proxy, coordinated attacks, and joint operations.

FINANCIAL SUPPORT

The Palestinian movement has provided substantial assistance to various revolutionary organizations such as leftist terrorist cells in Iran,[48] the Eritrean Liberation Front,[49] and the Japanese Red Army.[50] Other recipients include underground groups in Chad, Ireland, Panama, the Philippines, Sardinia and Corsica, and Thailand, to name a few.[51]

The main source of income for the Palestinian groups emanates from certain Arab states. In fact, following the Arab summit conference in Rabat in December 1969, it was reported,

> The Arab kings and presidents have decided to allocate 26 million pounds to meet the financial commitments of the Palestine Liberation Organization in the coming year, including 12 million pounds for the support of the Palestine revolution and 11 million pounds for the support of citizens' resistance in the occupied territory. It has been learned that Libya has decided to contribute 25 percent to the Palestine revolution budget.[52]

Libya, which considers itself "the only moral government in the world" and therefore stands "only for helping oppressed people, wherever they are,"[53] alone has allocated some $73 million directly to terrorist groups in recent years. For instance, according to Teheran sources, Libya, in 1976, had already disbursed $100,000 to Iranian terrorists and planned to allocate an additional $100,000 every three months.[54] The Libyan contribution obviously increased dramatically during the 1978-79 revolutionary struggle.[55]

Also, special bonuses have been offered by Libya to terrorist organizations for successful completion of operations. For the murder of the 11 Israeli athletes in Munich in September 1972, some $5 million was donated. Between $1 million and $2 million was paid by Mo'ammar el-Qadhafi, the Libyan chief of state, to the "international jackal" Carlos,[56] for the kidnapping of the Saudi Arabian oil minister, Sheikh Yamani, and other delegates in the OPEC raid of December 1975. Another participant in the operation, Hans Joachim Klein, the German terrorist, reportedly collected some $100,000 for his role. According to Egyptian sources, el-Qadhafi offered $16 million to the PFLP for the assassination of President Anwar Sadat.[57] More recently, a Norwegian terrorist received $1,000 from a terrorist organization supported by Libya for planting explosives in Jerusalem.[58]

Paradoxically, substantial financial aid to Palestinian groups is provided by moderate and antirevolutionary regimes: those of Saudi Arabia, Kuwait, and some oil sheikhdoms of the Persian Gulf. These countries, under the threat of terrorist activities in their own lands, are indirectly responsible for ideological and political violence elsewhere. Saudi Arabia, for example, is contributing $35 million to the Arab League's budget of $44 million for the PLO.[59] Indeed, special taxes are levied for the Palestinian movements as a whole, and government officials are called upon to contribute 5 percent of their salaries for the cause.

Aside from direct financial support by Arab states,[60] Middle East groups have obtained funds from Palestinians living inside and outside the region, blackmail activities (extortion and protection), kidnappings, hijackings, legitimate investments, and drug-smuggling operations. Regarding the latter source, it was reported as early as 1970 that several Palestinian groups purchased Chinese and Soviet arms with funds secured by smuggling large quantities of hashish to the United States through Canada.[61] In June 1978, members of a drug ring were convicted in Britain for their role in a similar activity. It was discovered that cannabis grown in Palestinian camps in northern Lebanon was smuggled into Syria, Turkey, Bulgaria, and Yugoslavia in foreign meat trucks, broken up into smaller loads, and hidden in cars and vans. Other Lebanese hashish was shipped out of Cyprus to Europe. Cash for the initial purchase of the drugs from a Syrian wholesaler in Sofia was provided by a large-scale car-stealing racket in Britain. The money earned from the sale of the drugs in various European cities was used to purchase arms in eastern Europe. These weapons were shipped back to the Middle East along the Sofia trail hidden in the same compartments that had held the hashish.[62]

To be sure, funds available to Palestinian groups and provided to non-Arab revolutionaries have not been the only shared source of money for terrorist operations. Movements outside the Middle East have also been generous with their foreign comrades. Terrorist groups in Argentina provide a case in point. They have collected hundreds of millions of dollars in the past several years primarily from ransoms for kidnapped business managers.[63] Some of that cash has been channeled to terrorist groups outside the country. According to one report, more than $2 million was traced to Europe, where it was spent by Chilean leftists who fled after the fall of President Allende in 1973.[64]

TRAINING

The majority of training camps available to terrorist groups are in the Middle East. They have been located at different times in Algeria, Iraq, Jordan, Lebanon, Libya, and the People's Democratic Republic of Yemen. Some camps are controlled by governments and others by various PLO groups, particularly Fatah and PFLP.

Libya, for example, administers camps at which many hundreds of terrorists annually undergo training, including the use of small arms and anti-aircraft missiles. It also provides naval and flight courses for revolutionaries. Libya often offers training in the techniques of executing specific terrorist operations abroad. For very advanced training, Libya sends her own and other volunteers to Syria and Algeria.

In general, thousands of Arab and foreign terrorists from some 15 countries have passed through Middle Eastern camps. Carlos, who joined the PFLP after being recruited in 1970, underwent his indoctrination and training in a Jordanian camp. He later sent other European and Latin American comrades to the Arab countries for training in sabotage, hijacking, and assassination.

Many non-Arab revolutionaries from the region have been trained by Palestinian groups. For instance, in 1972, Turkish authorities seized 14 nationals en route by boat to Turkey after completing training in Syria. The following year, an Israeli army unit detained a Turkish terrorist in a military operation at Neharral Berad, a Fatah training camp. In another Israeli raid on two training camps in Lebanon, nine Turkish terrorists were killed. They had been trained to carry out operations against Israeli and Turkish targets.[65]

Similarly, practical training in the use of arms was given to Iranian terrorists. Reporting on this linkage, a Lebanese newspaper stated,

> This aid first began in 1968, when a contingent of the Iranian revolutionary movement left Iran for training with the resistance movement. After their return to Iran, they began to train other members. Owing to the direct influence of the armed Palestinian struggle, revolutionary groups began to study armed struggle and to carry out armed actions inside Iran.[66]

Also, 18 members of the Cypriote Liberation Army (CLA) went to Lebanon for tactical training by Palestinians in preparation for "guerrilla warfare" against Turkish occupation forces.[67]

Among Asian terrorists, the Japanese Red Army (JRA), which developed links with the Palestinians in 1968, began receiving training at PFLP bases in Jordan in 1970. It was reported that the PFLP undertook the training at the time because it was impossible for the JRA to undergo such training in Japan.[68] Ukudaira Yassouda and

Okamoto, members of the JRA who participated in the Lod operation in May 1972 on behalf of the PFLP, were trained in Lebanon.[69] More recently, the Japanese hijackers in Dacca in September 1978 were reportedly outside Beirut and Baghdad.[70] Likewise, European terrorists underwent training in the Middle East. Members of the Baader-Meinhoff group, as well as other German revolutionaries, began to receive training in 1970 and 1971 at Fatah camps in Lebanon and Spain. Others were trained by the PFLP in South Yemen, including Peter Jugen Boock and Sieglinde Gudrun Hofmann, who were arrested and later released by Yugoslav police. These terrorists are believed to have participated in the shooting in July 1977 of Jurgen Pronto, chairman of the Dresdner Bank of Frankfurt.[71]

Italian terrorists, too, have been trained in the Middle East. A recent report relates that in the course of an investigation of arrested Red Brigade terrorists, the police found a map of Lebanon showing the location of a terrorist training camp. Besides geographical details, the map contained information about who to contact upon arrival as well as other instructions. A Libyan address was written on the back of the map.[72]

Other European terrorists trained in the region have been Irish, Dutch, and Norwegian. For instance, IRA sent comrades to train in South Yemen in the summer of 1976 and in southern Lebanon in the summer of 1978.[73] Several members of the Dutch Red Help were trained at a PFLP camp in South Yemen in the summer of 1976 in preparation for a series of attacks in Europe. Between 25 and 40 Norwegians were trained as terrorists by Palestinian groups in Lebanon in the summer of 1978.

According to some reports, several hundred U.S. citizens and residents of Arab descent have passed through training camps in the Middle East.[74] They have then returned to the United States "apparently to establish new contacts and perhaps to study various cities and airports for future operations."[75]

Other reports also indicate that terrorists are being trained outside the Middle East. "Guerrillas" have been sent to training camps in the Soviet Union and other Communist-bloc countries such as Bulgaria, China, Cuba, East Germany, North Korea, and Vietnam.[76] Recently, Czechoslovakia and Hungary have agreed to provide training to Palestinians who have joined the PLO since the end of the Lebanese civil war. During the summer of 1978, some 32 Palestinian pilots and 60 mechanics returned from advanced courses in east

European countries. Interestingly, Cuba, which provides terrorist training on the island, has also sent its advisors to the Middle East and Africa. For instance, Cubans were engaged in training members of the PLO in Lebanon[77] and Basque ETA separatists in Algeria.[78]

SUPPLY OF COMBAT MATERIALS

During the 1960s, terrorist groups had limited and often poor combat materials. In the past five years, however, modern military equipment, including Kalachnikovs, Katyushas, Dutch machine guns, portable antitank launchers of the RPG-7 type, and SA-7 anti-aircraft missiles, have reached underground movements. Although the major source of these weapons is Communist countries, the equipment is actually procured through various Arab countries and the Palestinian movement. For instance, in 1975, Libya signed a $2 billion arms deal with the Soviet Union. Some of these weapons reach terrorist groups with the direct involvement of Tripoli. According to documents found in a terrorist hideout in Teheran, Libya smuggled machine guns and hand grenades to Iran's desolated Persian Gulf coast for the use of opposition forces in the country.[79]

Palestinian groups frequently serve as intermediaries in the supply of weapons. On December 13, 1973, two Arabs, an Algerian, and ten terrorists belonging to the Turkish Popular Liberation Army were arrested in Paris. During the raid, the French police confiscated guns, grenades, letter bombs, booby-trapped books, and plastic explosives. This equipment had been smuggled in from the Middle East by the PFLP, which, with Turkish terrorists' assistance, planned to attack the Israeli Embassy in Paris as well as other targets.[80]

It has also been reported that, in November 1977, five tons of PLO hardware-mortars, rocket launchers, automatic weapons, and explosives were intercepted in Belgium. The arms were hidden in electrical transformers en route from Cyprus to the Irish Republic for the use of the IRA. Early in 1978, the IRA received a new supply of weapons from the Middle East, including a half dozen U.S. M-60 machine guns and explosives. This fresh equipment enabled the IRA to initiate a new offensive in the country.[81] During the same year, the Argentine Monteneros received Soviet-made RPG-7 rockets from Palestinian guerrillas.[82] Moreover, the weapons used by Red Brigade members in the kidnapping of Aldo Moro in March 1978 were comprised of a Czech Nagent pistol and an "unusual" Soviet machine gun.[83]

To be sure, the flow of military supplies is reciprocal. The Baader-Meinhoff group gave some M-26 hand grenades stolen from a U.S. military depot in West Germany to the Japanese Red Army and to Carlos. These hand grenades were used by the Japanese in a raid on the French Embassy in The Hague in September 1974 and by Carlos in an attack on a Paris "drugstore" during the same month. Some of these grenades and other weapons were stored by Carlos in his Latin-Quarter Paris apartment as well as in a villa outside the French capital, which was rented by the PFLP, the Turkish terrorists, and an Algerian leftist group. Both underground hideouts were subsequently uncovered by the French police.[84]

Similarly, during the 1975 attack on the West German Embassy in Stockholm, members of the Red Army used weapons provided by a female Italian terrorist who had stolen them from a Swiss national armory. Other stolen arms were discovered in terrorist hideouts in West Germany and Spain.[85] Finally, the IRA obtained three sets of U.S. electronic night-vision binoculars, which can detect infrared ray equipment used by the British army in after-dark surveillance. These binoculars were reported to have been stolen during a 1978 West German raid by "sympathizers."[86]

ORGANIZATIONAL SUPPORT

Organizational support, including communication and propaganda, forging of documents, and providing places of refuge, is another dimension of the international network of terrorist groups. They communicate with each other frequently and as the need arises. For example, on May 11, 1972, two days after the hijacking of a Sabena aircraft, Arafat received a cable from the Eritrean Liberation Front in which the "front expressed its condolences for the three Fedayeen killed by the bullets of the Zionist at Lod Airport."[87] Some of the movements also provide assistance in the field of propaganda. A case in point is the United Liberation Front for a New Algeria (FLUNA).[88] It is organizing a series of press conferences in which African, Arab, Asiatic, and Latin American groups will describe their "liberation struggles."[89]

Often, countries supporting guerrillas have provided similar assistance. A delegation from the Argentine Monteneros gave a press conference to the national news media of Mozambique on March 31, 1978. A speaker expressed the group's support of the struggle of the Rhodesian Patriotic Front, Polisario, the Revolutionary Front for the Independence of East Timor, and the PLO.[90] In October 1978, a series of radio broadcasts on behalf of SWAPO was carried by Dar es Salaam, Luanda, Lusaka, and Brazzaville. These communications stressed SWAPO's Marxist commitment to the control of economic interests and "armed struggle" for achieving that goal.[91] Finally, during the same year, Iran's Islamic Liberation Movement, the prime organizer of resistance to the shah, opened an information center in Beirut.[92]

Another dimension of organizational support is the forging of documents. The PFLP maintains a sophisticated workshop for this purpose, and it is likely that its international terrorist affiliates make use of this facility. The Palestinian terrorists also utilize documents stolen by other terrorist organizations. A Japanese courier who was detained in Paris upon his arrival from Beirut on July 26, 1974, had in his possession a quantity of forged passports and documents. Again, when some international-network hideouts were discovered in France in December 1973 and in June 1975, laboratories for forgeries and many documents, including passports, driving licenses, seals, official visas of various countries, and forged flight alteration notices for airline tickets, were found. The forged or stolen passports were of the following countries: Ecuador, Chile, Peru, Pakistan, West Germany, the United States, and Venezuela. It appears that terrorists can obtain official documents of almost any state in the world.

Indeed, 14 Palestinians carrying Latin American passports were arrested in Rabat, Morocco, for a conspiracy by Al Fatah to assassinate participants at the Arab Summit Conference.[93] In 1975, an Iranian terrorist seized in an attack on a Tel Aviv cinema had in his possession a forged British passport. The Iranian connection is also seen in a recent incident. On July 16, 1978, a West German terrorist suspect, Kristina Bersten, was arrested at the U.S.-Canadian border. She was carrying a false Iranian passport, one of several stolen by radical Iranian students when they occupied the Iranian consulate in Geneva in June 1976.[94]

A third form of organizational support is the providing of refuge havens for foreign terrorists released from prison or escaping from an executed attack. It is evident that some Arab countries have offered this type of assistance. The five German anarchists released following the kidnapping of Peter Lorenz in Germany were taken to South Yemen, where they were granted asylum. They later participated in attacks perpetrated by Hadad's terrorist organization. Also, in an Orly Airport attack, Palestinian terrorists selected 10 hostages from the group of innocent passengers, demanding and obtaining an escape plane. The government of Iraq gave the escape aircraft permission to land, and, after demonstratively arresting the terrorists, released them clandestinely and allowed them to join the camps of the PFLP in Lebanon.

Similarly, the five members of the JRA who participated in the raid of the U.S. Embassy at Kuala-Lumpur in August 1975 found refuge in Libya, together with five of their comrades who were released from prison in Japan as a result of the attack. Again, the six terrorists who carried out the attack on OPEC headquarters in Vienna in December 1975 were flown to Algeria; from there they continued on to Libya, where they were granted asylum. Finally, the assassins of Hans Martin Schleyer, the German industrialist, found refuge in Sabra, the Palestinian camp near Beirut, and in Iraq.[95]

ATTACKS BY PROXY

One pronounced feature of interregional terrorism is the frequent attacks by proxy carried out by one terrorist group in advancing the cause of other underground movements. This form of collaboration began as early as 1969.[96] On December 12 of that year, members of the Baader-Meinhoff group planted explosives in West Berlin at the El Al Airline office, American House, and at the U.S. Officers' Club.

Indeed, over the past 10 years, similar incidents have occurred. The following cases, selected at random, illustrate the nature of the threat.

A car of the Israeli meat company, Incade, was blown up in Ethiopia on April 29, 1970, by the Eritrean Liberation Front.

On March 25, 1971, members of the Movement of Youthward Brothers in War of the Palestinian People, a French pro-Arab group, threw stones and Molotov cocktails at the offices of the Bill Computer Company, a subsidiary of General Electric. In April of that year, five French citizens failed in their attempt to sabotage hotels in Israel. Questioning by the police led to the discovery of a network of 55 people, including Algerians, Palestinians, and French extremists. On May 23, 1971, the Israeli consul in Turkey, El-Rom, was assassinated by members of the Turkish Popular Liberation Army. Following the murder, Fatah expressed support for the Turkish extremist organizations, praised their antiregime activities, and emphasized its alliance with the Turkish fighters.

In another instance, three Japanese anarchists of the United Red Army were recruited to execute the Lod Airport operation on behalf of Palestinians on May 30, 1972, after they had been contacted several years earlier by PFLP's George Habbash. The Japanese trio was equipped with weapons provided by Italian terrorists in Rome. The latter sent them to Israel by Air France for an attack that brought death and injury to some 100 people, most of whom were Puerto Rican Christian pilgrims with no direct involvement in the Arab-Israeli conflict.

On June 3, 1972, an extremist Italian group bombed the offices of Honeywell, IBM, and Bank of America in Milan and a Honeywell factory in a Milan suburb. Leaflets found at the damaged sites referred to the "struggle of the Vietnamese people against American imperialism" and the victories "of the revolutionary and Communist army in Vietnam."

The overthrow of President Allende in Chile resulted in several attacks by proxy. On December 31, 1973, a leftist Italian group put explosives at three offices of ITT subsidiaries in Rome, causing heavy damage. Leaflets found in the areas stated that "ITT organized the coup in Chile and it is made up of Fascist and reactionary elements." Similarly, a French group called "We Must Do Something" claimed responsibility for the fire destruction of the Sonolar factory, a French ITT subsidiary, on March 1, 1974. It was a "welcome" for the newly arrived Chilean ambassador to France.

Several incidents related to various causes occurred in the following years. In January 1976, a San Francisco terrorist group planted a powerful bomb that heavily damaged a new financial-district skyscraper housing the Iranian consulate. The bomb exploded after a telephone warning to United Press International. The group said the bombing was carried out "in support of the Iranian people's struggle to rid themselves of the CIA-backed shah." The group proclaimed solidarity with revolutionary groups in Angola, Greece, Puerto Rico, and Iran as well as U.S. terrorist organizations. Two people who had been in an office on the fourteenth floor of the four-story Embarcader Center were slightly injured by flying glass from the blast, which caused $200,000 damage. On June 20, 1976, Germany's revolutionary Cells, operating on behalf of the PFLP, planted explosives at Frankfurt's AGREXCO offices. Bernard Hansuran, a German terrorist who planted a booby-trapped suitcase that exploded at Ben-Gurion Airport in May of 1976, worked on behalf of the PFLP. Two Dutch nationals, members of the Marxist-Leninist "Red Help" group, were dispatched in September of that year by the PFLP to study Air France's Bombay-Tel Aviv air route in preparation for a hijacking mission. Both were arrested and the terrorist plot was foiled.

On April 11, 1977, the Revolutionary Commandos of Solidarity, a Costa Rican group, exploded the offices of Pan Am and Henderson & Company, as well as a building housing the U.S. military mission in San Jose. The attack caused heavy damage but no injuries. Apparently, the bombing was a reprisal for the death of Carlos Aguerero Echeverria, a Costa Rican who was a leader of Nicaragua's FSLN. In May 1976, a Norwegian student was detained at Beirut airport en route to Frankfurt and Israel to carry out sabotage acts for the Popular Democratic Front for the Liberation of Palestine (PDFLP).

Finally, on January 19, 1978, a bomb exploded at a U.S.-owned Discount Bank in Paris. Pamphlets found in the area called for revenge for the October death of Andreas Baader, who had been held in a West German prison.

COORDINATED ATTACKS

Growing coordination in the planning and execution of attacks by terrorists groups is becoming apparent. Several examples will suffice.[97]

Black September terrorists who held several Western diplomats hostage in the Sudan in March 1973 issued an ultimatum that they would kill them within 24 hours unless members of the Baader-Meinhoff were released. The reason offered for this demand was that the German terrorists "supported the Palestinian cause."

Three Pakistanis, describing themselves as members of the Moslem International Guerrillas, a group known to be active in the Philippines and Indonesia, seized a Greek freighter in Karachi on February 2, 1974, and threatened to blow up the ship and kill its crew unless two Black September terrorists, who were sentenced to death for an attack on a crowd at Athens Airport that killed five people and wounded 53, were freed. Subsequently, the Arab guerrillas were deported from Greece to Libya and freedom.

On September 13, 1974, members of the Japanese Red Army attacked the French Embassy in The Hague and took hostage the ambassador and a dozen embassy personnel. The terrorists demanded the release of Suzuki Furuya, a member of their group who had been apprehended by French police at Orly Airport while carrying secret documents. Reportedly, Carlos and PFLP's Mukharbel did reconnaissance in The Hague prior to this raid. Several hours after the attack on the French Embassy began, Carlos was apparently involved in another operation linked to the Dutch incident. A hand grenade was thrown into "Le Drugstore" on Boulevard Saint Germail in Paris, killing two people and injuring 34. Telephone calls to news agencies indicated that the attack was in support of the Hague operation and that further violence should be expected. Subsequently, the Japanese terrorists in The Hague and their comrade in French hands were given "free passage" to the Middle East with a ransom of $300,000 paid by the Dutch government.

The most dramatic case is the October 1977 hijacking of a Lufthansa plane to Mogadishu by PFLP for the Baader-Meinhoff group to reinforce demands of the kidnappers of Hans Martin Schleyer, who was subsequently murdered. Interestingly, Japanese authorities believed that the Lufthansa incident and the JRA hijacking in Dacca a month earlier were carried out under a coordinated plan.

> . . . in both cases, the hijackers called themselves by numbers instead of names, and the plastic bombs used in both cases were of the same type. . . . The Japanese commandos forced all passengers to write their names and addresses and sent letters to them in May through July seeking their support. They also sent similar letters to Japanese imprisoned radicals. The hijackers in the Mogadishu incident also distributed envelopes among passengers and forced them to write their names and addresses on them. The German hijackers then told the passengers they would send letters to them, but the German commandos were later killed or arrested by the German authorities. . . . The Japanese and German hijackers treated the passengers in a similar manner. The hijackers collected passports, ID cards, and other personal belongings of the passengers, apparently to determine the order for killing them in case the hijackers' demands were not met.[98]

JOINT ATTACKS

A close examination of terrorist activities since 1970 reveals an increasing number of joint operations among different terrorist groups. In the first place, it is evident that some members of terrorist movements have joined the ranks of other groups and have "fought" alongside their "brethren." For instance, the Iranian revolutionary movement established a "Palestine Group" composed of 45 people and participated in operations against the "enemy" in Palestine. Also, Turkish and Japanese "volunteers" participated in Palestinian guerrilla operations during the Lebanese Civil War.[99]

Most joint terrorist attacks, however, have occurred outside the Middle East.[100] In September of 1970, an American, Patrick Joseph Arguello, head of a Nicaraguan underground organization, joined Palestinian Leila Khaled in an attempted hijacking of an El Al plane in London. On February 2, 1972, the Black September, with the participation of a Belgian teacher, Stefan van den Berrmatt, detonated gas works in Holland. In July of that year, a Japan Airline plane flying over the country was hijacked by the JRA and two Latin American terrorists carrying Peruvian passports. In the following month, the Black September and Italian extremists blew up oil tanks in Trieste.

On July 20, 1973, a Japanese jumbo jet was hijacked on a flight from Amsterdam to Tokyo by Arab and Japanese terrorists. Later, the plane was blown up at the Tripoli Airport in Libya. Another joint operation was carried out by the PFLP and the Japanese Red Army in Singapore on January 31, 1974. Four guerrillas seized a ferry in the harbor with five hostages aboard after making an unsuccessful attempt to blow up refineries of Royal Dutch Shell. The terrorists stated that their attack on the storage tanks was in support of the "Vietnam revolutionary people and for making a revolutionary situation after considering the situation of today's oil crisis." The Singapore government rejected the guerrillas' request for safe conduct to an Arab country. Meanwhile, PFLP terrorists in Kuwait took hostages at the Japanese Embassy there and threatened to kill them unless the demands of the guerrillas in Singapore were met. Subsequently, a Japan Airline plane took all the terrorists involved in both operations to safety in Aden.

The raid on the OPEC headquarters in Vienna in December 1975 was carried out by a combined squad of PFLP members, Germans, and Venezuelans. It was led by Carlos, who was accompanied by Gabriele Kroecher-Tiedman, a Baader-Meinhoff gang member released from jail in exchange for the release of a kidnapped West German politician.

Another example of this cooperation can be found in the hijacking of an Air France airliner to Uganda on June 27, 1976. Individuals belonging to several extremist underground organizations participated in that operation: the commander of the four-person terrorist squad that seized control of the aircraft after its take-off from Athens was a German, Ernst Wilfried Boese. An anarchist lawyer associated with Carlos and a member of the PFLP, after his defection from the Carlos network, Boese served two prison sentences, first in Paris and later in Germany, where he was in detention until 1975. A young German woman was also a member of the hijack squad.

When the plane reached Entebbe, the hijackers were joined by three other terrorists. One was Antonio Degas Bonia, a South American with an Ecuadoran passport, formerly head of the Carlos network in London. He took command of the operation from the moment the hijacked plane landed at Entebbe.

Finally, in April 1978, the Egyptian attorney general announced the exposure of an international network of terrorism in Egypt in which Palestinians and Swiss and Italian Red Brigade members worked together for Abu Nid'al, head of the pro-Iraqi Arab Liberation Front (this group was recently reported to have changed its name to the Palestine Liberation Front). This group allegedly was under "the control of an international network which operated throughout Europe and which extends its activities with the cooperation of radical subversive elements in the Arab World."[101] This group, apparently linked to previous terrorist attacks, seemed to be involved in a scheme aimed at carrying out a series of assassinations and acts of sabotage in Egypt in an effort to undermine the Camp David Middle East peace accords.

In spite of these and other instances of collaboration among terrorist groups, it would be a gross exaggeration to assert that most subnational movements belong to an international network and take orders from a single clandestine centralized body. Each group acts within very different traditions, and these differing traditions prevent a single transnational conspiracy from developing. However, widespread alliance to the lineage of revolutionary ideologists and strategists, as well as the sense of guerrillas' solidarity with other comrades waging an armed struggle for political and ideological ends, provides ample evidence of the existence of an expanding international violence zone. With the proliferation of modern weapons and further advances in communications, which would likely increase the level of collaboration among "have not" groups, the danger of terrorism will ultimately become unbearable.

Because of the factors that encourage terrorism, particularly its support by Communist and Third World countries and the existence of an international network of terrorism, the world can anticipate more explosions, hijackings, kidnappings, and assassination, possibly through the 1990s. Most liberal democracies favor control, at least in principle, but unless they can find ways to deal realistically with factors that promote terrorism, they will be hostages of global blackmailers forever.

In view of this probability, there is an immediate need for the business community to ponder the future with grave concern and to determine appropriate strategies to counter the terrorist threat to commerce, property, and profit.

NOTES

1. For recent studies on terrorism, see, for example, Yonah Alexander, ed., *International Terrorism: National, Regional and Global Perspectives* (New York: Praeger, 1976); Yonah Alexander and Seymour M. Finger, eds., *Terrorism: Interdisciplinary Perspectives* (New York and London: John Jay Press and McGraw-Hill, 1977); Yonah Alexander, David Carlton, and Paul Wilkinson, eds., *Terrorism: Theory and Practice* (Boulder: Westview Press, 1979); J. Boyer Bell, *Terror Out of Zion* (New York: St. Martin's Press, 1976), and *On Revolt* (Cambridge: Harvard University Press, 1976); David Carlton and Carlo Schaerf, eds., *International Terrorism and World Security* (London: Croom Helm, 1975); Richard Clutterbuck, *Kidnap and Ransom: The Response* (London and Boston: Faber and Faber, 1978); Ronald D. Crelinsten, Danielle Laberge-Altmejd, and Denis Szabo, eds., *Terrorism and Criminal Justice* (Lexington: Lexington Books, 1978); John D. Elliot and Leslie K. Gibson, eds., *Contemporary Terrorism: Selected Readings* (Gaithersburg, Md.: International Association of Chiefs of Police, 1978); Alona E. Evans and John F. Murphy, eds., *Legal Aspects of International Terrorism* (Lexington: Lexington Books, 1978); Richard W. Kobetz and H. H. Cooper, *Target Terrorism* (Gaithersburg, Md.: International Association of Chiefs of Police, 1978); Stefan T. Possony and Francis Bouchey, *International Terrorism – The Communist Connection* (Washington, D.C.: American Council for Freedom, 1978); Walter Laqueur, *Terrorism* (Boston: Little, Brown, 1977); Maurius H. Livingston, Lee Bruce Kress, and Marie G. Wanek, eds., *International Terrorism in the Contemporary World* (Westport:

Greenwood Press, 1978); *Terrorism: An International Journal* 1 (1977-78); Paul Wilkinson, *Political Terrorism* (London: Macmillan Press, 1974); and *Terrorism and the Liberal State* (New York: John Wiley, 1977).

2. See, for instance, Yonah Alexander, Marjorie Ann Browne, and Allen S. Nanes, eds., *Control of Terrorism: International Documents* (New York: Crane, Russak, 1979); and Robert H. Kupperman, *Facing Tomorrow's Terrorist Incident Today* (Washington, D.C.: Law Enforcement Assistance Administration, 1977).

3. "Terrorism and Business: Conference Report" (Washington, D.C.: Center for Strategic and International Studies Notes, July 1978).

4. For details, see Yonah Alexander and Herbert M. Levine, "Prepare for the Next Entebbe," *Chitty's Law Journal* 25 (1977): 240-42.

5. See, for example, National Foreign Assessment Center, *International Terrorism in 1977* (Washington, D.C.: Central Intelligence Agency, August, 1978); and *Executive Risk Assessment* 1 (November and December, 1978).

6. There are obviously terrorist groups that do not fit this classification. A case in point is Ananda Marg, an Indian religious terrorist group. It has an international membership with transnational support apparatus. It has conducted attacks on Indian diplomats on several continents.

7. Yonah Alexander, "The Various Ideologies and Forms of International Terrorism," unpublished report at the International Scientific Conference on Terrorism, Berlin, November 14-18, 1978.

8. See J. Bowyer Bell, *Transnational Terror* (Washington, D.C.: American Enterprise Institute, 1975). For a popular treatment, see Ovid Demaris, *Brothers in Blood: The International Terrorist Network* (New York: Charles Scribner, 1977).

9. The New York *Times*, January 4, 1974.

10. Alexander, "The Various Ideologies and Forms of International Terrorism."

11. Linkages between terrorist movements operating within one country also exist. For instance, the pro-Soviet Revolutionary Armed Forces of Columbia (FARC) and the pro-Castro National Liberation Army (ELN) have recently agreed on the urgent need for a coordinated plan of action and other strategic tactics in the country. Reported by Bogota Cadena Radical Super in Spanish, 1100 GMT, July 10, 1978.

12. The Monteneros profess allegiance to Peronist ideology of economic independence, social justice, and political sovereignty. For details, see, for example, Ernst Halperin, "Terrorism in Latin America," *Center for Strategic and International Studies Washington Papers* 4 (1976); "From Peron to Somoza," *The Washington Quarterly* 1 (Autumn 1978): 110-14; Rose E. Butler, "Terrorism in Latin America" in Alexander, *International Terrorism: National, Regional, and Global Perspectives*, pp. 46-61; Richard Gott, *Guerrilla Movements in Latin America* (London: Thomas Nelson, 1970); James Kohl and John Litt, *Urban Guerrilla Warfare in Latin America* (Cambridge: Massachusetts Institute of Technology Press, 1974).

13. *Granma*, December 5, 1970.

14. The Tupamaro of Uruguay never elaborated a detailed political and economic program; nevertheless, it is primarily concerned with armed struggle

against the system. For details, see Halperin, *Terrorism*; Butler, "Terrorism"; Kohl and Litt, *Urban Guerrilla Warfare*; Gott, *Guerrilla Movements*; and Robert Moss, "Urban Guerrillas in Uraguay," *Problems in Communism* 20 (September-October, 1971).

15. The Movement of the Revolutionary Left (MIR) in Chile includes Moscow-oriented Communists and Trotskyists. See Brian Crozier, ed., *Annual of Power and Conflict 1976-77* (London: Institute for the Study of Conflict, 1977), pp. 134-36.

16. The Argentinian People's Revolutionary Army was founded in 1970 at the Fifth Congress of the Trotskyite Workers' Revolutionary Party. It still remains a significant force in Argentine politics. See Crozier, *Annual*.

17. The National Liberation Army of Bolivia was originally set up by Che Guevara. See Crozier, *Annual*.

18. Lester A. Sobel, ed., *Political Terrorism* (New York: Facts on File, 1975), pp. 102-3.

19. Thomas P. Anderson, "The Ambiguities of Political Terrorism in Latin America," unpublished paper, February 1978.

20. The New York *Times*, October 19, 1976.

21. For a popular treatment, see Les Payne et al., *The Life and Death of the SLA* (New York: Ballantine, 1976).

22. See Sobel, *Political Terrorism*, pp. 137-42.

23. Ibid.

24. Statement by Lt. Thomas Lyons, a member of the Dade County Public Safety Dept., and Raul J. Diaz of the department's Organized Crime, Terrorist, and Security unit, before the U.S. Judiciary Committee's Subcommittee on Internal Security, May 1976. Quoted in Sobel, *Political Terrorism*, p. 141.

25. The New York *Times*, May 26, 1977.

26. The 23rd September Communist League had recently absorbed about a dozen guerrilla groups. For details, see Sobel, *Political Terrorism*, pp. 151-54.

27. The San Diego *Union*, September 7, 1978.

28. See J. Bowyer Bell, *The Secret Army: The IRA, 1916-74* (Cambridge: Massachusetts Institute of Technology Press, 1974); and Alan O'Day, "Northern Ireland, Terrorism and the British State," in Alexander, *Terrorism: Theory and Practice*, pp. 121-35.

29. The separatist ETA developed from a splinter of the Basque Nationalist Party and then itself split into Marxist and non-Marxist factions. For recent developments, see Sobel, *Political Terrorism*, pp. 240-46.

30. FLB is a Celtic group advocating separatist independence for Brittany. For a brief survey of terrorism in France, see Crozier, *Annual*, pp. 31-35.

31. For discussion of political violence in Britain 1971-77, see Richard Clutterbuck, *Britain in Agony* (London: Faber and Faber, 1978); and Gordon Carr, *The Angry Brigade* (London: Gollancz, 1975).

32. Sobel, *Political Terrorism*, pp. 240-46.

33. Reported by Dr. Hans Josef Horchem at a State Dept. Conference on International Terrorism, Washington, D.C., March 25-26, 1976.

34. Broadcast by Lisbon Domestic Service in Portuguese, 0800 GMT, December 15, 1978.

35. For details on these groups, see Jillian Becker, *Hitler's Children* (London: Panther, 1978); Richard Clutterbuck, *Guerrillas and Terrorists* (London: Faber and Faber, 1977); Albert Parry, *Terrorism from Robespierre to Arafat* (New York: Vanguard, 1976); Alexander, *International Terrorism: National, Regional and Global Perspectives*; and Laqueur, *Terrorism*.

36. The Palestinian movement represents the Palestinian guerrillas or the Palestine Liberation Organization (PLO). It serves as an umbrella organization for eight guerrilla groups, including small ones that oppose any negotiated settlement of the Middle East conflict. See David Pryce-Jones, *The Face of Defeat* (London: Weidenfeld and Nicolson, 1972); and A. W. Kawwali, *Palestine, A Modern History* (London: Croom Helm, 1978).

37. The PFLP crystalized under the leadership of Dr. George Habash in November 1967. This Marxist-Leninist group consists of from 1,000 to 1,500 members. It rejects a peaceful settlement in the Middle East. See The New York *Times*, February 21, 1978.

38. Wadi Haddad was the mastermind behind the most notorious international terrorist attacks during the past decade, including the OPEC raid in 1975 and the Entebbe operation in 1976. He died on March 28, 1978. Haddad was eulogized by George Habash who described him as one of the greatest fighters on behalf of the Arab cause.

39. These movements consist of Eritrean Liberation Front Revolutionary Council (ELF-RC) and the Popular Front for the Liberation of Eritrea (PFLE).

40. Broadcast in Arabic to the Arab world, 1800 GMT, July 1, 1978.

41. DFLP is a Marxist-Maoist group that split from PFLP in 1969. It is led by Nayef Hawatmeh, who is close to Syria. Membership is about 1,500 people. The New York *Times*, February 21, 1978.

42. FSLN is dedicated to the overthrow of the Samoza dictatorship in Nicaragua. For details, see Halperin, *Terrorism in Latin America*.

43. *Business Conflicts Report* (August 1978): 6.

44. Broadcast by Havana International Service in Spanish, February 5, 1978.

45. For recent activities of the Monteneros, see Halperin, *Terrorism in Latin America*; and Sobel, *Political Terrorism*, pp. 87-118.

46. Broadcast by "Voice of Palestine" (clandestine) in Arabic, June 21, 1978. This meeting was also cited in *Business Conflicts Report* (October 1978): 3.

47. *Berlinske Tidende* (Copenhagan), March 18, 1978.

48. *Al-Anwar* (Beirut), May 22, 1976.

49. *Al-Hakika* (Libya), June 16, 1972.

50. Funding was provided by the PFLP for the JRA operation in The Hague, September 13, 1974.

51. *The Times* (London), January 4, 1974.

52. Broadcast by Cairo Radio, December 25, 1969, BBC Monitoring Service.

53. Quoted by a high-ranking Libyan official of the Ministry of Foreign Affairs during an interview with the Bangkok *Post*, January 5, 1979.

54. The New York *Times*, May 23, 1976.

55. *Business Conflicts Report* (August 1978): 3, and *Near East Report* 23 (January 10, 1979).

56. Carlos gained attention as the "world's most wanted terrorist." A Venezuelan by birth, he joined the PFLP in 1970. For details, see Dennis Eisenberg and Eli Landau, *Carlos: Terror International* (London: Transworld, 1976).

57. *Newsweek*, June 25, 1975.

58. The Jerusalem *Post*, June 2, 1978.

59. Yonah Alexander, "Terrorism in the Middle East: A New Phase?" *The Washington Quarterly* (Autumn 1978): 116-17.

60. For details, see *Al-Gumhur al-Jadid* (Beirut), March 6, 1969; "Arab Terror in Europe," *Britain and Israel* 17 (October 1972); *JTA Daily News Bulletin*, March 29, 1977; Philadelphia *Inquirer*, April 10, 1977; and *The Guardian*, June 4, 1977.

61. *The Daily Telegraph*, September 4, 1970.

62. Alec Hartley, "PLO Arms Funded by Drug Smugglers," *The Guardian*, June 4, 1977.

63. For statistics and details, see "Executive Kidnapping – A Growing Threat," *Executive Risk Assessment* 1 (November, 1978).

64. The Philadelphia *Inquirer*, April 10, 1977.

65. *Al-Usbua al-Arabia* (Beirut), December 19, 1971.

66. *Al-Ahad* (Beirut), December 19, 1971.

67. Sobel, *Political Terrorism*, p. 102.

68. *Al-Usbua al-Arabia* (Beirut), December 19, 1971.

69. *Three Minutes at Lod* (Jerusalem: Israel Information Center, June 1972).

70. Broadcast by Tokyo Radio in English, 0313 GMT, July 12, 1978.

71. The New York *Times*, June 26, 1978.

72. *L'Europeo* (Milan), May 19, 1978.

73. *The Irish Times*, June 14, 1978.

74. The Jerusalem *Post*, June 2, 1978.

75. Andrew McKay, "Arab-U.S. Terror Link Admitted," New York *Post*, April 6, 1977.

76. See *Al-Jadid* (Beirut), May 15, 1969; *As-Safa* (Beirut), June 20, 1969; *Ad-Difa'a* (Amman), July 29, 1969; and Possony and Bouchey, *International Terrorism*.

77. Alexander, "Terrorism in the Middle East: A New Phase?" p. 17.

78. *Intersearch*, October 6, 1978.

79. The New York *Times*, May 23, 1976.

80. Ibid., December 14, 1973.

81. *The Times* (London), February 12, 1978; Chicago *Tribune*, February 23, 1978; *The Irish Times*, June 14, 1978.

82. *Business Conflicts Report* (October 1978): 3.

83. The Washington *Star*, April 21, 1978; *Time*, April 3, 1978; and *l'Europeo* (Milan), May 19, 1978.

84. Eisenberg and Landau, *Carlos*.

85. Sobel, *Political Terrorism*, p. 247.

86. *Intersearch*, October 6, 1978.

87. Sobel, *Political Terrorism*, p. 52.

88. FLUNA is composed of harkis (pro-French Algerians) and the Democratic National Council of the Armed Forces of the National's People's Army. These groups challenge the authority of the government of Algeria.

89. *El-Moudjahid* (Algiers), June 5, 1978.

90. Broadcast by Maputo Radio in Portuguese, 1400 GMT, March 31, 1978.

91. *Business Conflicts Report* (November 1978): 6.

92. *Near East Report* 23 (January 10, 1979).

93. *Al-Sabah* (Amman), October 27, 1974.

94. The Los Angeles *Times*, July 28, 1978.

95. Broadcast by Hamburg Radio, 1212 GMT, November 11, 1977; and *The Christian Science Monitor*, November 29, 1977.

96. For further details, see Charles A. Russell, "Transnational Terrorism," *Air University Review* (January-February, 1976): 26-35; and Demaris, *Brothers in Blood*.

97. Ibid.

98. Broadcast by Tokyo Radio in English, 0313 GMT, July 12, 1978.

99. *Al-Sha'ab* (Algeria), October 22, 1971; *Al-Usbue* (Beirut), May 31, 1973; and The Washington *Post* and *The Christian Science Monitor*, April 25, 1978.

100. For further details, see note 96.

101. Broadcast by Cairo Domestic Service in Arabic, 0525 GMT, April 23, 1978.

4
Supply Security of Coal and Uranium

James Cobbe

Energy is vital to modern economic life. Coal and uranium, the raw materials for nuclear energy, remain important sources of energy, especially for the manufacturing industry, throughout the industrialized world. In 1977 in the International Energy Agency (IEA) region (that is, the Organization for Economic Co-operation and Development less France, Finland, Iceland, and Portugal), solid fuels accounted for 28 percent of domestic energy production and nuclear energy for 5 percent; imports of solid fuels were 16 percent of domestic production thereof; solid fuels and nuclear energy combined amounted to 48 percent of energy used for electricity generation; and industry obtained 37 percent of its energy requirements from solid fuels and electricity. These are averages, and the numbers vary markedly from country to country as a result of differences in domestic energy resources and past policies.

The IEA's projection of how these figures will change by 1985, although based on data collected in 1978 before the recent round of

I wish to acknowledge the help of my research assistant, David Green, and the encouragement of Yonah Alexander, who showed more confidence than I that I could contribute something worthwhile on this topic. An earlier and shorter version of this chapter was presented at the Center for Strategic and International Studies conference on "Political Terrorism and Energy: The Threat and Response," Georgetown University, Washington, D.C., May 1980.

oil price increases and therefore understated, suggests that this dependence on coal and uranium will increase. The projected figures for 1985: solid fuels accounting for 30 percent of domestic energy production and nuclear for 12 percent; imports of solid fuels to be 17 percent of domestic production thereof; solid fuels plus nuclear representing 60 percent of energy used for electricity production; and industry obtaining 38 percent of its energy requirements from solid fuels and electricity.[1] Following Three Mile Island and other developments with respect to nuclear energy since 1978, more recent projections suggest that the shift to dependence on uranium may be slower, but that that to coal may be faster, than these numbers suggest.[2]

While all projections of future consumption of coal and uranium are somewhat speculative, Table 4.1 gives two alternative projections of OECD steam coal (that is, coal for energy use, distinguishing steam coal from metallurgical coal used for steel production), taken from the 1980 World Coal Study. Case A assumes 1.75 percent per annum growth in energy use, Case B 2.5 percent per annum. Even in the less rapid growth forecast, Case A, production of coal, dependence on coal, and international trade in coal all rise comparatively rapidly. The major exporters will probably be the United States, Australia, South Africa, and Canada, with smaller quantities of exports from China, India, Poland, and possibly such countries as Tanzania, Colombia, and Botswana.

Thus coal and uranium are important energy sources for the industrialized countries, especially for their manufacturing sectors (transport is overwhelmingly dependent on oil, and residential and commercial sectors also use oil and gas for more than 70 percent of their energy requirements). This dependence is expected to increase during the next decade in response to the major increase in the relative price of oil and the uncertainties surrounding oil's security of supply. It is of some importance, therefore, to investigate the vulnerability of coal and uranium supplies to politically inspired disruption.

In doing this, we need first to note that, at least with respect to coal, the United States and Canada are in a somewhat different position from western Europe and Japan. North America is a large exporter of coal, whereas Japan and western Europe are importers. This is relevant since coal moving in international trade may be more vulnerable to terrorist disruption than purely domestic coal.

TABLE 4.1
Projected Coal Requirements in OECD* Countries
(million tonnes of coal equivalent)

		2000		
Country	1977 Total Coal	Steam Coal Case A	Steam Coal Case B	Total Coal Case B
Canada	18.0	67.0	106.0	121.0
United States	432.0	975.0	1,590.0	1,700.0
Denmark	4.6	9.4	20.9	20.9
Finland	3.5	3.0	12.0	13.0
France	31.0	31.0	105.0	125.0
West Germany	79.0	125.0	153.0	175.0
Italy	2.4	19.5	48.5	60.5
Holland	1.5	20.0	34.0	38.0
Sweden	0.3	14.3	23.1	26.0
United Kingdom	91.0	117.0	158.0	179.0
Other Western Europe	33.0	96.0	121.0	175.0
Japan	10.0	64.0	132.0	224.0
Australia	29.7	124.0	149.0	166.0
Total OECD*	740.0	1,670.0	2,650.0	3,025.0

*Organization for Economic Co-operation and Development.

Source: World Coal (WOCOL), World Coal Study, as reported in *The Economist*, May 17, 1980, p. 89.

In order to assess the future supply security of coal and uranium, the hard-mineral energy sources, it is necessary first to understand some of the basic technical aspects of the chain of events from minerals in the ground to usable energy, to identify possible vulnerable points in the chains of supply.

MINING

Three general types of mining are usually distinguished: deep or underground mining, opencast or surface mining, and unconventional mining.

Underground mines involve systems of shafts and galleries, by means of which deposits deep below the surface are worked. Deep deposits are hard to locate, the capital cost of underground mines is high, and deep mines cannot operate without miners. Often workers prepared to go underground are in inelastic supply. An underground mine is vulnerable to output disruption in many ways. Apart from accidents and labor problems, underground mines are also obviously vulnerable to sabotage, although actual underground sabotage requires action by mine employees and could well be very hazardous for the saboteur and his colleagues. However, such surface installations as winding gear, ventilation equipment, and pumps also must work for the mine to work.

Opencast or surface mining is quite different. It is used when the deposit is sufficiently close to the surface to be extracted directly from above, without benefit of shafts. In coal mining, two subtypes of opencast mining are distinguished, associated with different types of deposit. Where coal, usually soft coal, is found in thick seams covered by an overburden of soil, sand, and friable rock, a form of direct attack is used, employing "bucket-wheel" machines. This type of mining is quite common in Europe. When the overburden is more difficult, it may have to be fractured by explosives, and the usual technique is "strip mining," using huge machines known as "walking dragline scrapers." These machines are highly specialized, often designed and built for the coalfield in question, and very expensive. Often only one is employed per coalfield, and there is no backup or standby because of the cost. In these circumstances, the entire opencast operation depends on the uninterrupted functioning of this single machine – which could, of course, be sabotaged.[3]

Unconventional mining refers to any method of getting out of the ground what is wanted, other than the standard deep or opencast methods. In general, unconventional techniques are designed for use on deep deposits, particularly those that are slanted or for other geological reasons hard to exploit, but in such a way as to avoid the necessity of physical removal of the mineral via shafts and galleries. An unconventional method of obtaining uranium has been expanding rapidly recently in the United States: in situ leaching. Chemicals that combine with uranium are applied to the site of the deposit; collected after they have leached through the ore, surrounding rock, and earth; and then processed to remove the uranium they have picked up. About 8 percent of U.S. uranium production was from in situ recovery methods in 1977. One advantage of this method is that it makes economically feasible the exploitation of grades of ore much lower than can be worked by conventional techniques – as low as 0.05 percent uranium according to some sources. The technique does, however, raise difficulties with respect to environmental protection. Most uranium mined in the United States is still produced by opencast methods, although underground mining is also used to some extent.[4]

As yet, unconventional methods of exploiting coal deposits are in the experimental stage. The most promising line of attack is techniques of in situ gasification. The objective is to extract at least some of the energy content of the coal deposit, without actually removing the coal. One way in which this might be done involves partial combustion of the coal in the ground and the collection of gas produced, which could then be burnt. This technique is likely to be extremely inefficient in terms of the proportion of the potential energy content of the coal recovered, but it might be economically competitive as a way to exploit deep deposits, expensive to extract by conventional techniques, with appropriate geological and locational characteristics.

POSTMINING PROCESSES

Energy is not immediately usefully available when either coal or uranium ore has been removed from the ground, although the type and range of further processes required differ markedly between coal and uranium. With coal, the two major processes required are normally, first, cleaning and sorting/grading (which in some cases may result in only half as great a tonnage of saleable steam coal as the tonnage of raw coal initially mined) and, second, transport. Transport is only necessary when the coal is to be used as a prime source of energy not at the mine, and it adds substantially to cost. Some transport techniques, such as slurry pipelines (in which pulverized coal is mixed with water to produce a slurry that can be pumped through pipelines), may require further processing both before and after transport. Also, some coal for certain purposes, such as "smokeless solid fuels" for domestic or industrial use, is processed into uniform briquets or pellets before use. Production costs for coal vary a great deal from country to country and from region to region within countries, reflecting differences in quality and type of deposit and differences in input costs (labor costs in particular). For low-cost producers, such as Australia, South Africa, the United States, and

India, the production cost at the mine may be as low as from $10 to $20 per metric tonne. Transport costs to distant importing regions may more than double this cost. In the Australian case, the 1980 World Coal Study estimated that a mine cost of from $12 to $20 per tonne translates to a cost, insurance, and freight (CIF) landed price in Rotterdam of from $32 to $43 per tonne. However, despite the expense of transporting coal over long distances, Europe and Japan are likely to greatly increase their imports in the future. Even after transport costs are added, the cost advantage of the deposits in the exporting countries over domestic deposits is great enough that imported coal is usually much cheaper than domestically produced coal. In the first half of 1979, the average production cost of hard coal in the European Community was $104 per tonne of oil equivalent, but the average price for steam coal imported into the European Community in the second quarter of 1979 was only $51 per tonne of oil equivalent, with a low price of $41 for some South African coal.[5] As shall be argued, coal supplies are probably most vulnerable to terrorist interruption in the transport stages, particularly at transfer points such as ports.

Energy derived from coal can be divided into three types. First and most important is electricity generated from conventional thermal power stations. More steam coal is used to generate electricity than is used for all other purposes put together, many times over. Second, coal is burnt directly to produce heat energy or steam power for industrial purposes. This use has been declining in recent decades, during which oil and natural gas were cheaper sources of heat, but it is now growing again in most industrial countries. It already accounts for about 9 percent of total OECD coal use and is likely to grow from 5 to 7 percent a year for the rest of the century. Especially fast growth is expected in energy-intensive industries such as cement production, chemicals, paper making, and oil refining. Since it has not usually been the practice to design plants that can be switched quickly from burning coal to burning oil or gas, this tendency may increase the vulnerability of industrial production to interruptions in coal supply. On the other hand, it is usually much quicker, easier, and cheaper to switch from coal to oil or gas than from oil or gas to coal, and the stocks of coal held at plants are traditionally often larger than their stocks of oil or gas, so that overall coal-fired industries may be much less vulnerable to fuel supply interruptions than oil- or gas-fired industries. (Stocks of oil and gas in the supply chain, however, are usually larger than total stocks of coal, as opposed to those at plants.)

The third use of coal for energy purposes involves the production of liquid or gaseous fuels from coal. Traditional "town gas" produced from coal, widely used in Europe until the 1950s, was very costly compared with natural gas and has virtually disappeared. Much research is being done on less costly coal gasification, and the production of liquid fuels from coal is practiced on a commercial scale in South Africa and is the focus of considerable research and development in the United States and elsewhere. It appears extremely likely that commercially feasible coal liquification or gasification processes will involve large-scale, complex, capital-intensive plants, which are likely to be vulnerable to determined terrorist attack even under security-conscious conditions. This is illustrated by the attacks on the Sasol I and II plants at Sasolburg and Secunda in South Africa in May 1980 by the African National Congress (ANC) guerrillas, in which Sasol I was extensively damaged. Oil or gas from coal plants is liable to be vulnerable to terrorist attacks, especially via rockets, under almost any circumstances, because of the presence of large quantities of inflammable and explosive substances and the relative fragility of the processing plant. Coal liquification and gasification plants are comparable to oil refineries and storage depots in terms of vulnerability to terrorist attacks; hence, programs for increased coal liquification and gasification reduce supply insecurity only partially, not wholly.

In the case of uranium, the fuel cycle from ore in the ground to usable energy is considerably more complex than with coal. There are six steps between ore in the ground and fuel ready to be used in a nuclear reactor. This first is mining, already described. Uranium ores contain little uranium; 4.0 percent is a very high grade, and 0.1 percent is not unusual. The average grade of ore mined by conventional techniques in the United States is around 0.15 percent uranium.[6] The next step is milling, a process in which the ore is crushed and then chemically treated to produce a mixture of substances rich in uranium oxides, usually known as "yellowcake" as a result of its color when pure and calcined. Mills are large, capital-intensive plants with long lead times from planning to operation – estimated in 1975 at from three to eight years.[7] In the United States, mill capacity is the binding constraint on yellowcake production. Mill development has been slowed in some places, including some in the United States, by environmental problems, particularly waste disposal (mills produce large quantities of "tailings" or processed ore that are normally still quite radioactive). The milling stage can be bypassed by in situ recovery methods, and this is one reason for the increasing use of such methods.

Naturally occurring uranium is only 0.7 percent U-235, the fissile isotope. The proportion of U-235 in uranium for use in reactors must be raised to around 3 percent (weapons-grade uranium must have 90 percent or more U-235). This is known as enrichment. However, uranium oxide cannot be enriched directly. First, it must be converted to uranium hexafluoride because enrichment processes all operate by exploiting the fact that the fissile U-235 has lighter atoms than the nonfissile U-238. This fact can only be used to advantage, however, if the uranium is in a compound in a gaseous state. Uranium hexafluoride, although a solid at room temperature, becomes a gas at temperatures that are sufficiently low to allow the enrichment process to be practical. There are only two conversion plants in the United States: an Allied Chemical plant in Illinois and a Kerr-McGee one in Oklahoma. Other conversion plants exist in Canada, England, and other European countries, and Australia is considering building conversion capacity to enable it to export its uranium in a more processed form.

The traditional enrichment process involves gaseous diffusion, based on the principle that the lighter molecules containing U-235 will pass through semipermeable membranes somewhat faster than the heavier molecules containing U-238. Gaseous diffusion was originally devised to produce weapons-grade material, and the plants are still generally owned by governments. In the United States there are three federal government controlled plants; France, South Africa, and the United Kingdom also have plants, but the United States, as late as 1976, probably controlled 95 percent or more of enrichment capacity outside the Soviet Union and China.[8] Gaseous diffusion is difficult because of the highly corrosive and toxic nature of uranium hexafluoride, is energy-intensive, and is very expensive. The endproduct for energy purposes is the enriched uranium hexafluoride, containing 3 percent U-235. A byproduct is depleted uranium, also known as the "tails." This still contains some U-235, typically from 0.2 to 0.3 percent, but it is currently useless as an energy source (at some point in the future it may be possible to convert the U-238 in depleted uranium into plutonium fuel in breeder reactors).

An alternative and potentially less costly approach to enrichment would be based on the centrifuge principle. Britain, Germany, and the Netherlands are jointly building a centrifuge-based plant, the United States government is scheduled to begin operation of one in 1986, and South Africa is also constructing one. Centrifuge methods, if successful, may cut the cost of enrichment by as much as 90 percent.

After enrichment, the uranium hexafluoride must be reconverted to more stable uranium oxide. The uranium oxide is then fabricated into fuel rods, generally consisting of dense pellets packed into thin-walled metal containers of various shapes. Reconversion and fabrication are generally performed at the same facility and involve fairly complex chemical and mechanical processes that require considerable care because of the radioactivity of the enriched uranium and the chemical properties of uranium hexafluoride. Seven commercial fuel reconversion and fabrication plants currently operate in the United States, with others overseas. The final product is the enriched uranium fuel rod, which, when loaded into a reactor, provides the source of energy for nuclear-generated electricity.

SOURCES OF VULNERABILITY: COAL

At first examination, coal seems a relatively secure source of energy from the point of view of terrorist disruption of supply. This impression is, however only partially correct. Coal supplies can be disrupted at two stages and in a variety of ways. Production at source can be disrupted, or transport can be disrupted. Coal transport is uniquely vulnerable because of the great weight and bulk of coal relative to energy content compared with other energy sources and because of the highly specialized transport facilities frequently used for coal nowadays.

Overall, disruption at source is not a very important risk with respect to coal supply since, in virtually all countries, coal comes from diversified sources, and it would be very remarkable if all sources were disrupted simultaneously. In this regard, it is interesting to note that the preferences of importing countries for sources of imported coal in the future, as revealed in the 1980 World Coal

Study, reflect a definite desire to continue a diversity of import sources in all cases.

Nevertheless, modern individual coalfields can be sufficiently large to be disruptive to supply conditions, at least locally, should one or a few of them stop production, and to cause at least short-term shortage conditions. It is also possible for the output of all the fields within a major exporting country to cease production, and this could be very disruptive to the international market and to those areas, notably Japan, east Asia, and OECD Europe, that are heavy importers. As noted, however, the five countries that are the current major exporters and that are anticipated to continue to supply the bulk of world exports are the United States, Australia, South Africa, Canada, and Poland. It is scarcely plausible that terrorist-related or politically inspired disruption could cut off exports from the United States, Australia, or Canada. For South Africa and possibly Poland, however, there is some risk.

How might terrorist activity disrupt coal production? Basically, there would seem to be two plausible approaches. One is sabotage, directly incapacitating key parts of the capital equipment or infrastructure of the mine. The other is more indirect, working somehow through the labor force. In general terms, the discussion that follows is not specific to coal, but applies generally to the production of any hard mineral, including uranium.

All large-scale mining is capital intensive; the capital equipment must be in operating condition for the mine to operate. The technical characteristics of mines often mean considerable lumpiness in parts of the capital equipment – a single walking-dragline scraper per open-pit operation, one winding gear per deep shaft, and so on. In other words, there is often at least one point in the array of capital equipment at which there is little or no redundancy. Put this piece of machinery out of action, and the mine stops production.

Fortunately, the paradox here is that the very vulnerability caused by lack of redundancy makes the risk from sabotage, in a sense, small. All machinery breaks down from time to time, so there is the expectation of the need to perform repairs and often there exists the capacity to do them quickly. Also, the fact that most coal-producing countries possess many mines implies that replacement machines can often be obtained and installed relatively quickly. So terrorist activity aimed at stopping coal production via sabotage is a strategy likely to produce only temporary and short-lived disruption of supply. The only exception to this is major underground sabotage of deep mines. In principle, terrorists could sabotage shafts or galleries in a major way, which could shut down an underground mine for months. However, performing such sabotage — which most likely would require a fairly large underground explosion or fire to be effective — would be both difficult and dangerous. It would almost certainly require the cooperation of, or participation in the actual terrorist act by, mine personnel, who would be putting themselves and their colleagues at considerable risk. Although possible, such sabotage seems unlikely, and its risk can probably be reduced by appropriate personnel procedures and normal standards of safety discipline underground.

The more indirect approach by which terrorism could disrupt coal supply would be through the labor force. Just as the mines cannot produce without their machines, neither can they produce without workers. Workers may withdraw their labor for two types of reasons. The first possibility is politically motivated strikes or their equivalent. Such strikes might be encouraged or fomented by terrorist-related groups, although they hardly represent terrorist acts as such. Labor problems are potentially most serious in deep mines since the skills and attitudes required of underground workers tend to be more specialized and scarcer than those needed to work surface mines. Nevertheless, labor problems are possible even in surface mines, and it is worth noting that since the mid 1970s in new opencast coal mines in South Africa (from which most of South Africa's coal exports come) all drivers of earth-moving equipment are Africans.[9] South Africa must be considered a somewhat insecure source of supply, since labor problems could easily disrupt production. However, even in that case, it would be unlikely for all mines to be affected simultaneously. Similarly, labor problems could disrupt Polish output for politically inspired reasons involving domestic conflicts. However, the link to terrorism as normally understood is tenuous at best.

The second way in which terrorism can affect labor requirements of mines is by intimidation, which is much more clearly a terrorist type of activity. It is conceivable that terrorist intimidation could disrupt labor supply to a coal mine in a country such as South Africa. However, it seems somewhat unlikely. Much more at risk are uranium mines in developing countries that rely on expatriate skilled labor, a point to which this chapter shall return.

Hence it seems reasonable to assume that production of coal is relatively immune to terrorist disruption. Countries, such as the United States, that are self-sufficient in steam coal or are net exporters face no serious risk from terrorism to the output of coal, since at worst terrorism could only hope to temporarily close a few mines. Countries, such as Japan and those of western Europe, that are partially dependent on coal imported from countries where there is more risk of widespread labor unrest of a political nature, such as South Africa and Poland, face a somewhat greater risk, but still very minor compared with other potential risks. This risk is well handled by geographical diversity in sources of supply of imports, including large proportions from relatively secure sources such as the United States, Canada, and Australia, and this policy is already followed by most importers.

Coal's greatest vulnerability seems to lie in transportation, and the most vulnerable coal seems to be that which moves by sea between countries since this involves more transfer points, which tend to be particularly vulnerable. As already noted, coal is heavy and bulky for its energy content. Inland, substantial quantities of coal rarely move by road; instead, coal is usually transported in "unit-trains" or by slurry pipeline. Both rail- and pipelines are to some extent vulnerable to sabotage by terrorists. Pipelines, however, are mainly vulnerable at pumping stations since the pipelines are usually buried. However, the disruption caused by such sabotage could be expected normally to be only local and temporary. Transportation of coal is perhaps more vulnerable at transhipment points between mine and transport mode, between transport modes, or at unloading points at power stations. This is because the equipment for loading, unloading, and transhipping coal in large quantities is complex and the process is usually highly mechanized. Sabotage at these points could conceivably cause somewhat longer-lived difficulties, but they would normally be only local and less serious if the main supply disruption were to only some power stations and an interconnected electricity grid permitted the importation of electric power to the affected area.

In summary, then, it is possible to identify various points at which coal supply could be vulnerable to terrorist attack, mainly in the form of sabotage. However, given the nature of coal supply (generally from many mines and/or several overseas sources) and use (mostly in electricity generation in many power stations) and the strong probability that terrorist disruption would only be short-lived, serious economic or social dislocation from terrorism aimed at coal supply seems unlikely. It would require coordinated sabotage at many points almost simultaneously, and even then the effects would probably not last long. Accordingly, on the assumption that terrorists are rational in some sense about their choice of action, it would seem likely that terrorist attacks on coal supply, except in special situations such as South Africa, are unlikely except as propaganda-generating actions, quite possibly of local concern only.

SOURCES OF VULNERABILITY: URANIUM

Although both coal and uranium can be described as hard-mineral energy sources, there are very considerable differences between them with respect to vulnerability to terrorist attack. These differences stem from four sources. First, the geographic pattern of production of uranium differs substantially from that for coal, with significant quantities of uranium mined in skill-scarce, less developed countries by foreign mining companies using foreign skilled labor. Second, uranium requires much more processing in several stages, between the mine and the fuel ready to go into the reactor. Third, uranium, unlike coal, is radioactive. Last, there is a tremendous difference between coal and uranium in the bulk and weight/energy content relationship.

In principle, the United States could be, and until recently was, self-sufficient in uranium. For commercial reasons, connected to relative cost conditions, price conditions in world markets, and the supply and demand situation, the United States has been a net importer of uranium since the mid 1970s, and this is likely to continue. Japan has essentially no domestic uranium resources, and the only significant deposits in Europe are in France (and they are insufficient for domestic needs).

Apart from Canada, South Africa is the largest exporter, followed by Niger, Gabon, and Namibia. In 1979, these four African countries produced some 13,800 tonnes of uranium, about 35 percent of market-economy world production. Production from these sources is projected to double by 1990, and active exploration or early development of identified deposits is also occurring in Botswana, the Central African Republic, Mauritania, Togo, and Zambia.[10] Frankly, none of these African countries can be regarded as particularly secure sources of supply.

Particularly disturbing is that uranium in low-income African countries is produced by foreign companies that mainly employ expatriate skilled labor and local unskilled labor. Potentially, such mines are vulnerable to disruption in a variety of ways not associated with coal mines in countries such as Australia.

Mine labor forces in developing countries typically consist of two components: a large, semiskilled or relatively unskilled, local contingent and a smaller, highly skilled, expatriate component. Typically, neither component can be quickly replaced. Relations between mining companies and their labor forces are of obvious importance from the point of view of continuous production. With respect to local labor, there are two possible sources of disruption to production. One is normal, wage or working-conditions related, industrial action. Such disruptions are typically short-lived in developing countries since it is difficult for either side or the government to sustain prolonged strikes. Nevertheless, discontented labor forces obviously tend to increase costs and may, in one way or another, increase the insecurity of supply. Disaffected workers are also more likely to connive, actively or passively, with politically motivated sabotage or other disruptive action. Experience in South African gold and coal mines also shows that, even in extremely authoritarian and "controlled" situations, mine workers who decide to turn on their employers can do a great deal of physical and financial damage in a short time. Restoring order can be very difficult — in some cases in South Africa, it involved considerable loss of life — and the intangible damage to worker morale and productivity can be serious and long-lived. Few governments outside South Africa would be willing to use the extreme measures used there to control disturbances by mine workers, so that in other places the consequences of permitting labor relations to deteriorate that far could be more serious to production.

The more directly political causes of disruption are threefold. First, local labor forces might disrupt production for political reasons through politically motivated strikes. This might seem unlikely for the very reasons that prolonged industrial-relations strikes seem unlikely: typically the strikers would not have the resources to sustain a prolonged period without income from wages. Although this is true, one should not discount the possiblity of events getting out of control, with an event intended originally as a symbolic demonstration of workers' political discontents resulting in violence and sabotage with far-reaching effects. One could conceive of such a scenario obtaining its initial impetus either from domestic political concerns or — and this is where the terrorism aspect is more pertinent — as a result of international connections, for example, as an expression of displeasure at the mining company's links with the West or South Africa.

Second, in many cases in Africa, mine production is considerably dependent on expatriate skilled workers. Nowadays, these workers tend to be hard to recruit and are sensitive to local conditions. Terrorism could be directed at such workers, with either the intention of obtaining publicity or of intimidating them and driving them away, thereby disrupting production and damaging the mining company and/or the local host government. One could argue that situations like these two alternatives have happened already in Chad and Shaba province of Zaire, respectively. Worker problems are not very closely connected with the general international situation, but are an outgrowth of local dissension and political instability within the country concerned. There is not much firms or Western governments can explicitly do about these problems. It is not possible to wholly ensure the physical safety of expatriate workers, and there are frequently severe negative consequences of attempts to improve physical security by isolation, compounds, and so on, even if that route is acceptable to host governments.

Last in this connection, general political instability in a host country may disrupt production via general disruption, for instance, of transport routes, supplies of inputs, and so on. Unfortunately, this has to be recognized as a real possibility in virtually all developing countries. If something approaching a low-level civil war breaks out in the host country, mining output will be at risk — because transport of inputs and outputs will be insecure, because local labor will be discontented and may break down into hostile factions, and because foreign skilled labor will be more difficult to recruit and retain.

After mining, uranium has to be milled, concentrated into yellowcake, converted, enriched, reconverted, and fabricated before it is ready to be used as fuel in a reactor. These processes all represent additional potential points of vulnerability, all enhanced by uranium's radioactivity. The radioactive nature of uranium, particularly after enrichment but even in yellowcake form, raises the possibility of environmental contamination following terrorist attack and, hence, of difficulties with public opinion and concern, which may cause delay and difficulty in getting damaged facilities back on stream.

For standard bulk-reduction reasons, milling is normally carried out at or close to the mine. Milling involves large-scale, highly specialized capital equipment, and, as noted, it takes a long time to get a mill from the planning stage into production. Successful sabotage of a mill would, therefore, quite probably reduce supply for some time, particularly since milling capacity has tended to be the binding constraint on production in recent years.

Conversion plants are also highly specialized, and there are very few of them in existence. There is no readily available information on how quickly conversion plants can be constructed, but they too appear to be vulnerable links in the chain. Enrichment is government-controlled in all countries and is subject to fairly tight security. Nevertheless, there are very few plants and, because of both their great complexity and specialization and the highly corrosive and toxic nature of uranium hexafluoride in its gaseous state, enrichment facilities must be considered vulnerable to terrorists with access to, say, rockets or mortars.

At the reconversion stage, there are rather more plants (seven in the United States as opposed to three enrichment facilities and two conversion plants), somewhat reducing vulnerability. On the other hand, at this stage the uranium is enriched, making the radioactivity aspect more crucial.

Last, there is the transport question. The value to bulk ratio of uranium, after milling and concentration, is high. The tonnages involved are small; hence supplies are not subject to disruption from terrorist attacks on transport facilities in the same way as coal or oil. In fact, yellowcake at times has been quite routinely transported by air between Africa and Europe.[11] Unfortunately, the radioactivity issue complicates matters. Uranium has to be moved around — mine to mill, mill to conversion plant, conversion plant to enrichment facility, enrichment facility to reconversion and fabrication plant, and then to power plants — and the public in many industrialized countries, particularly the United States, has shown itself very sensitive to risks of radioactive contamination of the environment. A terrorist group seeking publicity, rather than trying to inflict serious economic damage, might well be tempted to hijack a cargo of uranium in transit and then threaten, or execute, a dispersion of the cargo in a population center. This might well cause serious local dislocation from public panic and would almost certainly be a well-publicized media event. The possibility suggests that the security of uranium shipments deserves attention.

However, as in the case of coal, it seems unlikely that terrorist attacks on uranium supply could produce serious economic dislocation. Given the nature of nuclear power generation, even successful, coordinated, widespread attacks on uranium supply, which could conceivably reduce supply by a significant proportion for several years, would only slowly work through into a reduction in electricity generated from uranium. In most nuclear power reactors, from one-quarter to one-third of the fuel rods are replaced annually. Hence a physical shortage of new uranium for new fuel rods would only slowly reduce the capacity to generate electricity from nuclear reactors, and one would anticipate that alternative (albeit probably more costly) sources of electricity could be substituted for nuclear, given the lead times involved.

Probably more serious are the possible indirect effects of successful terrorist attacks on the uranium supply chain. If such attacks resulted in the release of radioactive materials or the misappropriation of enriched uranium (even if not nearly of weapons grade), repercussions on public opinion and on the legislative and regulatory environment for the nuclear power industry and the uranium supply chain itself would follow. This could raise the cost of nuclear power and slow its development, possibly with wider implications for economic conditions if other sources of energy were disrupted, increased in cost, or uncertain in supply.

PRECAUTIONARY MEASURES

Terrorists do not necessarily want to inflict serious economic damage. Depending on the nature of the terrorist group and its aims, it may be quite content with a substantively symbolic attack that results in a spectacular propaganda success. Because of this, there is little reason for business or government to take much solace from the conclusion that terrorist attack does not appear to represent a serious threat to energy supplies in the form of coal and uranium. This is particularly true for business. Conceivably, a terrorist group with no interest in energy or the economic consequences could carry out a sabotage act to make a point about a related concern. For example, groups disapproving of the use of water for a slurry pipeline might sabotage the pipeline, causing serious loss to the coal mines, pipeline companies, and utilities burning the coal. Such possibilities, whether remote or not, suggest that some attention to precautionary measures would be wise throughout the coal and uranium industries. Because of the radioactivity issue and its potential for propaganda purposes, this is especially true of the uranium supply industry.

In general terms, the recommended precautionary measures amount to little more than intelligently applied common sense. For the energy companies themselves, there are four major elements: intelligence, physical security, personnel policies, and contingency planning. Intelligence means, in this context, less romantic undercover work than simply paying intelligent and informed attention to the political climate and conditions in every locality where a potentially vulnerable facility is located. The intention is to possess an early-warning capability for possible problems, which may then be countered in advance either by the public relations function of the firm, by actual changes in firm policy, or by enhanced physical security.

Absolute physical security is, in most situations, an impossibility, a chimera that should not be pursued. The objective should be to raise the cost of successful attacks, to avoid inviting attack by the complete absence of protection, and to know how to increase physical security quickly if it seems appropriate. Similarly, personnel policies are worth some attention since it is clearly undesirable to employ potential terrorists or saboteurs. Within the United States, it may be difficult to do much about this without infringing upon employees' civil rights, but in most cases the risk is probably minor. Personnel policies, viewed more broadly to include labor relations generally, are probably much more important for mining companies overseas, especially in developing countries.

Last, there is contingency planning, with three necessary components. The first is with respect to enhanced physical security to counter a perceived threat of terrorist action. Second, there is planning for how to deal with an actual attack in terms of restoring the flow of output. Third and of most importance to the uranium industry, there is planning of how to handle the public relations aspects of a terrorist attack.

For energy users, rather than producers, precautionary measures are very limited. There are really only three options. One is stockpiling — keeping on hand sufficient coal or uranium to last for the duration of the disruption considered sufficiently probable. For coal, this may be feasible at reasonable cost; for uranium, it is less likely to be. Second is diversification of supply. This is obvious, often overlooked, and may raise costs. Last, there is contingency planning — where could we get alternative supplies if normal supplies were cut off?

Finally, for governments, many of the same measures apply as for energy users, with one addition. For countries that import coal or uranium, a diversity of suppliers with no one supplier dominant obviously reduces risk. Similarly, stockpiling buys insurance, though at a cost, as do some contingency planning and investments (for example, good interconnections in electricity supply, a diversity of prime energy sources used in electricity generation, furnaces that can burn a variety of fuels, and so on). Law and regulation can also be used to encourage or enforce such measures as well as physical security measures. With respect to uranium, such official enforcement of physical security, particularly of material in transit, might be very desirable.

NOTES

1. All data in these two paragraphs are from IEA/OECD, *Energy Policies and Programmes of IEA Countries, 1978 Review* (OECD: Paris, 1979).

2. *World Business Weekly*, February 11, 1980, p. 25.

3. Ari Sitas, "Rebels Without Pause: The MWU and the Defence of the Colour Bar," *South African Labour Bulletin* 5 (October 1979): 51-52.

4. J. H. Taylor and M. D. Yokell, *Yellowcake: The International Uranium Cartel* (New York: Pergamon Press, 1979), p. 14.

5. Answer to a Written Parliamentary Question to the Commission of the European Communities, cited in *European Community* (London) (January/February 1980): 11.

6. Taylor and Yokell, *Yellowcake*, p. 13.

7. Ibid.

8. Ibid., p. 15.

9. Sitas, "Rebels Without Pause," pp. 51-52.

10. Roger Murray, "Uranium: The Search Continues," *African Business* (April 1980): 12.

11. The output of the Rossing mine in Namibia, for example, is reported to have been airfreighted to the United Kingdom since 1978. *New African* (April 1980): 6.

5
Terrorism and the Energy Industry

Richard J. Kessler

The U.S. energy industry remains highly vulnerable to terrorist attack, and this vulnerability will increase as energy supply sources become more concentrated. Indeed, even today, a highly organized and technically sophisticated group of terrorists could bring the U.S. energy system to a halt and thereby contribute to its economic collapse.

However, it is not at all certain whether this vulnerability should be a subject of concern. There is a gap between susceptibility to disruption and its likelihood.

This chapter examines the issue of the vulnerability of the U.S. energy industry to terrorist attack, with two qualifications.

First, only the domestic energy industry is examined. The present international energy environment is such that terrorist attacks must be considered not only possible but inevitable. Second, short-run terrorist attacks, effecting minimal damage, are not considered relevant. The terrorist threat is only considered in terms of its ability to cause a great and long-term disruption of U.S. energy supplies.

Four diverse examples of the U.S. energy industry are briefly studied: the nuclear power sector, electrical utilities, liquified energy supplies, and the oil pipeline system. These sectors are examined within the context of three main issues: vulnerability, probable antagonists, and available countermeasures.

Within these issue areas, there are a variety of critical questions. In terms of vulnerability: Where is the system vulnerable? How vulnerable is it? What are optimal targets, maximizing vulnerability and disruptions? What weapons are needed to disrupt these targets? Considering antagonists: Who could affect a disruption? What are the characteristics of terrorists? When and by whom in the past has the energy industry been targetted? What causes terrorism? For the issue of countermeasures: What countermeasures can be taken? By whom should these countermeasures be taken? What is their cost? Who should bear the cost?

This chapter is not a prescription for terrorism. Many relevant details have been omitted. But the information used here is public record, and more detailed information can easily be obtained.

NUCLEAR POWER INDUSTRY

In popular literature, the nuclear power industry is often the target of terrorist attack. But in comparison with other sectors of the U.S. energy industry, it is probably the least vulnerable.

One study has concluded that "(a) major attack on a nuclear site would tax the skills of the most professional and highly trained commando unit. . . . Very few illegal action groups have the organization, training, or level of skilled persons necessary to carry out a major attack on a nuclear site."[1]

Discussion of the terrorist threat to nuclear power has focused on possible penetration of nuclear-weapons storage areas and on stealing weapon-grade plutonium.[2] Sophisticated countermeasures have been taken to guard against these possible threats – threats, which, for the most part, can only be envisioned by imaginative novelists.

Nor is it likely that a terrorist attack on nuclear power facilities, even if successful, would have a major impact on U.S. energy supplies. Nuclear power provided only 11.8 percent of U.S. electrical energy consumption in 1977, and, even under optimistic projections, will contribute only 22 percent by 1990. The disruption of one facility, as evidenced by the shutdown of Three Mile Island (TMI), does not lead to power outages elsewhere.

The real vulnerability of the nuclear power industry is in, as the TMI incident also illustrates, the increased operating costs caused by a shutdown.[4] The long-term effects of TMI on the financial viability of the U.S. nuclear power industry have not been fully assessed, but they will certainly be great and may result not only in a diminished public acceptance of nuclear power but also in a decrease in the contribution of nuclear power to U.S. energy needs. Should terrorists, for whatever reason, target nuclear power plants for disruption, the effect in terms of the public's and investors' perceptions may be the equivalent of a meltdown.

ELECTRIC UTILITIES

As in the nuclear power industry, the major danger to the electric power industry from terrorist attack results from the increase in operating expenses. Table 5.1 illustrates the estimated costs of a proposed 756-kilovolt (kv) transmission line. Damage to any part of the system can be extremely costly to the utility, although the expense is ultimately borne by the consumer.

The utility system is also highly vulnerable and, in the past, has been the subject of frequent attacks. (See Appendix 1 for a

TABLE 5.1
Transmission System Unit Cost Estimates

765-Kilovolt Transmission Line	*Cost (in thousand of dollars)*
Single-Circuit Steel Lattice Towers	337/mile
Four 954 MCM ACSR conductors per bundle	
Right of Way	
200-foot wide 24.24 ac. $2,063 ac.	50/mile
765 kv Circuit Breaker	
Includes bus structure, relaying control,	
and communications	1,690
1,500 mva, 765/345 kv, (3-1ϕ) Auto Transformer	5,000
500 mva, 765/345 kv, Auto Transformer	2,500
600 mva, 765 kv, 3-1ϕ Reactor	3,190
Series Capacitor $780,000/Substation + 14.20/KVAR	

Source: Economic Regulatory Administration, Office of Utility Systems, *The National Power Grid Study, Volume II: Technical Study Reports* (Washington, D.C.: Department of Energy, September 1979), DOE/ERA-0056-2, p. 135.

selected list of incidents.) Transmission-line structures can easily be destroyed and are often located in isolated areas where a saboteur can work at leisure.

Unlike nuclear power, damage to utilities and their transmission systems will not result in a long-run reduction in electric power generation. In addition, a disruption will not necessarily result in a short-run reduction in electric power supplies because of the system's ability to powerwheel.

In the past, the electric power system has shown great flexibility in emergencies. For example, during the winter of 1978 coal strike, 15 billion kilowatt hours (kwh) were transmitted from New England, Florida, the Dakotas, and Oklahoma into the Midwest. Another emergency illustrates the high degree of coordination that would be needed by any terrorist group trying to cause a major electric power outage: in April 1974, 300,000 square miles of the Midwest were hit by a series of tornados, damaging more than 100 transmission circuits. It would be difficult for any group to deploy with the random effectiveness of a tornado.

However, the extensive U.S. transmission system (more than 359,000 circuit miles) is its weakest link as well as its strongest. There are now three major, unconnected networks of extra high voltage (EHV) transmission facilities in the United States: in the eastern two-thirds of the United States from the Atlantic to the Rockies, in Texas, and in the West Coast area. The development of a national power grid, connecting high-capacity lines of the West Coast system with the eastern Missouri River basin and the Mississippi River basin systems, may simplify the terrorist objective of identifying the critical transmission links and destroying them, especially since the continued development of economies of scale in the transmission of electric power is increasing maximum transmission voltage. A key terrorist target would be to identify the transmission line interconnecting points that now enhance the system's power transfer capability.

LIQUEFIED ENERGY GAS

Liquefied energy gases (liquefied natural gas, liquefied petroleum gas, and naphtha) provide approximately 3 percent of U.S. energy consumption.[5] Liquefied natural gas (LNG) is a mixture of hydrocarbons, from 65 percent to 99 percent methane, and ethane, propane, and butane. Liquefied petroleum gas (LPG) is propane and butane, processed from natural gas or crude oil. Naphtha is a generic term for various mixtures of hydrocarbons extracted from crude oil during refining.

One cubic meter of LNG makes 424,000 cubic feet of a highly flammable natural gas/air mixture. One cubic meter of LPG makes a slightly larger flammable volume. Naphtha is between kerosene and gasoline in volatility.

Because of the extreme volatility of these gases, there has always been concern about vulnerability to terrorist attack. Once spilled from container vessels, liquefied energy gases (LEG) vaporize rapidly, becoming highly flammable and explosive. The only major LNG spill in the United States occurred in Cleveland on October 20, 1944. Fires and explosions initiated by the collapse of a 4,200 cubic meter tank killed 130, injured 225, and caused $7 million in property damage. The disaster effectively stopped LNG use in the United States for nearly 20 years.

The typical LNG storage tank now holds 95,000 cubic meters, sufficient to produce about 2 billion cubic feet of natural gas. The typical LNG tanker holds 125,000 cubic meters. Some LNG ships hold up to 165,000 cubic meters. The largest LPG ships can hold 100,000 cubic meters.

About 85 percent of LPG is held under pressure in bulk storage in underground salt domes or mined caverns. It is mainly transported through 70,000 miles of high-pressure pipeline (see Figure 5.1). In addition, there are 16,300 rail tank cars and 25,000 transport and delivery trucks. A large LPG truck holds 40 cubic meters. LPG is odorless, colorless, and, since it is heavier than air, will flow toward the lowest point. Once in a sewer system, for example, an LEG explosion can occur miles from the point of release. An explosion of naphtha released by a former employee of a rubber company in Akron, Ohio, on June 23, 1977, resulted in the destruction of 6,625 feet of sewer pipe and cost more than $10 million to repair.

LPG trucks are single-walled and pressurized, while LNG trucks have inner and outer tanks with insulation between them. LPG trucks are more vulnerable to cracks and punctures, but LNG trucks are considered more vulnerable to sabotage. The 40 cubic meters of LNG in one truck, once vaporized and mixed with air in flammable proportions, are sufficient to fill more than 110 miles of a six-foot diameter sewer line.

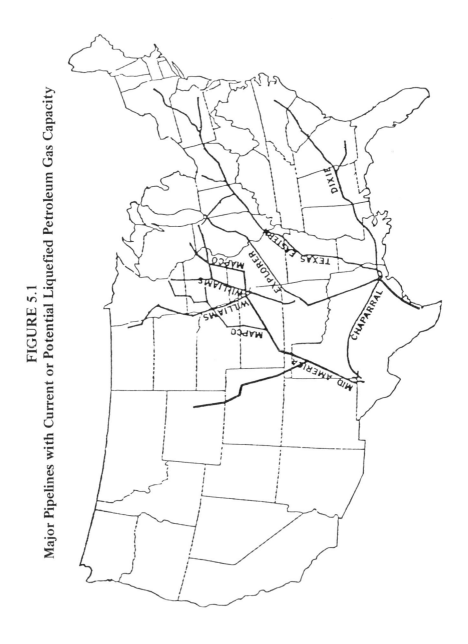

FIGURE 5.1

Major Pipelines with Current or Potential Liquefied Petroleum Gas Capacity

LEG are also vulnerable to sabotage at holding terminals. A General Accounting Office study has concluded that "(l)ittle attention has been paid to sabotage at LEG facilities, and most of them are inadequately protected."[6] Currently, LEG are contained in three types of tanks: steel, aluminum, and concrete. Despite being double-walled, the steel tanks provide no protection against even small nonmilitary weapons. Tests have shown that present protective dikes surrounding tanks are inadequate to contain the LEG if the tanks were breached. The steel straps anchoring the tanks to their concrete foundations are also vulnerable to destruction. But concrete tanks are resistant to bombs, including those from shaped charges.

LEG facilities and transportation systems are highly vulnerable to sabotage, but the effects of sabotage are not yet fully understood. While a large release of LEG may result in a vapor-air cloud that could detonate, it is uncertain what conditions would be necessary to cause a detonation.[7] However, present fire-fighting equipment cannot extinguish a large LEG fire. While a terrorist attack against this target would not disrupt the U.S. energy system, it could cause extensive and costly damage.

PETROLEUM PIPELINE SYSTEM

The most vulnerable segment of the U.S. energy supply system is in the petroleum pipeline network. This vulnerability results from three factors: the extreme dependence of the United States on pipelines to distribute petroleum and natural gas, the time required to repair damaged pipelines, and the ease of access to critical links in the system. Relative to all other energy targets, the U.S. pipeline system should be considered the ideal terrorist objective.

There are three major pipeline systems in the United States: the Capline, the Trans-Alaskan Pipeline System (TAPS), and the Colonial pipeline system. Their operation can be halted at numerous points with relative ease. Their disruption could cause incalculable damage to the U.S. economic system, particularly if it occurred during critical seasonal periods, such as winter.

The Capline is a 40-inch diameter pipe running 632 miles from St. James, Louisiana, to Patoka, Illinois. With maximum daily capacity of 1.2 million barrels, it annually delivers 400 million barrels and supplies the Midwest with 25 percent of its requirements (see Figure 5.2).[8]

FIGURE 5.2
Capline Pipeline

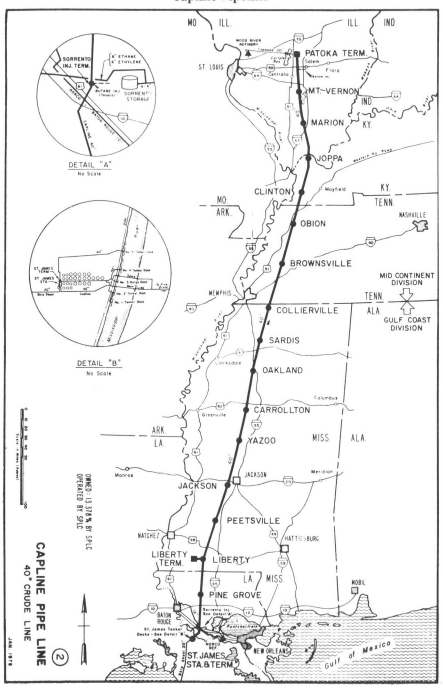

92

There is no adequate alternative to this system. An additional 216 barges would be needed on the Mississippi River to equal the pipeline's daily flow.[9] The entire system is controlled by a computer at St. James, with 16 pump stations to boost the flow and five intersecting pipelines to distribute the crude to refineries.[10]

The TAPS is a 48-inch diameter pipe extending 800 miles from Prudhoe Bay to Port Valdez. With a daily capacity of 1.2 million barrels, it provides 400 million barrels annually. This system is controlled by computer at Port Valdez and has eight pump stations (see Figure 5.3).[11]

The Colonial pipeline system is a 30- to 40-inch diameter pipe stretching 1,600 miles from Houston, Texas, to Linden, New Jersey. It has a daily capacity of 2.1 million barrels and delivers 600 million barrels annually. The entire system is controlled by computer at Atlanta, Georgia, and has 81 pump stations (see Figure 5.4).[12] The eastern United States is heavily dependent on this system; damage to it at certain positions could halt the flow of petroleum to the East.[13] For example, 90 percent of Washington, D.C.'s gas, heating oil, commercial oil, and aviation fuel flows through two underground pipelines.[14]

The time required to repair damage to any pipeline varies, depending on the size of the damage, its complexity, weather conditions during repair, required safety measures, and the availability of skilled repair crews. For example, damage to a Tapline pump station could take nine months to fix.[15] Some booster pumps are constructed to each system's specifications and might require six months to a year to replace.[16] Damage to pump stations or to the automated control facilities could result in as much as a one-third reduction in throughput.[17]

Pipelines are currently constructed and maintained with little regard to their vulnerability to sabotage.[18] The one exception is Tapline, which has an extensive and sophisticated surveillance system.[19] One study has identified 126 "hit points," which if damaged or destroyed could halt product movement.[20] Pipelines are vulnerable at several points: input terminal, pump stations, river crossings, and intersystem linkups.[21] The lack of skilled repair and operating personnel as well as the shortage of easily obtainable critical spare parts are other reasons for their vulnerability.[22] This vulnerability does not mean that the system will be disrupted, only that it can be. The Tapline has already been damaged by sabotage.

FIGURE 5.3
Trans-Alaska Crude Oil Pipeline System

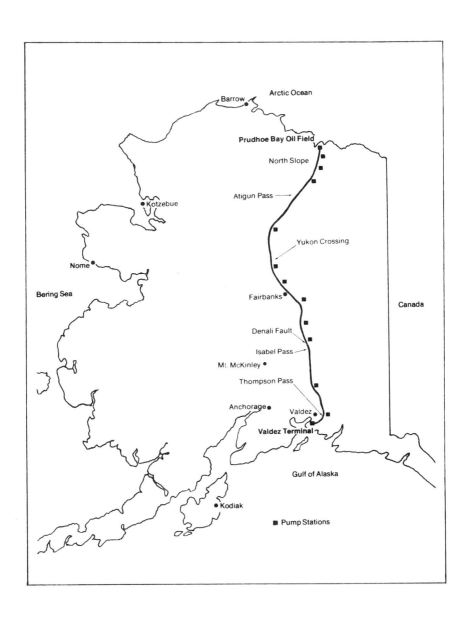

FIGURE 5.4
Colonial Pipeline Company System Map

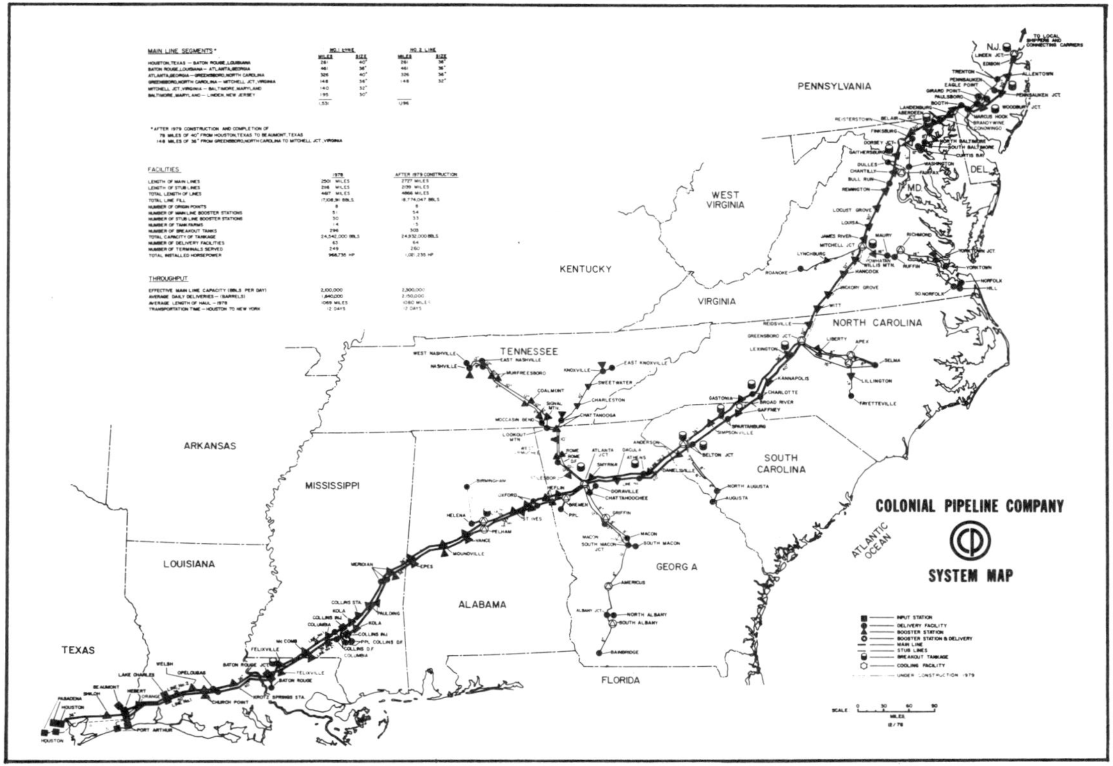

Still, most pipelines are capable of sustaining some destruction and continuing to operate. The major danger would result from multiple and simultaneous attacks along the system.

THE TERRORISTS

When examining the feasibility of energy supply system disruptions, there are two critical questions: Can it be done? Are there groups capable of doing it?

Every system has its weak points. A skilled and dedicated group could engineer the disruption of any segment of the U.S. energy industry. This does not mean that such a group will develop or seek such a target nor that we should develop a "wartime" type of security system to guard against such a group.

A study of terrorist incidents 1966-75 found that very few targetted energy systems for attack (see Table 5.2) . Unlike other targets, the energy industry is a high-technology target, requiring specialized knowledge to attack. In the past, most U.S. terrorism has been directed against lightly protected, low-technology, highly symbolic targets. Sophisticated weapons have not often been employed in these ventures.

However, attacks have not been indiscriminate. In general, they have avoided causing a high number of casualties and have been

TABLE 5.2

U.S. Terrorist Attacks against Energy Targets, 1966-75

	Target (percent of total U.S. terrorist attacks)		
Type of Group	*Public Utilities*	*Fuel Tanks/ Pipelines*	*Microwave Towers*
Ad Hoc	17	—	—
Criminal	—	5	—
Separatist	7	—	—
Reactionaries	—	—	2
Violent-Cause-Oriented	16	—	—

Source: BDM Corporation, "Analyses of the Terrorist Threat to the Commercial Nuclear Industry," contract no. AT (49-24)-0131, McLean, Virginia, September 30, 1975, p. 47.

covert. Unhappy or former employees of companies have posed the greatest threat. In attacks against the energy industry, terrorists have provided little warning or follow-up contact. They have also shown the capability to deploy explosives to cause maximum damage.[23]

There are a variety of terrorist types operating in the United States. These include foreign governments, foreign subnational groups, domestic criminals, domestic right- and left-wing revolutionaries, domestic issue-oriented groups, dissident employees, and psycho- or sociopathic individuals.

Which groups are most likely to target the energy industry for attack? Is there a transformation through which each must go before reaching such a stage? Given the history of terrorism against the energy industry, what are the attributes, capabilities, and motivations of future terrorists?

In the past, a pattern of terrorist violence has been observed. Initially, there is a bargaining stage: terrorist actions are carried out with demands for change. The second stage is one of terrorist action coupled with political statements. This is followed, if the group does not believe it's gaining sufficient attention, by greater acts of violence aimed at social paralysis. Finally, there is large-scale violence with a number of casualties.[24]

An attack against a major sector of the domestic energy industry would require a highly motivated group with an "insider's" knowledge of the industry's operations as well as access to sophisticated explosives. The group would have identified itself to the authorities during earlier efforts to articulate its demands. Disruption of U.S. energy supplies is not an objective with which a terrorist organization begins; it is one with which it ends.

CONCLUSIONS: COUNTERMEASURES AND THE FUTURE

Should the energy industry anticipate large-scale terrorist action against it during the 1980s, and, if so, what can it do about such action?

Small-scale targetting of the industry has probably existed since its inception. The type of low-level violence characterized by the bombing of microwave transmission towers in the western United States during the 1960s and by the bombings of California public utility plants 1970-72 will, undoubtedly, continue. Protests and efforts to disrupt nuclear power plants will also continue.

A variety of security measures can be implemented at little or no cost to counter this low-level violence. Such measures would, and already do, include controls over facility entry: improved controls over locks and keys, fencing installation, 24-hour lockups, records of entrance to key facility components, restricted access to key sectors (such as computer rooms), and visitor identity checks. While these measures do not prevent "insider" knowledge, they do facilitate identification of any insider involved in an attack. In addition, employee security training can help prevent unwanted entry as well as provide an early warning of intended terrorist activity. Separation of critical facilities can prevent an explosion or fire in one from damaging another. Finally, security checks on ease of entry can help tighten defense of the overall system.

More difficult attacks aimed at disrupting an entire energy sector rather than a minor component will probably not occur in the 1980s. However, if there is a change in the political and economic environment of the country — that is, an economic depression and a loss of political efficacy, resulting in social decay — there will probably be an escalation of violence.

Much of this violence could be directed against the energy industry, especially as energy is widely perceived as a major U.S. problem. The movement to large-scale, capital intensive plants (as in oil-shale development) and delivery systems (as in coal-slurry pipelines and the Alaskan gas pipeline) will no doubt make these industries inviting targets. The attack against the South African Sasol plants in May 1980 may be an indicator of what could occur in the United States, especially since synfuel development is likely to replace nuclear power as the popular protest issue of the 1980s.

There is no doubt that much more work needs to be done in this area before terrorist threat can either be dismissed or accepted. A major study on energy and terrorism should be undertaken with the following objectives: an assessment of the system's vulnerability to terrorism, a determination of the probable impact of a major supply disruption, an assessment of the characteristics of likely antagonists, an evaluation of the adequacy of industry and government measures against terrorism, and an assessment of the adequacy of planning to minimize the effects of a disruption.

NOTES

1. BDM Corporation, "Analysis of the Terrorist Threat to the Commercial Nuclear Industry," report to the Special Safeguards Study, Nuclear Regulatory

Commission, contract no. AT (49-24)-0131, McLean, Virginia, September 30, 1975, p. 69.

2. See *The Defense Monitor* 4 (February 1975): 8; Mason Willrich and Theodore Taylor, *Nuclear Theft: Risks and Safeguards* (Cambridge: Ballinger, 1974); Augustus R. Norton, "Nuclear Terrorism and the Middle East," *Military Review* 57 (April 1976): 3; Louis René Beres, "Terrorism and the Nuclear Threat in the Middle East," *Current History* 70 (January 1976): 27; "If Terrorists Go After U.S. Nuclear Bombs," *U.S. News and World Report* 86 (March 12, 1978): 43-45.

3. U.S., Energy Information Administration, Assistant Administrator for Applied Analysis, "Commercial Nuclear and Uranium Market Forecasts for the United States and the World Outside Communist Areas," DOE/EIA-0184/24, Department of Energy, Washington, D.C., January 1980, p. 12.

4. See U.S., General Accounting Office, "Three Mile Island: The Financial Fallout," EMD-80-89, Washington, D.C., July 7, 1980: "The nuclear accident at Three Mile Island raised serious questions about the financial ability of the electric utility company owners to clean up and repair the damaged reactor facilities while continuing to provide reliable electric service to customers."

5. This discussion is largely taken from the U.S. General Accounting Office (GAO) study, "Liquefied Energy Gases Safety," EMD-78-28, Washington, D.C., July 31, 1978 (vol. 1, "Liquefied Energy Gases Study"; vol. 2, "Appendixes"; and vol. 3, "Federal Agency Comments."

6. Ibid., vol. 1, p. 11.

7. The Department of Energy is currently conducting research to determine whether destructive detonations of LEG are possible. The semantics are important:

A detonation is a combustion (burning) wave moving supersonically; combustion is so rapid that a high temperature is reached before the mixture has much chance to expand, thus producing a high pressure that is independent of the presence of confining walls. . . . Deflagration is a flame front moving at subsonic speed, generally building up little pressure unless the mixture is confined in a closed or nearly-closed structure. . . . Explosion usually denotes any gaseous expansion which produces a large noise.

GAO, "Liquefied Energy Gases," vol. 1, chap. 13, p. 1.

8. U.S., General Accounting Office (GAO), "Key Crude Oil and Products Pipelines are Vulnerable to Disruptions," EMD-79-63, Washington, D.C., August 27, 1979, p. 7.

9. Ibid., p. 36.

10. Ibid., p. 7.

11. Ibid.

12. Ibid., p. 11.

13. U.S., Department of Interior, "Vulnerability of Total Petroleum Systems," Defense Civil Preparedness Agency, Washington, D.C., May 1973, p. 5.

14. The Washington *Post*, March 4, 1979.

15. GAO, "Key Crude Oil," p. 15, n. 1.

16. Ibid., p. 24.

17. Ibid., pp. 22-23. The reduction in throughput depends on terrain and the distance over which petroleum is carried. Destruction of computer control facilities and reliance on manual operation also reduce throughput because manual operations are, by nature, slower and because there now exists a lack of skilled personnel.

18. U.S., Library of Congress, Congressional Research Service, "National Energy Transportation, Volume III, Issues and Problems," Washington, D.C., March 1978, pp. 159-61.

19. 49 Code of Federal Regulations (C.F.R.) vol. 49, section 195.436, requires operating companies to protect facilities against vandalism and unauthorized entry but not against terrorism.

20. Stanford Research Institute, "Potential Vulnerability Affecting National Survival," Menlo Park, California, September 1970.

21. GAO, "Key Crude Oil," p. 15.

22. Ibid., p. 22.

23. BDM, "Analysis of the Terrorist Threat," p. D-38.

24. Ibid., p. ix.

APPENDIX I

Incidents at Public Utility and Petroleum
Company Facilities, 1974-77

A selected list of 20 incidents occurring at public utility and petroleum company facilities from 1974 through May 1977 follows.

Colorado, March 1974

The Mapleton Power Substation of the Public Service Company of Colorado in Adams County was the target of a bombing on March 8. A large pipe bomb or similar device was placed next to a transformer at the substation and detonated. Extensive damage, estimated at $250,000, occurred.

Pennsylvania, June 1974

At 9:29 p.m., June 13, the Pittsburgh Police Department was notified of a telephone warning received by the Gulf Oil Corporation that a bomb was in the corporation's facility. The caller said that he was with a terrorist group and that a bomb was in the building and would detonate in 17 minutes. An explosion occurred on the twenty-ninth floor of the oil company building, resulting in from $300,000 to $500,000 in damages. A communiqué issued by the same group claimed credit for the bombing as a reprisal for the oil corporation's operations in an African country.

Oregon, October 1974

During October, 11 power transmission towers in four different locations were discovered to have been bombed. Three were in the Maupin area, three near Brightwood, three near Parkdale, and two near Sandy. At least three of the towers were toppled as a result of the explosions. Damage was estimated at more than $200,000.

Source: U.S., General Accounting Office, "Liquefied Energy Gases Safety: Appendixes," EMD-78-28, Washington, D.C., 31 July 1978, Appendix IX.

A series of extortion letters mailed to the Federal Bureau of Investigation at Portland and to a Portland area daily newspaper demanded payment of $1 million and threatened a "blackout" of Portland if demands were not met.

Kentucky, November/December 1974

During November and December, 20 natural gas transmission lines and two natural gas cooling towers belonging to a Kentucky-West Virginia gas company were targets of bombing incidents in various areas of Kentucky. The gas pipelines varied in diameter from 2 inches to 20 inches. Dynamite bombs were used in each of the incidents, which caused an estimated $92,650 in damage. In many areas, service was disrupted. The motives are believed to have stemmed from labor disputes. There were no injuries or deaths.

California, March 1975

Facilities belonging to a gas and electric company were the targets of bombings on March 20, 27, and 29. During the early morning of March 20, three towers at San Bruno were bombed. Damage was slight, and service was not interrupted.

At approximately 11:05 the same evening, three more towers were bombed in Alameda County. Pipe bombs were utilized, and damage was estimated at $500.

Shortly after midnight on March 27, detonation of five more pipe bombs occurred at utility stations in San Jose. These attacks caused extensive damage to three power transformers and two oil switches. The resulting loss of power affected 35,000 people. Damage was set at from $80,000 to $100,000.

On March 29, a transformer at Rancho Cordova was bombed. Damages cost $20,000.

California, April 1975

At 9:00 p.m. on April 4, a telephone warning was received by a San Francisco television station that a bomb was located in a building owned by Standard Oil of California. A second warning call was received at 9:30 p.m. by a telephone operator, during which the caller stated that a bomb would detonate at 10:00 p.m. At approximately 9:34 p.m., an explosion occurred at the building mentioned in the threat. Damage to the building and surrounding area was estimated at $300,000.

California, September 1975

On September 26, a major oil company was the target of a bombing claimed by an extremist group. An estimated $100,000 in damage was done to two 5,000-barrel oil storage tanks at an oil company facility near Coalinga. A crude, highly explosive device was utilized. The tank closest to the bomb contained 3,000 barrels of water.

Washington, December 1975

An anonymous male caller representing an extremist group telephoned the Seattle Police Department at 11:30 p.m. on December 31 and advised that there were bombs at a Seattle power transformer and at a supermarket chain office in Bellevue. At approximately the same time, an explosion occurred at the distribution-center office building of the supermarket chain in Bellevue. About 15 minutes later, a bomb exploded next to a water tower and pumping station near the same building. In the same time period, an explosive device detonated at a Seattle city light substation. All of the explosions were caused by pipe bombs with timing devices. Total damage to the three locations was estimated at $102,500. A subsequent communiqué from the group stated that the attacks were in support of striking city electrical power workers and of farm workers who had been exploited by the supermarket chain.

California, May 1976

One person was killed and one other injured while they allegedly attempted to place an explosive device inside the locked, fenced area of a hydroelectric power station. At approximately 11:00 p.m. on May 15, the two men entered the unguarded facility with a bomb, which detonated prematurely, resulting in the casualties. A third suspect, who escaped injury, was acting as a lookout. Minor property damage was estimated at $1,500.

California, October 1976

An extremist group's demands for assistance to poor and working class people were demonstrated when it attempted to bomb a gas and electric power facility in Mill Valley on October 1, the management of which the group accused of insensitivity to the needs of under-privileged persons. Two explosive devices were found and rendered safe by San Francisco police.

California, January 1977

On January 19, a bomb exploded at a utility company in Sausalito. A newspaper received a communiqué from the Eugene Kuhn Unit of the New World Liberation Front (NWLF). The communiqué claimed that the bombing was in retaliation for an elderly man's death, which had resulted from his electricity having been turned off.

California, January 1977

On January 22, in Olema, an improvised explosive device damaged a local utility company. A telephone caller said the NWLF was responsible.

California, January 1977

On January 27, in Monte Vista, a utility company was the scene of four pipe bombings. The NWLF claimed responsibility.

California, February 1977

On February 2, at Cool, an improvised explosive device caused damage to a utility station.

Utah, March 1977

On March 7, in Dutch John, a small improvised explosive device was found on the roof of a power plant dam.

New Mexico, March 1977

On March 10, at Albuquerque, a newly installed power transformer sustained $2,000 in damage during a bombing incident.

New York, April 1977

On April 3, in New York City, a projectile was found at an oil company facility. A military mortar round, it was dismantled in place by bomb technicians.

California, April 1977

In Oakland, on April 14, transformers at a utility company substation sustained $25,000 in damage caused by a bombing. The blast caused a brief power outage.

California, April 1977

In Sonoma, on April 17, four pipe bombs exploded at a utility substation, disrupting power. The Eugene Kuhn Unit of the NWLF claimed responsibility in an anonymous telephone call.

Michigan, May 1977

At an oil company in Birmingham, on May 2, $100,000 worth of damage was caused by a bombing in the company parking lot. One vehicle was destroyed and several others damaged.

6

Security Risks to Energy Production and Trade

Lisa Maechling
Yonah Alexander

In terms of volume, oil is the principal commodity traded internationally. In 1980, countries exchanged close to 30 million barrels of petroleum a day (mmbd) or just over half of all the oil produced worldwide (57 mmbd). Approximately half of these oil shipments comes from the Middle East, a fifth from Africa (north and west), and the rest from Southeast Asia, South America, and the Soviet Union. The Organization of Petroleum Exporting Countries (OPEC), founded in 1960, represents most of the oil-producing states of the Middle East, Africa, and Southeast Asia. (Algeria, Bahrain, Egypt, Iraq, Kuwait, Libya, Qatar, Saudi Arabia, Syria, and the United Arab Emirates form OAPEC; Ecuador, Gabon, Indonesia, Iran, Nigeria, and Venezuela are non-Arab members of OPEC.) Thus more than two-thirds of the oil in international trade comes from OPEC nations.

In order to handle the tremendous oil traffic that passes among nations, oil companies have developed a complex logistical system. This delivery network depends not only on uninterrupted oil recovery but also on the unimpeded operation of storage facilities, oil ports, pipelines, and refineries. In effect, oil production, transport, and consumption are parts of a continuous process that starts in oilfields and ends thousands of miles away at gasoline stations, utilities, and factories.

Certain events — from the Arab Oil Embargo of 1973 to the Iranian Revolution of 1979 and the Iran-Iraq War of 1980 — have

107

exposed the vulnerability of oil trade to political and military forces beyond the control of companies involved in the market. Other forms of energy production or distribution, especially electric generation, are also subject to potentially crippling attacks. Without warning, terrorist attacks, military assault, or government interdiction could bring energy delivery to a halt. Interference in one part of the system is likely to disrupt other aspects of production and transportation. For example, destruction of oil ports in the Iran-Iraq war forced a shutdown of production. In effect, when one critical link in the distribution chain falls apart, others can quickly fracture.

In the past, oil companies had the flexibility to overcome a variety of logistical disruptions so that no single accident could force that segment of the system — production, refining, tanker trade, or pipeline transmissions — to be entirely shut down. Companies have become accustomed to random accidents because petroleum is a highly flammable substance. A refinery fire, for example, could immobilize processing for weeks, while fires at offshore oil wells can burn for months. To lower the risks of fires and explosions, companies have instituted a range of safety measures to control temperatures and chemical mixtures at the wellhead and in refineries, storage areas, pipelines, and tankers. While such precautions cannot totally prevent accidents, they help to safeguard the system against severe or prolonged damage.

The prospect of increasing military or terrorist assaults on energy systems worldwide raises two important questions: should companies — or governments — devise safeguards beyond those currently maintained by companies to protect key aspects of the oil production and transportation system from sabotage; is a comprehensive security plan for the logistical network for oil, gas, and electricity even possible? While these questions do not have easy answers, it is possible to characterize the principal risks to the energy logistical system and to draw some conclusions about how — or if — the network can be made more secure.

ISOLATED TERRORIST ATTACKS

Over the past 20 years, oil operations worldwide have become the object of sabotage. As long as these incidents occur at roughly the same frequency as accidents, companies are able to handle the damage of isolated bombings on pipelines and other installations. Since many of these attacks have effects similar to — and not always as damaging as — accidental fires and explosions, companies have been able to manage these crises with their own methods. However, the prospect of increased terrorist assaults on critical aspects of the system has aroused governmental concern at home and abroad. Will these attacks increase; who should be responsible for safeguards, the companies or governments?

In the decade between 1970 and 1980, there were close to 450 instances of sabotage committed against oil-related enterprises worldwide (see Appendix I).[1] A large proportion of those attacks were made on pipelines, both in fields and in lines that transmit oil from fields to storage facilities and tankers. The most serious single incident occurred on May 11, 1977, in Saudi Arabia. Unknown saboteurs set fire to the ARAMCO-operated production center, causing $100 million in damage to network pipelines.[2] Other noteworthy attacks on U.S. oil industry personnel, facilities, and operations abroad include the following incidents, selected at random.[3] Members of the People's Revolutionary Front in the Philippines detonated bombs at the headquarters of Esso and Caltex in Manila in 1971, damaging the offices and killing a Filipino employee. In 1972, unidentified attackers sabotaged facilities of the Kuwait Oil Company, which is partially U.S.-owned. During the same year, European terrorists, cooperating with members of Al Fatah, sabotaged the Gulf Oil refinery in Rotterdam. In 1973, members of the Revolutionary People's Army (ERP) kidnapped a general manager of Esso in Argentina; he was later released for a ransom of $8.5 million. During the same year, members of the Lebanese Revolutionary Guard attacked Caltex-Mobil facilities in Sidon, destroying an oil storage tank, badly damaging two others, and slightly damaging a fourth. Texaco and Mobil oil pipelines in Venezuela were dynamited in 1976. Palestinian terrorists damaged the equipment of a U.S. oil company in the West Bank during the same year. In 1977, a Portuguese revolutionary group in Lisbon threatened to blow up Gulf Oil's offshore drilling complex in Cabinda. In Iran, the Peoples Strugglers (Mujaheddin e Khalg) assassinated a Texaco executive working with the Oil Services Company of Iran (ESCO) in 1978. In 1980, terrorists killed the general manager of Texaco in Colombia after holding him hostage. Similar incidents have involved companies such as Amoco (Argentina), Esso-Pappas (Greece),

Esso (Germany), Tenneco (Ethiopia), Texaco (Italy), and Texas Petroleum (Colombia).

A second significant example is that of ECOPETROL in Colombia. During 1977, 14 incidents involved the state-owned corporation. All were part of a rapid resurgence in rural guerrilla and urban terrorist activities throughout Colombia that year. The attacks, initiated by various groups including the April 19 Movement (M-19), were related to a labor strike against ECOPETROL. The corporation had considerable monetary losses, and the severity and length of terrorist operations and sabotage resulted in spot shortages of crude oil for refineries and in national shortages of gasoline.[4]

A third illustration of the nature of the terrorist threat to the foreign oil industry is the June 1980 bombings of fuel storage tanks at two major oil-from-coal plants at Sasolburg (southwest of Johannesburg). Final damage estimates exceeded $7.5 million. These incidents suggest that terrorist groups in South Africa are entering into a new phase of sabotage and urban terror. The attacks were well planned and coordinated on strategic targets. Not only were the attacks aimed at South Africa's Achilles' heel — its oil supplies — they were also intended for maximum propaganda impact. The outlawed African National Congress (ANC) has claimed responsibility for the attacks. This group, according to official South African sources, is receiving weaponry and military training from the Soviet Union, East Germany, and Cuba. In southern Africa itself, East Germans and Cubans give logistical aid to ANC and also assist as military instructors.[5]

To be sure, there have also been numerous oil industry related incidents abroad that point to unconfirmed sabotage. Supertanker sinkings in mysterious circumstances exemplify these cases.[6] One dramatic incident took place in December 1976. A Liberian-registered oil tanker that ran aground on the Nantucket Shoals 27 miles off the Atlantic Coast produced what was described as the worst Atlantic Coast oil spill in history. The U.S. Coast Guard said that a telephone caller who identified himself as a crew member of the ship told the Coast Guard's New York headquarters that the tanker might have been run aground deliberately. The chief of the Coast Guard office of merchant marine safety said that the information had been referred to the Liberian government maritime office in New York and that the Liberian office was to investigate. The Coast Guard representative said that the Coast Guard itself was not investigating because the tanker broke up in international waters, where the U.S. government has no authority to investigate except at the request of the foreign government involved. The vessel piled onto the Nantucket Shoals while running from Venezuela to Salem, Massachusetts. The tanker was 10 miles off its course. None of the 38 crew members and officers was injured.

More recently, in April 1980, two incidents occurred. The first involved a Liberian-registered supertanker, the 239,400-ton *Albahaa B*, owned by Wellem Ship Management, Ltd., of Hong Kong. It exploded and sank off Africa's east coast near Tanzania. Six crew members were missing, and 37 were picked up. The ship was in ballast and heading for the Persian Gulf after delivering full cargos of oil. The second incident involved another Liberian-registered supertanker, the 238,889-ton *Mycene*, owned by the Mycene Shipping Company of Monrovia. It sank off the coast of Senegal, Africa's westernmost point. One crew member was missing, and 32 were rescued by a Dutch ship.

Although these suspected sabotage cases and the confirmed terrorist attacks directed at U.S. and foreign oil industry targets abroad are a major cause for concern, no critical interruption of imported U.S. petroleum has so far occurred. The fact remains, however, that the operation of oilfields and the movement of oil are extremely vulnerable. In the Middle East, threats to oil facilities along the Persian Gulf coast are posed by Shiite minority workers in Saudi Arabia, by expatriate groups in Iraq and Yemen, and by other disaffected tribal groups within each country. In addition, regional weaknesses can be exacerbated by endemic violence in Turkey, internal unrest in Syria, civil war in Lebanon, Palestinian terrorists, and the resurging, unsettling influence of Islam.[7]

In assessing the ability to guard oil and other energy installations, it is important to distinguish between defense of the system and protection of the territory in which operations take place. This point is especially pertinent to the debate over U.S. military involvement in the Persian Gulf. It is one thing to protect the region from Soviet incursion or internal upheaval; it is another to believe that such military intervention could keep oil flowing to the West. Indeed, a central thesis of this chapter is that the oil logistical system is indefensible by conventional military means and that the United States and its allies must find another strategy for lowering the risks of politically inspired attacks on key oil operations.

INTERFERENCE IN OIL PRODUCTION AND TRADE

The worldwide oil production and distribution chain has several weak links that could fracture under pressure. First, oil is a finite resource whose depletion is in sight. Unless companies can explore for new reserves, known reserves will decline. Thus, denial of access to oil producing areas can pose a long-term threat to world oil supplies. Furthermore, when oil recovery methods are interrupted suddenly or are poorly controlled, the productivity of oilfields can be impaired. In short, the oil tap cannot be turned off and on arbitrarily without technical and economic consequences. Second, transportation facilities, especially oil-loading ports, computerized pump stations, and storage tank farms, can be easy targets of air attack. Destruction of these facilities could bring all other oil operations to a standstill. In order to understand the intricacy of oil production and distribution — and of other energy networks — it is useful to first describe how different operations work and where they can go wrong.

Oil production, like any other form of mineral extraction or industrial activity, is subject to a combination of physical, economic, and technical factors. While the petroleum will always be in the ground, the economic conditions may not always exist to recover the oil. Production may at first be relatively inexpensive as oil flows under its own gravity. The costs, however, increase as engineers apply artificial pressure to the oil reservoir in order to maintain the flow. Since technology also operates in a marketplace, some recovery methods may be too costly to use under certain financial or market conditions. Thus, any political actions that can throw an economy or market into chaos may have a long-term impact on oil production.

Contrary to popular belief, an oil reservoir is not an underground lake full of petroleum. If it were, the oil would be easy to suck out. Instead, the reservoir resembles a hard sponge from which oil must be "squeezed." Rock formations (petroleum literally means "rock oil") hold oil, water, and gas, trapped in microscopic pores. In order to extract the oil, engineers must apply pressure to the rock — the oil reservoir — and drive the oil down into wells from which it rises, under the force of gravity, to the surface. In short, pressure maintenance is the key to oil production.[8]

In the Middle East, many — but not all — oilfields flow under natural pressure, that is, under the weight of the oil, gas, and water in the formation.[9] Depending on the thickness of the crude oil, the proportion of water, gas, and other substances in the petroleum (there are nearly as many types of oil as there are types of geological formations in which oil is found), the natural pressure can force out approximately a quarter of all the oil in the reservoir. However, as the weight of the remaining gas and fluid begins to decrease, so does the flow of oil.

The level of pressure at which the natural flow of oil starts to drop off is the "bubble point." At this point, natural pressure has been sufficiently relieved to allow oil and gas to separate in the reservoir. If the natural pressure falls below the bubble point, oil starts to be "left behind" in the reservoir. This oil can be produced only if pressure is maintained in the reservoir.

In order to keep pressure up artificially above the bubble point, engineers inject water, steam, or gas — pressure maintenance operations known as secondary recovery methods. As natural pressure continues to decrease, engineers increase the level of waterflooding, steam, or gas injections so that the overall pressure is somewhat higher than the original pressure. Through waterflooding, the most common secondary recovery method, engineers can help to extract an additional 5 to 25 percent of the petroleum in place. Usually for every barrel of oil produced, a barrel and a half of water is injected.

Saudi Arabia produces a substantial portion of its oil by means of waterflooding. To support production of 8.5 mmbd, Saudi Arabia must use at least 11.4 mmbd of water.[10] Furthermore, since the region lacks fresh water, the Saudis use salt water, which must be desalinated before it is injected into the reservoir. Despite these efforts, salt water still can contaminate wells and field equipment such as drilling bits, pipelines, and casements. Thus, desalinization plants have become a crucial component of Saudi oil production and destruction of such facilities could impair oil recovery significantly.

Even when water flooding is successful, over half of the oil in the reservoir can be left behind because of inadequate pressure. Thus, in many fields — especially those in the United States that have been producing oil for decades — producers have embarked on exotic tertiary recovery projects to force out some of the remaining oil. One method injects such chemicals as heavy polymers, surfactants, or carbon dioxide into the reserve. Such methods can boost the total recovery rate to 65 percent. However, it may not be economical to apply some of these costly techniques unless the real price (that adjusted for inflation) reaches a level sufficiently high to compensate for the expense.

Any field that has already produced a considerable amount of oil requires continuous and proper application of pressure in order to keep up the flow of oil. If such a field were suddenly shut down and recovery operations ceased, the cost of restoring production could be far greater than the cost of maintaining steady recovery. First, the field may require total repressurization at vast expense to the producer. Second, other constraints, such as inadequate or poor water supply, could limit production. Third, other substances or equipment for tertiary recovery methods could be inaccessible – especially in countries in which political chaos has disrupted normal trade and economic activity.

The 1979-80 political turbulence in Iran and in Iraq could have long-term effects on those nations' oil production. Together, they have close to 90 billion barrels of proved oil reserves, and in 1978 – the last year of normal production – they recovered nearly 9.0 mmbd (5.2 in Iran, 3.4 in Iraq). However, despite their resource potential, neither country may ever again reach the level of output achieved before war and revolution threw their economies into chaos.

Before the Iranian revolution, the shah had planned massive secondary recovery programs to reverse the decline in oil production that was already underway. In 1977, output briefly peaked at 8 mmbd, but it dropped thereafter because of declining pressure. These recovery projects were abandoned when the shah was deposed. The revolutionary government of the Ayatollah Khomeini expelled foreign technicians and pursued a policy of having an "all Iranian" oil industry.[11] Although the new government planned to keep production at 4 mmbd, output was down to 1.7 mmbd by mid-1980 and to 1.2 mmbd in the beginning of 1981. Productive capacity 1981 was estimated to be only 3.0 mmbd. In order to raise capacity much above this level, Iran would need to institute major water-flooding, gas-injection, and other tertiary recovery methods.

Iraq is in a far better position to bring oil production back to normal levels. First, Iraqi production is for the most part still in the primary stage of recovery – flowing under natural pressure – and hence many of the fields do not yet require waterflooding or other forms of artificial pressurization. Indeed, Iraq produces most of its oil from a few giant oilfields (those holding 500 million barrels of proved reserves or more), the largest of which are Rumaila, on its border with Kuwait, and Kirkuk, on its border with Iran.[12] Since Iraq has not depleted its oil resources as rapidly as have some other Middle East countries, notably Iran, it continues to produce from fields that are the most economical to develop.

The major constraint on Iraqi production in the near term stems from the destruction of its export facilities. Without the means to transport oil out of the country by tanker, Iraq cannot produce much more than 2.0 mmbd — the total capacity of its pipelines to Turkey, Syria, and Lebanon.[13] More than any other event to date, the Iran-Iraq war showed how vulnerable key transport facilities — both pipelines and tanker loading terminals — were to military attack and how a breakdown in the delivery system could bring total production to a halt. In order to understand the mounting risks involved in oil transport, it is necessary to trace the course of an oil cargo from field to market.

VULNERABILITY OF PETROLEUM TRANSPORT

Petroleum transport and production are part of a continuous process. When oil is produced, it flows from wells through pipelines to field storage tanks. From these tanks, oil continues to move by pipeline to storage tanks at refineries or oil ports. These pipelines must be entirely filled before oil can be transmitted through the line. Pumps, frequently operated by computer, force the oil through the pipe at from 3 to 5 miles an hour. While the flow of oil from fields to tankers can be slowed down, it cannot be stopped without bringing to a halt the flow of oil from the wellhead.

Oil loading terminals form a critical link in the oil delivery system. At the producer end, terminals have been constructed to receive oil from specific fields as well as blends of oil from different fields. Blended or segregated supplies of oil are stored in tanks on shore from which pipelines carry oil out to loading terminals. These terminals are either fixed docks, with berths into which tankers can slip to be loaded, or offshore terminals. The offshore facilities consist of large circular moorings that can handle either one or many ships at a time. In either case, submarine pipelines carry the oil from shore to the terminal, which acts as a conduit for transmitting the petroleum into the tanker. Pump stations for these underwater lines rest on floating platforms, servicing a network of moorings.

In the Persian Gulf, most of the loading terminals are offshore, where greater depths can accommodate supertankers. The exception is the large, fixed, deep-water ports at the north of the gulf constructed by Iran, Iraq, and Kuwait. Three fixed docks — Kharg Island, Khor-al-Kafka, and Khor-al-Amaya — were severely damaged by air attack during the Iran-Iraq war.[14] While Kuwait's principal oil port, Mina-al-Ahmadi was not destroyed in the war, it remains a vulnerable target. If this giant port (consisting of 14 berths for supertankers of from 250,000 to 400,000 deadweight tons) were destroyed, Kuwait would have only two offshore moorings at which tankers could be loaded. While offshore facilities are less easy targets for air attack than are large fixed docks, they can be sighted and hit. In short, all the oil loading terminals in the gulf are "sitting ducks" for air attack.

Table 6.1 describes the characteristics of the major oil loading terminals in the Persian Gulf and the Mediterranean that serve the principal Middle East and North African producers. As the table indicates, the depth of the harbor and the size of the tanker that the terminal can accommodate control the maneuverability of tankers and, thus, the flow of oil exports. Very large or ultralarge cargo carriers (VLCCs, ULCCs) of from 250,000 to 500,000 deadweight tons (dwt) cannot receive shipments at most terminals in the Mediterranean because the harbors are too shallow. Similarly in the Persian Gulf, supertankers cannot load oil at the older fixed docks at Ras Tanura, which only handle tankers of 70,000 dwt. Thus, whereas tankers of roughly 80,000 dwt or less can move anywhere, supertanker traffic (on which world oil trade depends) would be immobilized if the special offshore loading facilities were destroyed.

The exposure of oil loading terminals in the Persian Gulf suggests that the most effective way to cripple oil trade from the Middle East would be aerial attack on the principal oil ports and offshore loading terminals up and down the gulf. Any defense system devised to ensure continuous oil operations should treat as a top priority the placement of anti-aircraft weaponry in or around these loading facilities. At this time, such weaponry is absent or inadequate, according to strategic experts.

Estimates of how long it would take to repair these terminals range upward from a year. Since the oil loading terminals are without question the "Achilles' heel" of the international oil logistical

TABLE 6.1
Oil Loading Terminals in the Persian Gulf and the Mediterranean

Country, Port		Type	Berths/Buoys (mbm, sbm)	Controlling Depth (feet)	Maximum Tanker (dwt)	Tanker Capacity (million barrels)
PERSIAN GULF						
Iran						
Kharg Island		artificial sea island,	10 berths	68	250,000	1.86
			1 berth	68	75,000	0.56
		fixed	1 berth	68	100,000	0.74
		offshore	2 mbm	98	500,000	3.70
Iraq						
Khor-al-Kafka		fixed	1 berth (Mina-al-Bakr)	69	350,000	2.60
Khor-al-Amaya		fixed	3 berths	69	330,000	2.40
al-Fao		fixed	1 berth	35	33,000	0.24
Kuwait						
Mina-al-Ahmadi		fixed	12 berths	63	250,000	1.86
			2 berths	90	400,000	3.00
		offshore	2 sbm	93	500,000	3.70

(continued)

Table 6.1, continued

Country, Port	Type	Berths/Buoys (mbm, sbm,	Controlling Depth (feet)	Maximum Tanker (dwt)	Tanker Capacity (million barrels)
Saudi Arabia					
Ras Tanura	fixed	10 berths	46	70,000	0.50
	sea island	8 berths	64	327,000	2.10
Juaymah	offshore	6 sbm	107	500,000	3.70
Zulaf	offshore	1 sbm	90	450,000	2.90
Qatar					
Um-Said	offshore	1 sbm	39	300,000 (partially loaded)	—
United Arab Emirates					
Abu Dhabi					
Jabal Dhanna	offshore	4 mbm	47	320,000 (partially loaded)	—
Dubai, Sharjah	offshore	unknown	no limit	no limit	no limit
Oman					
Mina-al	offshore	2 sbm	92	500,000	3.70
Fahal		1 sbm	48	100,000	0.70
		1 sbm	39	300,000 (partially loaded)	—

MEDITERRANEAN

Algeria					
Arzew	offshore	2 mbm	49	90,000	0.70
	fixed	1 berth	42	50,000	0.37
		1 berth	48	90,000	0.70
Ad Oran	fixed	1 berth	38	60,000	0.40
Skikda	fixed	1 berth	45	50,000	0.37
Bejaia	fixed	1 berth	41	85,000	0.60
La Skhirra	fixed	2 berths	50	120,000	0.80
(Tunisia for Zarzatin oil)					
Egypt					
Alexandria (receiving oil only)	fixed	unknown	33	30,000	0.20
Suez/Port Said (canal)	fixed	unknown	35	30,000	0.20
			53	150,000	1.00
Lebanon					
Tripoli (Iraqi oil)	fixed	3 berths	60	140,000	1.00
Syria					
Banias (Iraqi oil)	offshore	4 mbm	53	120,000	0.80

(continued)

Table 6.1, continued

Country, Port	Type	Berths/Buoys (mbm, sbm)	Controlling Depth (feet)	Maximum Tanker (dwt)	Tanker Capacity (million barrels)
Turkey					
Dortyol	fixed	2 berths	65	330,000	2.40
(Iraqi oil)		2 berths	53	150,000	1.00
Libya					
Ras Lanuf	offshore	3 mbm	55	130,000	0.90
		1 sbm	72	255,000	1.90
Zuetina	offshore	3 sbm	70	250,000	1.80
		2 mbm	50	120,000	0.80
Marsa-el	offshore	1 mbm	40	65,000	0.50
Brega		1 mbm	49	100,000	0.70
		1 sbm	65	300,000	2.20
Essidir	offshore	3 mbm	35	100,000	0.70
		1 sbm	62	255,000	1.90
Tobruk	fixed	jetty	54	100,000	0.70
	offshore	1 mbm	45	65,000	0.50

mbm = multiple buoy mooring
sbm = single buoy mooring
dwt = deadweight tons
7.45 barrels to a long ton

Source: An international oil company that prefers to remain anonymous.

system, every effort must be made to secure these key installations (see Table 6.2).

The other major weak point in the logistical system is the Strait of Hormuz at the mouth of the Persian Gulf. This waterway is about 25 miles wide, while the channel through which supertankers pass (with drafts of from 50 to 100 feet) is only two miles wide. Each day as many as 300 vessels of various size pass through the strait, including tankers carrying roughly 60 percent of the world's oil cargos.[15] There has long been speculation that the strait could be closed to traffic by a blockade, by mines, or by a few sunken or damaged tankers in the middle channel.[16] While the sinking of two or even three tankers in the strait would not prevent passage of other vessels, the psychological impact of such an event would send insurance fees for vessels in the gulf skyrocketing. These commercial responses by oil companies and insurance brokers would result in a significant slowdown in oil flowing through the gulf. The crippling impact that terrorist action of this sort would inflict is devastating, even though it would not directly result in any reduced capability.

By far the greatest threat to the strait would be the placement of mines or even the false declaration that the channel had been mined. One estimate suggests that "only 200 mines would be required to close the 25-mile strait. Another 50 mines might be added to this requirement to hedge against technical failures, misplaced drops and similar errors."[17] Mines could be placed by either submarines or aircraft. The threat of mining could be as disruptive as actual mining. If planes or ships appeared to be mining the strait — with large

TABLE 6.2
Crude Oil Imports, First Half of 1980
(millions of barrels a day)

	United States	Japan	West Germany	France	Italy	Canada
OPEC	4.2	3.9	1.6	2.1	1.6	0.4
Non-OPEC	1.5	0.6	0.4	0.2	0.3	0.2
Total	5.7	4.5	2.0	2.3	1.9	0.6

Source: U.S., Central Intelligence Agency, *International Energy Statistical Review* 24 (February 1981): 5-8.

chunks of concrete for example – ships would refuse to pass through the channel until a minesweeper declared the region safe.

In the event that the oil terminals were destroyed or that the Strait of Hormuz was closed, Middle East producers would have only a limited capability to send oil out by pipeline to ports in the Red Sea or the Mediterranean. Because of interterritorial disputes and political upheaval in states through which these lines pass, most of these lines do not run at full or even partial capacity at this time.

As previously noted, the pipeline system has been the object of frequent attack in the past. Because pipelines and pump stations are the most exposed equipment used for petroleum transmission, they are the object of sabotage. While the lines can be repaired in a relatively short period of time, destruction of pump stations can put the entire system out for weeks or months, depending on the availability of replacement parts. The destruction of pump stations for pipelines in Iraq was a principal cause of the cutback in Iraqi exports from the Mediterranean during the Iran-Iraq war. Although pipeline disruptions may not cripple the entire distribution system, they pose a risk to the smooth flow of oil from the Middle East and other major producing areas, including the United States.

MIDDLE EAST OIL PIPELINES

There are five major crude oil lines from the Persian Gulf to the Mediterranean, but only three have operated in recent years. Together, five lines have the capacity to pump 4.6 mmbd, slightly more than a quarter of total Middle East oil output. Three lines run from the Kirkuk oilfields of Iraq to Banias, Syria; Tripoli, Lebanon; and Dortyol, Turkey —all ports on the eastern Mediterranean. The line to Turkey can pump from 500,000 to 700,000 barrels a day, while the parallel lines to Banias and Tripoli can pump 700,000 and 500,000 barrels a day, respectively. Thus, Iraq has the capacity to export roughly 2.2 mmbd – two-thirds of its oil output – by pipeline to the Mediterranean.

The other east-west lines in the area transport crude oil from Saudi Arabia. In the 1950s, the American-Arabian Oil Company (ARAMCO) built a 754-mile line from the Qaisuma fields through Jordan to Sidon, Beirut, which could pump 470,000 barrels a day. Today, however, the Saudis ship only a small quantity of oil through this line to Jordan.

The other Saudi crude oil line has been under construction since 1977 and is close to completion. In 1981, Petromin, the state oil company, will begin to operate the pipeline from the Abqaiq oilfield to the refinery and port complex at Yanbu on the Red Sea.[18] The line has an initial capacity of 1.85 mmbd and could eventually transport 2.35 mmbd, or about 20 percent of Saudi output. The line will feed oil to the refinery at Yanbu (capacity of 170,000 barrels daily) and Jeddah (54,000 barrels daily). The rest will be available for export.

From Yanbu, oil shipments are likely to go north through the Red Sea to the Suez Canal or through the Suez-Mediterranean pipeline (Sumed) to Alexandria. The Sumed line, which is still under construction, will have the capacity to move 200,000 barrels a day. Until its completion, however, cargos will go by small tanker through the Suez Canal and on to Europe by the Mediterranean.

For political, economic, and physical reasons, it is unlikely that the pipeline/Mediterranean port network will become a major outlet for Middle East oil, either replacing the Persian Gulf route or taking some of the pressure off it. First, the Mediterranean ports are considerably smaller than the Persian Gulf loading ports, and therefore they cannot accommodate supertanker traffic. Furthermore, the cost of using smaller tankers for crude shipments through the Mediterranean to Europe would be higher than moving the same volume of oil to Europe and other markets by supertanker. Second, political tensions among the Arab states in the region could interfere with operation of pipelines and ports. This is particularly true of relations among Iraq, Syria, and Lebanon. In the past, Syria has tended to obstruct exports of Iraqi crude from Banias by posting excessively high tariffs. The line to Tripoli was closed for six years because of political upheaval within Lebanon. While the line to Turkey remained open during the Iran-Iraq war, it does not have the capacity to handle all of Iraq's exports. Moreover, Turkey's own political dispute could interfere with Iraqi oil movements by pipeline.

Thus, because of the limited capability of Middle East pipelines and the Mediterranean ports, oil producers and importers must continue to rely on supertanker traffic out of the Persian Gulf for supply through the 1980s. As long as the Middle East remains a major oil producer and exporter, the Persian Gulf will remain the primary channel through which supply moves. While this area can and must be defended by conventional forces, it is debatable whether the key operations in the region can be effectively guarded against attack.

As one noted expert on the subject has stated, "The problem today is that the Strait of Hormuz is essentially unguarded. . . .

> The shah is gone, and although Oman now has one of the better armed forces in the region, it is small and inadequately equipped. Without external help, Qaboos probably could not have succeeded in defeating the Dhofar rebels, small in number though they were. If there is a renewal of the revolt, the Sultan's chances of quelling it are slim. With this situation in Oman, and the uncertain future of the Iranian revolution, local threats to the waterway are a real possibility.[19]

In the past, Oman has proposed a regional security plan that envisaged an alliance of gulf states and the cooperation of Western states, including the United States, West Germany, and Great Britain. This plan was rejected for obvious reasons. A Western presence in the gulf could do more to provoke the sorts of terrorist attacks feared by Oman than to prevent them. While it is beyond the scope of this chapter to look at the political and strategic factors involved in Persian Gulf security (see Chapter 8), the point is that the strait and the entire gulf region are vulnerable to either terrorist or military attack at any time.

At least two strategic analysts have commented on the indefensibility of oil installations in the Persian Gulf. Jeffrey Record has noted:

> The difficulty of defending oilfields and oil shipping routes inside the Gulf against direct assault by terrorist or regular armed forces constitutes another obstacle to successful U.S. military intervention in the Persian Gulf. The spatial vastness of the Gulf's major oilfields, the exposed nature of wells, pipelines, pumping stations, storage tanks, refineries, and loading piers; and the vulnerability of large, slow-moving, and unarmed tankers to aerial attack, artillery fire, and even small, hand-held rocket launchers — all dictate a reliance on means other than the direct employment of military force to protect oilfields and facilities.[20]

John M. Collins, a well-known expert on U.S. and Soviet military capability (see Chapter 1), also comments:

military forces needed to seize and secure a lodgment on Persian Gulf shores could cope with cratered airfield runways and ruined port facilities, but could neither restore petroleum installations nor operate the system. Highly skilled civilian manpower and special materials would be required for such purposes. . . . Successful saboteurs could impede or perhaps even stop the flow of oil at its source in the fields, at pipeline choke points at terminal facilities or after products have been pumped aboard tankers.[21]

Collins goes on to note the peculiar vulnerability of the sophisticated equipment that Saudi Arabia requires for its petroleum recovery and petrochemical operations.

Saudi Arabia's machinery presents special problems, generally being the biggest in the world: the biggest gas separators (50 of them); the biggest pumping stations (2 million barrels each per day); the biggest water-injection plants (400 million cubic feet daily from Abqaiq field alone); the biggest storage tanks, the biggest oil port and the biggest desalinization plant (except for one in Kuwait). One-of-a-kind items that would be time consuming and expensive to replace.[22]

Collins concludes that, given these complicated aspects of oil production and transport in the region, "restoration requirements would exceed U.S. capabilities, unless damage was quite restricted."[23]

Such analyses suggest that conventional military operations in the Persian Gulf could be irrelevant to the task of protecting oil installations and that some other security measures, sharply different from traditional military tactics, are required. An effective security system for the oil installations in the Persian Gulf may, in fact, be impossible. However, if the West's vital objectives in the region are to preserve the flow of oil as well as to protect the region from Soviet or dissident forces, the oil producing states, the United States, and U.S. allies must address the inadequacy of current safeguards.

THE U.S. OIL DISTRIBUTION SYSTEM AS A TARGET OF TERRORISM

The history of the domestic U.S. oil system records that all segments of the industry, including management, extraction, processing, and distribution, have been subjected to sabotage and terrorist attacks. The oil system is a high-technology industry that has its vulnerable points. So far, terrorist operations have been limited in scope and not indiscriminate, owing to the perpetrators' desire to demonstrate their tactical capabilities rather than to commit a major violent act for its own sake.

The earliest incident involved teamsters in 1859 who, in a disagreement over wages, bombed the first oil pipeline constructed by Colonel Drake.[24] Over a century later and in another labor-management dispute, a Tenneco Oil Company maintenance supervisor was killed by a worker during a strike.[25]

More recently, in 1974, the Weather Underground bombed the Gulf Oil offices in Pittsburgh and caused $450,000 worth of damage, claiming the action was in protest of Gulf's having fomented a Portuguese war in Angola.[26] In an extortion case in 1975, after a bomb exploded at an oil company facility in Carteret, New Jersey, threatening letters demanding a total of $45.5 million were sent to Gulf, Texaco, Exxon, Union, Phillips, Standard, and Amoco oil companies.[27]

To be sure, there have also been violent incidents for which the motivation remains unclear. A case in point is the 1978 bombing of the Trans-Alaska pipeline by unidentified saboteurs. The Alyeska Pipeline Service, which operates the pipeline, reported that about 15,000 barrels of oil were spilled. The pipeline was shut down for 21 hours — 12 for repair and 9 for federal approval to restart.[28]

This type of sabotage to the industry could stem from the efforts of organizations protesting utility rates, of disgruntled employees or local dissidents, or of persons advocating avowed patriotic or ideological causes, such as nationalists seeking separatism from the United States, or individuals furthering minority causes.[29] Americans for Justice, the New World Liberation Front, Puerto Rican Armed Forces of National Liberation (FALN), the Red Guerrilla Family, and Sam-Melville Jonathan Jackson Unit are some of the groups that have been involved.[30]

1970-79 has been the most active decade in terms of the number of incidents. Data compiled for Argonne National Laboratory for the period 1970 to mid-1980 show that a total of 71 attacks targetted the domestic oil industry (see Appendix I). They consisted of 27 operations against pipelines, 18 involving offices, 15 affecting petroleum storage, 6 directed against refineries, and 5 aimed at oil wells.[31] The most frequently attacked companies were Alyeska

Pipeline Service Company, Aramco, Esso Caribbean, Exxon, Gulf, Gulf and Western, Mobil, Phillips, Socony Mobil, Standard, and Union. High risk regions at which facilities and operations of the industry were affected included Alaska, Boston, California, Michigan, New Jersey, New York, Pennsylvania, and Puerto Rico.[32]

Although this record consists of a relatively small number of incidents, effecting minimal damage, experts suggest that future escalation in terms of frequency and magnitude is not only possible but may be inevitable.

The industry's production, distribution, and storage facilities are considered by experts as prime targets for any disaffected group that possesses knowledge of a particular system and the will to act. Skill and weaponry are less important elements in the equation once saboteurs know the system's pressure and access points.

As one expert on terrorism in the energy industry has noted, the logistical system is "designed for most economic service and not maximum security. . . .

> Most plants, offshore platforms, central oil and gas processing facilities, pipelines and refineries are totally exposed and are highly vulnerable. River crossings, which, if destroyed, could take months to repair are, by law, identified by large roadway signs as if to invite destruction. Power units, serving a refinery complex, are usually located along main highways and protected by nothing more than a chain-link fence. Although such substations are usually "looped" and alternate service can usually be routed to replace destroyed transformers, still there are numerous places where it is not always possible to restore electric service before an emergency plant shutdown becomes necessary.[33]

These extremely vulnerable targets provide easy access, by their very nature. Their operation could be halted at numerous points, as previously noted. Yet at this time, there is relatively little protection for these facilities. On the one hand, companies do not wish direct government involvement in security matters because it could interfere with company management. On the other hand, government — local, state, or federal — does not have the resources in terms of skill or staff to provide safeguards for the vast logistical network made up of pipelines, terminals, pump stations, river crossings, and intersystem linkups.

The pipeline complex should be regarded as the "ideal" terrorist aim. Specific objectives could include the 632-mile long Capline pipeline, supplying the Midwest with 25 percent of its requirements;[34] the 800-mile long Alaskan pipeline (TAPS), which contains a million barrels of oil at any given time;[35] and the 1,600-mile long Colonial pipeline, upon which the eastern United States depends.[36]

A recent warning of this peril was given in a report issued in 1979 by the U.S. General Accounting Office, an investigative arm of Congress. It asserted that "the petroleum industry is not adequately emphasizing the physical security of some key pipeline systems. And neither industry nor the Federal Government has plans for dealing with the critical impact of petroleum shortages should key pipelines become seriously damaged and disruptions occur."[37] So far, both the public and private sectors have ignored this assessment.

Although pipeline systems still remain the most attractive targets for future terrorist attacks, mention should be made of another important vulnerability of the industry: offshore facilities. Some experts suggest that these targets hold more potential for terrorist attack than onshore oil systems, although a lack of easy media accessibility to these areas serves as some protection against perpetrators who seek publicity for their activities.[38] They say there are more than 8,000 offshore oil platforms in operation off U.S. coasts, with the number of these facilities expected to increase substantially in the 1980s as this country makes an effort to reduce its dependency on foreign imports. Industry and government should note this likely proliferation, coupled with the fact that offshore oil targets are susceptible to attack from the surface, from underwater, and from the air. For example, well-placed explosives or precision-guided munitions could seriously damage or even destroy the "fortresses at sea." The relative ease with which such an operation could be carried out makes offshore oil facilities especially inviting targets. A determined group might also capture a facility and hold its crew hostage or threaten to blow up the rig and cause a major oil spill unless its demands were met.

Finally, in connection with the vulnerability of the oil industry, it is worth considering briefly the potential of liquefied gases, which provide approximately 3 percent of U.S. consumption.[39] Whether liquefied natural gas (LNG),[40] liquefied petroleum gas (LPG),[41] or naphtha,[42] liquefied gases are extremely volatile. For example, a major disaster of an LNG spill in Cleveland in 1944 killed 130 people, injured 225, and resulted in $7 million in property damage.

This isolated tragedy halted LNG use in this country for some 20 years.

LPG, once spilled, can become highly flammable and explosive. Held under pressure in bulk storage in underground salt domes or mined caverns, LPG is mainly transported through 70,000 miles of high-pressure pipeline. The LPG industry also uses 16,300 rail tank cars and 25,000 transport and delivery trucks. The vulnerability of these facilities and transportation systems, as well as those of LNG, must therefore be considered. An attack on liquefied energy gases would not seriously disrupt the U.S. energy system, but it could inflict extensive and costly damage.

Whether terrorist groups in this country, domestic or foreign, are likely to exploit the vulnerabilities of the entire oil industry in the foreseeable future cannot be supported by hard evidence at this time. What is clear is that only groups with certain attributes and capabilities could succeed. Richard J. Kessler (see Chapter 5) has realistically observed:

> An attack against a major sector of the domestic energy industry would require a highly motivated group with an "insider's" knowledge of the industry's operations as well as access to sophisticated explosives. It would also be a group which had previously identified itself to the authorities during earlier efforts to articulate its demands. Disruption of U.S. energy supplies is not an objective which a terrorist organization begins with; it is one with which it ends.[43]

Electric Utilities

Since 1970 there have been more than 150 attacks directed against electrical utilities in the United States and abroad.[44] Power lines, electric power substations, electrical control systems, transmission towers, power facilities, electrical transmission lines, electrical installations, utility towers, and powerline poles have been targetted from California to the Philippines, from France to Colombia. Approximately 40 percent of all utilities attacked between 1970 and 1980 were electrical.[45] Transmission line structures, for instance, are particularly vulnerable because they are often located in isolated areas where terrorist groups can attack them with relative ease.

The threat in the United States was assessed recently by energy analyst Kessler (see Chapter 5):

. . . the extensive U.S. transmission system (over 359,000 circuit miles) is its weakest link as well as its strongest. There are now three major, unconnected networks of extra-high-voltage (EHV) transmission facilities in the U.S.: in the eastern two-thirds of the U.S. from the Atlantic to the Rockies, in Texas, and in the Far West. The development of a national power grid, connecting high-capacity lines of the West Coast system with the Eastern Missouri River Basin and the Mississippi River Basin systems may simplify the terrorist's objective of identifying the critical transmission links and destroying them, especially as the continued development of economies of scale in the transmission of electric power is increasing maximum transmission voltage. A key terrorist target would be to identify the transmission line interconnecting points which now enhance the system's power transfer capability.[46]

One of the most active groups in the United States involved in attacking electrical utilities is the New World Liberation Front. For example, in March 1978, it bombed a Pacific Gas and Electrical Company substation in a San Francisco suburb, causing more than $1 million in damage.[47] More recently, in September 1980, the group exploded a bomb outside the same utility in Berkeley.[48]

Although no major disruptions to the electrical industry have occurred so far, incidents abroad have been more costly. One dramatic example of the industry's vulnerability was the September 1978 terrorist operation in the Philippines. The Moro National Liberation Front blacked out almost one-half of Mindoro as a result of attacks on 10 power facilities owned by the government.[49] And in November 1980, elements of the Movement of the Revolutionary Left (MIR) or the newer Militias of Popular Resistance bombed nine high-tension towers carrying power between Santiago, Valparaiso, and Vina del Mar and other high-tension towers near San Bernardo, Chile. These bombings were particularly significant: they cut off power to a substantial portion of Santiago, Valparaiso, and Viña del Mar. According to police reports, an estimated 30 terrorists participated in the operations. As a tactic, the destruction of electrical powerlines and substations appears to be gaining favor among Latin American revolutionary groups, with similar activities occurring in El Salvador, Colombia, Guatemala, and Peru.[50]

Damage to utilities and their transmission systems does not necessarily result in long-run reduction in electric power generation. Yet, damage to any part of the system can be extremely costly to repair. Moreover, the psychological costs in terms of terrorist propaganda are even higher. Consider, for example, the April 1980 Puerto Rican blackout. An explosion in the Palo Seco electrical plant knocked out the island's entire electrical distribution system. It cost millions of dollars in damage and business losses. Puerto Rican separatists claimed credit for this incident.[51]

The Nuclear Energy Industry

The vulnerability of the nuclear energy industry is of increasing concern.[52] As a consequence of the oil embargo and the political unreliability of some oil producing countries, industrial nations have been motivated to develop alternative sources of energy. Nuclear power has figured largely in these efforts. Currently, more than 300 nuclear power plants are either operating, under construction, or planned in 26 countries – the vast majority in the United States. Thus, as the world moves deeper into the plutonium economy, the potential dangers of diversion, theft, or seizure of fissionable nuclear material produced by private industry becomes greater.[53] There have already been hundreds of nuclear-related incidents, with serious implications for U.S. national security. Over the past several years, thousands of pounds of low-enriched uranium and plutonium have either "disappeared" or remain unaccounted for at the nation's nuclear installations. According to one estimate, more than 50 tons of fissionable material have been "lost" at dozens of facilities operated by the Department of Energy.[54]

Moreover, since 1970 there have been more than two dozen terrorist attacks against nuclear facilities in other countries. For instance, in 1973, members of the People's Revolutionary Army (ERP) seized the nearly completed Atucha nuclear station in Argentina. The attackers escaped after painting a political slogan on the building, stealing weapons, and wounding several guards.[55] Also in 1978, the Basque separatist terrorist organization (ETA) bombed the partially built nuclear plant at Lemóniz, Spain, the second largest plant in Europe. The bombing killed two workers, injured 14, and caused $8.1 million in material damage to the plant.[56] The following year, after Swiss voters rejected an antinuclear initiative, antinuclear extremists exploded a bomb at a building on the site of a nuclear power station at Kaiseraugust, Switzerland.[57]

More recently, reports of an attempted sabotage, in the name of the antinuclear movement, of $30 million worth of atomic fuel supplies at the Surry plant in Virginia and of a Puerto Rican terrorist threat to blow up the Indian Point nuclear power station near Peekskill, New York, have again focused attention on the vulnerability of nuclear power plants and their auxiliary facilities.[58] Against the backdrop of the Three Mile Island tragedy, these activities force one to think about the unthinkable — the prospect of a major nuclear disaster — with grave concern.

The impact of such developments on the future of the nuclear industry, and perhaps even on the survival of civilization, is staggering in its implications. If a minor terrorist attack against a nuclear facility led to the release of even minor quantities of radioactive materials, mass public panic could lead to the immediate closing and/or military occupation of all nuclear facilities. If such a closure occurred in concert with a major shortfall in global petroleum supplies, an energy crisis of staggering magnitude could result.

Moreover, to the extent that a diversion of highly fissionable materials by a terrorist group could be verified, the implications of a possible suspension of civil liberties to deal with such a threat could threaten the very foundations of the U.S. political system.

Coal and Uranium Mining

Coal and uranium mining are also subject to terrorist attacks.[59] Admittedly, potential threats to solid fuels are less spectacular than in the case of electric and nuclear utilities, but these threats become more important as the contribution of solid fuels to total energy consumption increases. Disruptions in the mining of coal and uranium can lead to higher energy costs and serious local production problems. The extraction, processing (particularly of uranium), and transportation phases of mining these solid fuels are most vulnerable to terrorism. On a comparative basis, facilities in western Europe and Japan are more exposed than plants are in North America or Australia.

Politically inspired disruptions, which may not be terrorist attacks, are the most visible threats to the mining of coal and uranium. Problems in labor relations because of working conditions or national events can lead to strikes that explode uncontrollably.

General instability within a country can also inspire terrorist acts at a mine site.

Although terrorist acts against coal and uranium facilities are rare and generally have only a temporary effect, it is imprudent to discount their occurrence, for they hold disastrous consequences for individual firms.

A recent warning signal was the February 1981 attack on a British coal ship off the Northern Irish coast. Seven members of the Irish Republican Army boarded the *Nelly M*, put its crew on a life raft, and blasted a hull before escaping. The explosion left the vessel partially submerged.[60]

CONCLUSIONS

In the past, terrorist or military attacks on energy facilities worldwide were relatively infrequent. While a few assaults caused considerable damage, they were not severe enough to suspend operations for any length of time. Since the early 1970s, however, the oil logistical system and other energy production and distribution networks have become susceptible to assault. As energy becomes the subject of more heated political debate (as is the case of nuclear power) or the instrument of political conflict (the "oil weapon" wielded by Arab countries), energy systems could become a prime target of sabotage.

This chapter has pointed out the vulnerability of energy distribution systems in the United States — specifically, of electric utilities and petroleum pipelines — and the physical insecurity of the oil logistical network centered in the Persian Gulf. U.S. companies have little security for their plants and transport facilities due to the simple reason that, so far, isolated attacks have been infrequent and relatively ineffective. Any group that set out to disrupt the flow of oil and gas or to destroy electric generators would require not only skill and determination but also a political cause for which it was willing to run the risks of such a mission. Thus, as long as the political climate of the United States remains relatively stable, it is unlikely that companies or local governments will step up security for major energy installations.

By contrast, the political instability of the Persian Gulf jeopardizes oil exports at any given time. The Iran-Iraq war and the Iranian revolution vividly revealed how vulnerable the major oil installations were to air attack and sabotage. This chapter has emphasized that the oil loading terminals along the Persian Gulf are the "Achilles' heel" of the international oil distribution system. At the present time, these terminals are poorly protected. Even if these ports and moorings were surrounded with anti-aircraft weaponry, a low flying plane could, in "hari kari" fashion, nosedive into the docks and destroy them. Furthermore, the docks themselves lack sufficient patrol to prevent access to terrorists. One journalist has reported how he was able "to drive onto one of the piers with a forbidden camera and approach an Iraqi tanker on foot without once being stopped or searched by the single guard on duty."[61]

While the Persian Gulf states believe that they alone should be responsible for the security of the region, they are the first to admit that they lack the staff or resources to defend the installations and, simultaneously, the territory in which they are placed. As one Saudi security official has stated, "We can't protect every inch of pipeline. It would take all our troops."[62] Because of the vast distances covered by the logistical network, it is to some extent indefensible. Yet, unless some greater effort is made to tighten the security of critical installations such as the oil ports, the Arab states and their Western clients cannot reduce the risks of sabotage and export interruptions that slack security presently engenders.

If the oil consuming states cannot count on the oil producing countries of the Persian Gulf to step up security for export facilities, what can they do to safeguard the flow of oil? Very little. First, overt assistance from the United States and other Western countries could provoke internal terrorist attacks on installations. While Western companies are currently designing security systems specifically suited to oil installations, debate continues within Arab countries over whether to purchase this equipment. However, without such defense systems in place, the oil ports and offshore moorings remain susceptible to attack.

If war broke out in the Persian Gulf, these petroleum facilities would be first to be destroyed. Military intervention by the United States and its allies after the fact would not be able to restore the flow of oil. Indeed, it is debatable whether the West and the Arab states would have the technical and economic resources to rebuild the vast oil infrastructure and to bring production back to the pre-war level.

With these considerations in mind, the United States must assume that military actions – both preventive and reactive – may be able to defend the territory or the political regimes of the Persian Gulf against internal upheaval and against the Soviet threat but that military actions may not be able to keep the oil logistical system intact and exports flowing to the West. If the threat to the logistical system is a function of the political instability of the region – a climate in which terrorist organizations thrive – other measures must be devised to "defuse" the charged political atmosphere of the region. Chapter 8 examines some of the diplomatic and foreign policy measures that the United States can take to help stabilize the Persian Gulf and, thus, to lower the risk of politically inspired attacks on the oil logistical system.

NOTES

1. Robert K. Mullen, "Potential Saboteurs to DOE Programs: Attributes and Inferences," report prepared for Argonne National Laboratory, Argonne, Il., September 1980, p. 35.

2. Edward F. Mickolus, *The Literature of Terrorism* (Westport: Greenwood Press, 1981), p. 698.

3. For details on oil-related incidents, see Lester A. Sobel, ed., *Political Terrorism* (New York: Facts on File, 1975); Brian M. Jenkins and Janera Johnson, "International Terrorism: A Chronology, 1968-1974," R-1597-DOS/ARPA, prepared by the Rand Corporation of Vienna, Va., March 1975; Marjorie Ann Browne and Allan S. Nanes, "International Terrorism," Library of Congress, Congressional issue brief no. IB 74042, September 1978.

4. Risks International, *Regional Risk Assessment: Latin America* (April 1979); and Mullen, "Potential Saboteurs," pp. 46-47.

5. Government of South Africa, unpublished documents, no date.

6. This section is based on unpublished material prepared by the Rand Corporation of Vienna, Va.

7. For details see *Annual of Power and Conflict* (London: Institute for the Study of Conflict, 1980), pp. 126-39, 404-9; and selected country studies of the region prepared by Foreign Area Studies, Washington, D.C.: American University, 1979-80.

8. For a brief but clear description of oil production, see *Facts About Oil* (Washington, D.C.: The American Petroleum Institute, 1979), pp. 13-15.

9. For a brief discussion of the extent of primary, secondary, and tertiary recovery worldwide and in the Middle East, see Richard Nehring, "Giant Oil Fields and World Oil Resources," a Rand Corporation report, R-2284-CIA, June 1978, pp. 77-78; and U.S., Senate, "The Future of Saudi Arabian Oil Production," a staff report to the Subcommittee on International Economic Policy of the Committee on Foreign Relations, Washington, D.C., April 1979.

10. Nehring, "Giant Oil Fields."

11. See Joseph P. Riva, Jr., "Iranian Oil Resources and Production," in *Economic Consequences of the Revolution in Iran*, a compendium of papers submitted to the Joint Economic Committee of the U.S. Congress, Washington, D.C., November 19, 1979, p. 112.

12. Nehring, "Giant Oil Fields," p. 146.

13. See "Oil Logistics Stakes are High in Iran-Iraq Flare-Up," *Petroleum Intelligence Weekly* 19 (September 29, 1980): 2.

14. "Iraq Oil Repairs May Take a Year," *Financial Times* of London, October 7, 1980.

15. "Vital Mid-East Oil Route Made Safer," *Christian Science Monitor*, October 30, 1979, p. 1.

16. See Barry M. Blechman and Arnold M. Kuzmack, "Oil and National Security," *Naval War College Review* 26 (May-June 1974): 12-13.

17. Ibid.

18. See "Saudi Arabia Set to Become World's Largest LPG Exporter," *International Petroleum Times*, June 15, 1980, p. 31.

19. Alvin Cottrell and Robert J. Hanks, *Maritime Access and Maritime Power* (Beverly Hills: Sage, 1981), p. 105.

20. Jeffrey Record, *The Rapid Deployment Force and U.S. Military Intervention in the Persian Gulf* (Cambridge: Institute for Foreign Policy Analysis, February 1981), p. 29.

21. John M. Collins, *U.S.-Soviet Military Balance: Concepts and Capabilities, 1960-1980* (New York: McGraw-Hill, 1980), p. 391-92.

22. Ibid.

23. Ibid.

24. For general overviews of terrorism in the United States, see, for example, Hugh Davis Graham and Ted Robert Gun, eds., *Violence in America: Historical and Comparative Perspectives* (Beverly Hills: Sage, 1979), chap. 12; Samuel T. Francis and William T. Poole, "Terrorism in America: The Developing Internal Security Crisis," Heritage Foundation *Backgrounder* 59 (August 7, 1978); and Brian M. Jenkins, "American Terrorism: More Bombast or Bomb Blasts?" *TVI Journal* I (1979): 2-8.

25. Washington *Post*, January 19, 1980.

26. Edward F. Mickolus, *Transnational Terrorism: A Chronology of Events, 1968-1979* (Westport: Greenwood Press, 1980), p. 459.

27. Ibid., p. 542.

28. New York *Times*, February 17, 1978; and U.S., General Accounting Office (GAO), "Key Crude Oil and Products Pipelines Are Vulnerable to Disruptions," EMD-79-63, Washington, D.C., August 27, 1979, p. 30.

29. For a psychological analysis of terrorist groups, see, for example, Frederick J. Hacker, *Crusaders, Criminals, Crazies: Terror and Terrorism in Our Time* (New York: W. W. Norton, 1976); and Charles A. Russell and Bowman H. Miller, "Profile of a Terrorist," *Terrorism: An International Journal* I (1977): 17-34.

30. For a detailed description of these and other U.S. terrorist groups, see National Advisory Committee on Criminal Justice Standards and Goals,

"Disorders and Terrorism," report of the Task Force on Disorders and Terrorism, December 1976, pp. 517-21. For a more recent listing of U.S. terrorist groups, see *Domestic Terrorism* (Washington, D.C.: National Governors Association, 1978), pp. 4-5.

31. Mullen, "Potential Saboteurs," p. 35.

32. For details on oil-related incidents, see, for instance, Sobel, *Political Terrorism*; Jenkins and Johnson, *International Terrorism: A Chronology, 1968-1974*; Browne and Nanes, "International Terrorism"; and various reports prepared by U.S. government agencies, including the Department of State, U.S. Information Agency, and the Central Intelligence Agency (unclassified).

33. Maynard M. Stephens, "The Oil and Natural Gas Industries: A Potential Target of Terrorists," in *Terrorism: Threat, Reality, Response*, ed. Robert Kupperman and Darrell Trent (Stanford: Hoover Institution Press, 1979), p. 222.

34. The Capline is a 40-inch-diameter pipeline running from St. James, Louisiana, to Patoka, Illinois. It has a maximum daily capacity of 1.2 million barrels.

35. TAPS is a 48-inch-diameter pipeline extending from Prudhoe Bay to Port Valdez. The system's present daily capacity of 1.2 million barrels can be expanded to 2 million barrels.

36. The Colonial system is a 30- to 40-inch-diameter pipeline stretching from Houston, Texas, to Linden, New Jersey. It has a 2.1 million barrel daily capacity.

37. See GAO, "Key Crude Oil," p. i. See also *The Trans-Alaska Pipeline* (Problems Posed by the Threat of Sabotage and the Impact on Internal Security) (Washington, D.C.: Government Printing Office, 1976).

38. See, for instance, M. M. Stephens, "Oil and Natural Gas Industries – A Potential Target of Terrorists," in Kupperman and Trent, *Terrorism: Threat, Reality, Response*, pp. 200-23; and John F. Ebersole, "International Terrorism and the Defense of Offshore Facilities," *Coastguard Proceedings* (September 1979): 54-61.

39. New York *Times*, January 26, 1978. For extensive studies see U.S., General Accounting Office, "Liquefied Energy Gases Safety," EMD-78-28, Washington, D.C., July 31, 1978, three volumes.

40. LNG is a mixture of hydrocarbons of from 65 percent to 99 percent methane, with amounts of ethane, propane, and butane.

41. LPG is propane and butane, processed from natural or crude oil.

42. Naphtha is a mixture of hydrocarbons extracted from crude oil during refining.

43. Remarks made by Richard J. Kessler at a conference on "Terrorism, Business, and Hostage Negotiations in the 1980s," sponsored by the Institute for Studies in International Terrorism, State University of New York, November 20, 1980. See Chapter 5 of this book.

44. This figure is based on various data bases and chronologies. It is impossible to arrive at an absolute figure because many national governmental policies preclude the publication of such data.

45. The term "utility" refers to (1) firms engaged in the production, refining, and dispensing of petroleum products, to include their offices, refineries,

pipelines, storage areas, tankers, and so on; (2) organizations producing electrical power from nonfossil fuel sources, including their offices, reactors, and other pertinent facilities; (3) firms involved in the production and distribution of electrical power derived from conventional fuels or water power, including offices, transmission equipment, powerlines, and so on; (4) corporations engaged in the operation of telephone communication systems, to include offices, communication lines, relay systems, and so on; (5) firms involved in the operation of water purification and distribution systems, including purification plants, pipelines, offices, and related activities.

46. Kessler, "Terrorism, Business." For more extensive details, see U.S., Department of Energy, Economic Regulatory Administration, Office of Utility Systems, *The National Power Grid Study*, vol. 2: *Technical Study Reports,* DOE/ERS-0056-2 (Washington, D.C.: Department of Energy, September 1979).

47. New York *Times*, March 15 and 18, 1978.

48. Risks International, *Quarterly Risk Assessment* (July-September 1980): 33.

49. Unpublished chronology prepared by Library of Congress analyst Allan S. Nanes, 1978.

50. Risks International, *Executive Risk Assessment* 2 (November 1980): 25-26.

51. Washington *Post*, April 12, 1980.

52. See, for example, U.S., Senate, Subcommittee on Internal Security of the Senate Judiciary Committee, "Terrorist Activity: International Terrorism," Washington, D.C., May 14, 1975, p. 197. The New York *Times* of March 12, 1978, reported that danger from "urban terrorists" and "sabotage" was cited by New York City in a legal argument when it sought to establish a local right to block the use of a 250-kilowatt research reactor by Columbia University on its Morningside Heights campus. For recent studies on the general problem, see Louis René Beres, *Terrorism and Global Security: The Nuclear Threat* (Boulder: Westview Press, 1979); William Epstein, *The Last Chance: Nuclear Proliferation and Arms Control* (New York: Free Press, 1976), pp. 19-22; and "Nuclear Terrorism and Nuclear War," a report to the Pugwash International Symposium on Nuclear War by the Year 2000, Toronto, May 4-7, 1978; Mason Willrich and Theodore B. Taylor, *Nuclear Theft: Risks and Safeguards* (Cambridge and London: Ballinger and Croom Helm, 1975); Ted Greenwood, Harold A. Feireson, and Theodore B. Taylor, *Nuclear Proliferation: Motivations, Capabilities and Strategies for Control 1980s Project* (New York: McGraw-Hill, 1977), pp. 99-107; Abert Wohlstetter, *Moving Toward Life in a Nuclear Armed Crowd?* (Los Angeles: Pan Heuristics, 1976); David M. Rosenbaum, "Nuclear Terror," *International Security* (Winter 1977): 140-61; and A. Dunn, "Nuclear Proliferation and World Politics," *Annals of the American Academy of Political and Social Science* (March 1977): 96-109.

53. *Gist* (October 1976); S. Burnham, ed., *The Threat to Licensed Nuclear Facilities* (Washington, D.C.: Mitre Corporation, September 1975), pp. 72, 95-96; and P. A. Karber, "Analysis of the Terrorist Threat to the Commercial Nuclear Industry," BDM/w-75-176-TR, draft working paper B, summary of findings, report to the U.S. Nuclear Regulatory Commission prepared by the BDM Corporation of Vienna, Va., September 1975.

54. L. Douglas DeNike, "Radioactive Malevolence," *Bulletin of the Atomic Scientists* 30 (1974): 16-20. For details on other theft incidents, see "Radioactive Plates Stolen from the Lab," Los Angeles *Times*, October 3, 1974; "Radioactive Needle Sought After Theft Suspect is Arrested," Los Angeles *Times*, November 28, 1974; "Cesium Sources Stolen, Found; Damage Reported," *Nuclear News* (February 1975): 59; U.S. Atomic Energy Commission news releases, October 29, 1974, and November 13, 1974. For other examples of missing or lost material, see Homer Bigart, "Engineers Pursue Lost Radium Hunt," New York *Times*, August 19, 1966, and "Second Shipment of Radium is Lost," New York *Times*, September 6, 1966; and Donald P. Gessaman, "Plutonium and the Energy Decision," *Bulletin of the Atomic Scientists* 37 (1971): 33-35.

55. *La Razón*, March 26, 1973, p. 4; *La Nación*, March 26, 1973, p. 3; and *Applied Atomics*, March 28, 1973, p. 4.

56. New York *Times*, March 18 and 22, 1978; and *The Guardian*, March 18, 1978. For recent developments related to ETA antinuclear activities, see Washington *Post*, February 11, 1981.

57. *International Herald Tribune*, February 20, 1979.

58. New York *Times*, October 29, 1979.

59. James Cobbe, "The Threat to Mining and Uranium," paper presented at Center for Strategic and International Studies conference on "Political Terrorism and Energy: The Threat and Response," May 1, 1980.

60. New York *Times* and Washington *Post*, February 8, 1981.

61. Walter S. Mossberg, "As Mideast Heats Up, U.S. Frets Over Peril to the Saudi Oil Fields," *Wall Street Journal*, January 21, 1980, p. 1.

62. Ibid.

APPENDIX I

Sabotage to Domestic and Nondomestic Energy-related and Military Targets, 1970 to Mid-1980

	Domestic	*Nondomestic*
Powerline	55	48
Powerstation/substation	43	21
Pipeline	27	54
Military aircraft	20	—
Office	18	11
Petroleum/gas storage	15	15
Nuclear energy peripherals and support	15	32
Laboratory	13	1
Warship	11	—
Refinery	6	12
Oil well	5	1
Hydroelectric facility	4	2
Missile complex	4	—
Mine	2	2
Coal train	1	—
Nuclear weapon association	1	—
Oil tanker	—	3
Oil trains	—	1
Nuclear waste freighter	—	1
TOTAL	240	204

Source: Robert K. Mullen, "Potential Saboteurs to DOE Programs: Attributes and Inferences," report prepared for Argonne National Laboratory (September 1980), p. 35.

7

Megadeath: Radioactive Terrorism

N. Livingstone

Today the problem is not making miracles — but managing them.

Lyndon Johnson

The magic Nibelungen Ring that gave all power to its possessor but carried with it a fatal destructive curse finds its modern counterpart in nuclear power, which contains so much promise and yet so much cause for apprehension. Today there is a broad public debate raging both in the United States and abroad regarding nearly every facet of nuclear power. In addition to public concern over the design and safety of nuclear reactors, questions regarding the storage of radioactive wastes, and fierce opposition to proceeding with the development of the fast-breeder reactor, there is also widespread concern that terrorists, seeking ever greater heights of terror, will ultimately undertake antisocial acts involving radioactive materials or nuclear facilities.

The question of radioactive terrorism is, in many respects, inseparable from the issue of the growth of the nuclear power industry since, as Amory B. Lovins and his associates have observed, nuclear power is the "main driving force behind proliferation,"[1] and inherent in proliferation is the collateral issue of how to adequately protect nuclear material and facilities from malevolent nonstate actors. According to James D. Watson, a Nobel Laureate in medicine,

I fear that when the history of this century is written, that the greatest debacle of our nation will be seen not to be our tragic involvement in Southeast Asia but our creation of vast armadas of plutonium, whose safe containment will represent a major precondition for human survival, not for a few decades or hundreds of years, but for thousands of years more than human civilization has so far existed.[2]

A New York *Times* editorial observed, "Once so promising in the first enthusiasm of the atomic era, nuclear power generation is becoming something of a monster, with dangers to people and to the environment so awesome as to raise serious doubts that this is indeed the best energy source of the future."[3] On the other side of the issue, the proponents of nuclear power note that this is a period of economic, social, and political dislocation and that during such periods people tend to look for scapegoats to lash out at in an effort to express their disaffection and confusion. Nuclear power, it is alleged, is one such target. It is frightening, people do not understand it, so they reject it. Proponents maintain that the nuclear industry's safety record has been nearly perfect and that the threats associated with nuclear power generation have been greatly exaggerated. Moreover, they contend that nuclear power is an indispensable source of energy that the world cannot overlook or do without.

To date, the United States has suffered no major accident or terrorist event involving a nuclear weapon, nuclear-powered vessel, nuclear power generating plant, or other facility engaged in the reprocessing or enrichment of special radioactive material, although there have been several potentially serious situations when disaster was narrowly averted: a 1961 incident at an experimental reactor in Idaho, the near "runaway" at the Enrico Fermi power plant outside Detroit in 1966, the 1975 fire at the Brown's Ferry, Alabama, nuclear power plant and, of course, the 1979 accident that resulted in extensive contamination of the Three Mile Island nuclear power plant in Pennsylvania. Reports from the Soviet Union, however, suggest that a major nuclear accident occurred in the 1950s in the Ural Mountains when nuclear wastes exploded, decimating a large region. If confirmed, it would be the most serious peacetime incident in history.

While there have been no publicly acknowledged U.S. terrorist incidents involving radioactive materials, there have been several hundred threats or actual acts of violence against licensed nuclear facilities in this country. In at least three instances, actual bomb material was discovered. Moreover, confidential sources within the Nuclear Regulatory Commission state that there have been at least six actual terrorist or criminal incidents involving nuclear materials in the United States; however, details are not available.

NUCLEAR POWER AND PUBLIC POLICY

At the very heart of the nuclear security problem is the surging demand for energy. At the present time, the daily world consumption of energy is equivalent to approximately 120 million barrels of oil. Nearly 60 percent of the world's energy comes from oil and natural gas; an additional 25 percent comes from coal; and the remaining 15 percent is derived from a variety of sources including hydroelectric power and the burning of wood and wastes. Despite the wide publicity accorded to nuclear energy, only a tiny fraction of the world's energy needs are currently satisfied by the output from light water reactors. Nevertheless, this situation is unlikely to persist since world demand for energy will soon outstrip the globe's rapidly diminishing fossil fuel resources.

Some experts predict that by the year 2000, world consumption of energy will be equivalent to 300 million barrels of oil per day. In view of the fact that oil and gas will account for less than a third of this anticipated daily consumption at the turn of the century, and coal for perhaps another third, there will be a shortfall of at least 80 million barrels of oil per day. While coal represents an alternative in many parts of the world, there are pollution and health problems associated with its use, and for many nations reliance on foreign coal supplies is little more desirable, as a matter of national policy, than reliance on foreign oil supplies. Moreover, despite optimistic projections by proponents of solar, wind, tidal, and other alternative energy sources, virtually all authorities agree that it is unlikely that such sources will account for more than 5 percent of the world's energy needs in the year 2000. Coupled with the output from hydroelectric facilities and the burning of wood and wastes, there will still be a shortfall of nearly 75 million barrels of oil per day by the end of the century. The construction of the first experimental fusion reactor is still more than a decade away, and the initial commercial fusion power reactors are unlikely to go on line before 2020.

Moreover, it was the conclusion of the Nuclear Energy Policy Study Group, which undertook a year-long study, under the sponsorship of the Ford Foundation, of the issues surrounding the nuclear policy debate, that fusion will not be an economically viable alternative to the breeder reactor in the foreseeable future, if ever.[4] Even if promising new energy technologies are developed in the years ahead, the problem facing the world today is still how to get from here to there.

Although it is embroiled in bitter controversy, nuclear power is the only proven new energy technology that promises to contribute significantly to filling the anticipated energy shortfall of the next half century. Lacking viable alternatives, the technologically advanced nations are irrevocably committed to its development.[5] While forecasts of the number of operational nuclear power plants by the end of the century have been scaled down, reactor construction is proceeding at a strong pace, propelled by the drive for alternative sources of energy and status politics. By 1984, it is anticipated that some 32 countries will have at least one > 20 Mega-Watts electric (MWe) reactor and that there will be somewhere in the neighborhood of 497 operational reactors in the world, each producing > 20MWes of power or more.[6] More than a dozen of the nations expected to possess operational nuclear reactors by the end of the 1980s are not fully stable polities and are experiencing or can be expected to experience periods of internal turmoil. This list includes South Africa, the Philippines, Pakistan, South Korea, Iran, India, Argentina, Mexico, Taiwan, Iraq, Brazil, Egypt, Israel, and Libya.

According to one study, by 1985,

> The plutonium produced in electric power reactors outside the U.S.A. and the U.S.S.R. would, if chemically processed, be sufficient to produce some tens of thousands of atomic bombs per year. By the year 2000, the plutonium expected to have been produced as a by-product of nuclear electric power would be enough to make several million bombs of the size that destroyed Nagasaki.[7]

Even if these figures turn out to be high in light of recent construction delays and order cancellations, they indicate the magnitude of the safeguards problem created by nuclear power proliferation and the greatly enhanced opportunities for diversion, sabotage, and improper use that this will present. Another recent international study ominously concluded that there was no way to prevent a sevenfold worldwide increase of "weapons-usable" plutonium over the next decade and, at the same time, that the prospect of developing an advanced nuclear fuel cycle that would not have plutonium as a byproduct is all but nil until well into the next century.[8]

The United States is powerless to prevent other nations from building nuclear power reactors since it has no monopoly on nuclear technology and is but one of the exporters of nuclear materials and technology (others are the Soviet Union, Sweden, France, Canada, West Germany, Switzerland, and the United Kingdom); hence any unilateral attempt to delay or control proliferation would be met with failure. In this connection, President Jimmy Carter's 1977 call for a global pause in projects to enrich uranium, to reprocess plutonium, or that use plutonium as a nuclear fuel went unheeded. Not one of 40 nations to which the proposal was addressed endorsed it. Moreover, the Nuclear Non-Proliferation Treaty confirms "the inalienable right of all of the parties to the treaty to develop research, production and use of nuclear energy for peaceful purposes without discrimination."[9] After being rebuffed in its efforts to slow down the pace of nuclear development, the United States has pressed instead for the adoption and strengthening of international safeguards through multilateral agreements and by attempting to restrain the proliferation of the most sensitive areas of the nuclear fuel cycle, namely reprocessing and enrichment facilities. In addition, the Carter Administration brought political pressure on nuclear exporters among its allies in cases in which it contended that the recipient country either did not have adequate safeguards or was located in an unstable region of the world. To date, however, such efforts have, at best, been moderately successful. The conclusion of a nuclear agreement between West Germany and Brazil, despite U.S. objections, is evidence of the futility of U.S. efforts.

The nuclear genie is out of the bottle, and this fact demands that effective international safeguards be developed to prevent nuclear material from being acquired by terrorists for antisocial purposes. According to Senate Majority Leader Howard Baker,

> The most urgent problem confronting the world in the near future may be a renewed effort to establish a realistic regulatory system to accommodate the expanding membership of the nuclear club. We are

confronted not only with the requirement for inspection and regulation of national nuclear arsenals, but also the awesome reality that through theft or terrorism, or through simple industrial endeavor, non-national groups may in our lifetime gain access to, or create, a nuclear explosive capability.[10]

Nations are not expressly required to adopt safeguards programs providing for the physical security of nuclear facilities and materials. Prudence would dictate that they do so, but no means of international evaluation exists to ensure that programs are adequate or that they keep pace with technological developments. Any country that desires U.S. technology or nuclear material, however, must undergo a physical security review to determine the effectiveness of its safeguards and must agree to legal and technical limitations on its use of that technology and materials to make radioactive weapons. The safeguards required by the United States before it will export nuclear material are administered by the International Atomic Energy Agency (IAEA). The signatories to the Nuclear Non-Proliferation Treaty agree to accept the IAEA safeguards pertaining to the export of nuclear materials and to refrain from exporting such materials unless the export "shall be subject to the safeguards required by this article."[11] Nevertheless, the IAEA regards its chief function as materials control and accountability, maintaining that physical security safeguards aimed at preventing diversion of fissionable material by terrorists is the domestic responsibility of the individual nation. Few other nuclear exporting nations, moreover, demand the same level of materials accountability and physical security as the United States, and this often puts the U.S. nuclear industry at a competitive disadvantage against western European firms. Even U.S.-required safeguards, however, can legitimately be criticized for emphasis on preventing the diversion of nuclear material by governments desirous of fabricating bombs rather than on its theft by terrorists or other nonnational groups.

It is not the purpose of this chapter to advance any conclusions pertaining to the efficacy of nuclear power in the modern world, but rather to assess the validity of the terrorist threat with respect to nuclear materials and facilities and, correspondingly, to judge the vulnerability of nuclear installations and transportation modes to terrorist assault. The threat can be broken down into three categories: the theft or construction of a nuclear weapon by terrorists or other nonstate actors, the antisocial use of radioactive materials, and the sabotage or seizure of a nuclear power generating plant.

First, let us examine the possibility that terrorists may one day be able to build or otherwise obtain a nuclear weapon that they could use either to blackmail or inflict widespread damage on a target society.

HOW DIFFICULT IS IT TO MAKE A NUCLEAR DEVICE?

Three things are required to build a nuclear weapon: accurate instructions, laboratory and machining facilities, and — most importantly — fissionable material. In this connection, it has frequently been asserted that, from a technical standpoint, the design and production of a serviceable but "dirty" nuclear weapon of a rudimentary nature is, relatively speaking, "no longer a difficult task."[12] "To design a bomb, nobody has to start from scratch; you no longer need, as you did in the pioneering years, a bunch of high-powered, hardworking physicists to figure out how to make a nuclear weapon," concludes Nigel Calder. "There are few 'trade secrets' left, notably how to use a small fission device to trigger a very large fusion explosion, but not many."[13] Given the requisite fissionable material and "using information that is widely published and materials and equipment available from commercial sources," observes Theodore Taylor, "it is quite conceivable that a criminal or terrorist group, or even one person working alone, could design and build a crude fission bomb that could be carried in a small automobile and that would be likely to explode with a yield equivalent to at least 100 tons of high explosive."[14] While those like Taylor have a tendency to understate the difficulty and time it would require, there is no question that it is possible for a technologically competent individual or group to at least design a workable fission device.

In recent years, there have been any number of widely publicized instances of university students designing viable nuclear weapons,[15] and there was even a threat against Orlando, Florida, devised by a 14-year-old boy who provided rudimentary but basically accurate diagrams of a bomb. Moreover, the now defunct Atomic Energy Commission conducted an experiment in which two young physicists with no experience beyond their Ph.D. degrees were challenged to design a nuclear weapon and to predict its yield. Given access to a small computer and an unclassified library, they finished the design of the weapon in six months. Experts judged that not only would the device work but that the two physicists had predicted the yield of their weapon within 10 percent.

In the words of Willrich and Taylor, "Every educated person already knows the single most important fact about how to make nuclear explosives: they work."[16] Moreover, the technical information needed to fabricate a nuclear device is readily available. This fact was vividly underscored in 1979 when several U.S. publications published classified information detailing the manufacture of a nuclear weapon. One authority has suggested that anyone with a master's degree in both physics and chemistry could probably design and, with the necessary materials, build a crude but credible nuclear device. According to Thomas Schelling, those with the skills and information needed to design and construct a bomb "reside in dozens of countries; they are not all under surveillance; and there is no master list of who they are."[17] Former senator Stuart Symington estimated in 1975 that from 100,000 to 1,000,000 people throughout the world possessed the information necessary to build a nuclear weapon.[18]

While it must be conceded that precise and accurate technical information on how to build a nuclear device has been widely disseminated and therefore is relatively available to those who might contemplate the antisocial applications of a nuclear weapon, the ability of terrorists to actually produce an operational device has been grossly exaggerated. The machine shop, laboratory, and other technical facilities necessary will not be that easy to come by, nor will such a project likely go unnoticed under most circumstances. But perhaps the greatest obstacle to be overcome is the acquisition of the necessary fissionable material.

BLACKMARKET IN FISSIONABLE MATERIAL?

To construct a fission device (A-bomb) would require from at least seven to ten kilograms of bomb-grade plutonium (Pu^{239}), which in mass would approximate the size of a grapefruit, or approximately 30 kilograms of uranium-235, or from 10 to 20 kilograms of uranium-233 oxide, which is derived from the element thorium but is far less common.[19] It is highly unlikely that a terrorist group could produce its own plutonium or bomb-grade uranium in view of the fact that to do so it would require "the technology to separate uranium isotopes by means of centrifugation,"[20] a very demanding task. Nevertheless, the authors of a recent article in *Foreign Affairs* suggest, "Non-nuclear commercial centrifuges may also be adaptable to uranium enrichment."[21] However, hundreds, perhaps even thousands, of commercial centrifuges and tons of uranium would be required to produce enough material for even one bomb. The process would be extremely costly and laborious and could take years of patient work just to accumulate a threshold amount of highly enriched uranium.[22] Thus, for the present, terrorists desiring to construct a bomb will have to look to other sources to obtain the necessary fissionable material.

The Atomic Energy Act makes it illegal for anyone in the United States to "transfer, receive, deliver, acquire, own, possess or import" special nuclear material without federal permission. Nevertheless, there have been a number of attempts to sell bomb-grade fissionable material on the international market. In 1977, for example, a Washington commodities dealer was contacted by two European business managers who purported to have 239 pounds of enriched uranium for sale, at a price of $2,650,000 per kilo (for a total of $288 million), more than 30 times its normal market value. The offer was investigated by both the CIA and FBI, but their findings have never been revealed. All purported attempts to sell bomb-grade material have reportedly been hoaxes or deliberate efforts to defraud the prospective purchaser. Indeed, several would-be illicit purchasers of "blackmarket" nuclear material have been unwitting victims of elaborate swindles, including Libya's Colonel Qadhafi.

At present, there is no known blackmarket in stolen fissionable material, despite the fact that gram for gram it may well be the most valuable substance on earth, or, at the very least, second only to interferon. Although its controlled market value is somewhere in the neighborhood of $100,000 per kilogram to bona fide purchasers, the price that an illicit buyer might be willing to pay for enough material to make a bomb is almost unlimited.

In view of the terrible risks for civilization that possession of a nuclear weapon by terrorists would entail and the highly interdependent nature of the world today, which affords little refuge from the effects of the detonation of such a weapon, the criminal underworld in the West, irrespective of the profits to be made, has shown little inclination to get involved in conspiracies either to divert fissionable material or to promote its sale to willing buyers. Indeed, agents of Libya's strongman, Mo'ammar el-Qadhafi, have allegedly contacted underworld sources in Europe, especially those in France, in efforts to secure enough fissionable material to build a "Moslem bomb." The French underworld, including the infamous Corsican Brotherhood, has readily cooperated with authorities to thwart efforts by third parties to create a blackmarket in fissionable material, recalling the patriotism of the French underworld during World War II when it gave active support and sustenance to the French Resistance.

More than 8,000 pounds of fissionable material is unaccounted for in the United States since World War II, but the U.S. government has traditionally been quite reluctant to publicly discuss the possibility of diversions. Nuclear Regulatory Commission officials admit that they often have not even informed Congress of missing nuclear material for fear that the information would become public and create a serious panic or that the knowledge would stimulate an unmanageable number of bogus blackmail attempts. Nevertheless, it is known that diversions of nuclear material have occurred. Evidence suggests that Israel has carried out at least five separate hijackings and that in at least three, if not all, of the incidents, it was aided by the acquiescence, if not the outright collaboration and complicity, of the government that was the target of the theft. Fearful of public and international reaction if either sold Israel nuclear material, in the late 1960s both France and Germany transferred enriched uranium to Israel for its nuclear program under the cover of carefully staged hijackings. Similarly, Israel diverted approximately 381.6 pounds of highly enriched uranium from a reprocessing plant at Apollo, Pennsylvania, with the assistance of the firm's president, Zalman A. Shapiro, who was reportedly identified by the FBI as an Israeli foreign agent. In addition, some 220 tons of European-owned uranium oxide, carried in drums labeled "plumbat," disappeared in ocean transit from Antwerp, Belgium, to Genoa, Italy, in the late 1960s, also presumably winding up in Israel.

Despite extensive concern by members of the U.S. intelligence community, Congress, and the Atomic Energy Commission, investigations into the Apollo diversions were suppressed at the highest levels of the U.S. government, and the inevitable conclusion is that the whole affair was, like the European diversions, simply a cover for U.S. cooperation with Israel in the development of nuclear weapons, more than likely at the top-secret atomic research center at Dimona, in the Negav Desert. It has generally been conceded for some time that Israel possessed, if not actual nuclear weapons, then surely the capability to assemble them quickly. The mysterious double flash recorded by a U.S. spy satellite on September 22, 1979, in a remote area of the Atlantic Ocean near South Africa was regarded by many experts as the signature of a nuclear test and, therefore, as irrefutable proof of Israel's nuclear capability. Israel, incidentally, is not a signatory to the Nuclear Non-Proliferation Treaty.

In 1980, it was revealed that 24 pounds of plutonium, enough to manufacture two relatively small bombs, disappeared from the Savannah River, South Carolina, reprocessing plant between 1976 and 1978. This is in addition to 303 pounds of plutonium missing from the plant between 1955 and 1976. Most nuclear plants and other facilities have experienced some loss of nuclear material, but not amounts equivalent to the loss at Savannah River. Nuclear experts, however, maintain that a 1 percent loss is normal and should not be cause for alarm. Considering that spent fuel from nuclear power plants must flow through approximately 50 miles of pipes before the plutonium is separated and purified, "It is inevitable that small quantities of the material will adhere to the walls of the pipes it passes through. Just a coating of less than one hundred-thousandth of an inch on the interior walls of pipes would account for the entire plutonium difference at Savannah River," explained a Department of Energy representative.[23]

The inability to account for such material indicates the inadequacy of current instrumentation in terms of measuring nuclear inventories, and this, in turn, makes it difficult, if not impossible under some circumstances, to differentiate between normal losses and actual diversions. The dangers associated with such instrumentation limitations are obvious. "For employees having continual access to the fissile material," R. B. Leachman writes, "undetected theft of the 10-kilogram (the amount required to fabricate a bomb) explosive quantity is then possible over a reasonably short period of time (for example, one year) by diverting quantities that are within the plant uncertainties."[24] The Nuclear Regulatory Commission has sought to develop and implement more advanced measurement techniques, but the recent losses at the Savannah River plant and at other facilities suggest that this problem is far from being solved. Moreover, since one of the most likely diversion scenarios involves the falsification of numbers in the records kept by nuclear facilities, measurement systems not only need to be made more sophisticated but should also provide for dual independent measures that can be compared with each other to ascertain any irregularities.

THE THREAT: WHO AND WHY?

The reasons someone might attempt to steal nuclear material are varied. First, the profit motive may be a paramount consideration, including a blackmarket sale of material by the thieves or hijackers or the ransom of the stolen material back to the party from which it was taken. Second, once a group has in its possession radioactive material, it could, if the material were of bomb-grade quality, attempt to fabricate a nuclear weapon. Even low-grade non-fissile quality material could be used either to contaminate some physical target or in an attempt to poison a target population. Third, the known disappearance or theft of nuclear material would be enough to lend credibility to any nuclear hoax, especially if the thieves were able to back up their threat with a sample of the stolen material or with accurate diagrams of the weapon they had constructed. No threat of this kind could be taken lightly, even if there were reason to believe that the extortionists would not carry out their threat or that the particular group possessed neither the resources nor the professional skills necessary to fabricate even a "dirty" low-yield bomb.

For many years, conventional wisdom held that only an insane person would try to divert enough fissile material to build a nuclear bomb. In defining five categories of potential nuclear thieves in 1973, for example, Ralph Lapp placed "one or more individuals acting on their own in an irrational manner" at the top of the list.[25] While the chief threat today clearly and unequivocally comes from nations desirous of joining the nuclear club, and despite the fact that the "threat of nuclear action by terrorists appears to be exaggerated,"[26] the dramatic increase in global terrorism in recent years has given security planners serious concern as they ponder potential threats to nuclear facilities and the possible antisocial use of radioactive material. Terrorist groups have demonstrated greatly enhanced skills and organization since the mid-1970s and are both better financed and armed than at any previous time, all of which makes them a far more formidable, and therefore more likely, threat to the safeguarding of nuclear material. According to the 1974 Atomic Energy Commission "Special Safeguards Study,"

> It is our opinion that the kidnapping of Patricia Hearst does not represent an isolated and passing incident, but is rather the precursor of a wave of such incidents. If not firmly and competently met, these kidnappings may lead to a rise of urban terrorist groups in this country of a sort without precedent in our history. These groups are likely to have available to them the sort of technical knowledge needed to use the now widely disseminated instructions for processing fissile materials and for building a nuclear weapon. They are also liable to be able to carry out reasonably sophisticated attacks on installations and transportation.[27]

It should be noted, however, that there is little reason to conclude that terrorists who have practiced conventional terrorism in the past will suddenly shift to nuclear terrorism in the future. The possibility nonetheless exists, however remote, that a technologically competent terrorist group, frustrated or embittered by slow progress in achieving its goals, will promote a radioactive incident designed to resolve their grievances or to strike back at their oppressors once and for all. Even a fairly moderate and not exceptionally bloodthirsty revolutionary such as Che Guevara spoke impassively of the circumstances that would justify the resort to nuclear terrorism or warfare.

> . . . rivers of blood will have to flow. The blood of the people is our most sacred treasure, but it must be spilled in order to save more blood in the future. What we affirm is that we must follow the road to liberation, even if it costs millions of atomic victims.[28]

Any individual who could make such a statement certainly would not shirk from the employment of radioactive weapons if it were within his capability and served his purposes.

In summary, all evidence suggests that criminal groups will continue to engage in the same profitable illegal activities that they do today, not only because the theft of fissionable material would be an extremely difficult undertaking, but also because any criminal diversion of such materials would probably stimulate an unprecedented crackdown on organized criminal elements, severely affecting traditional criminal activities. The threat to steal or divert nuclear material, therefore, comes from small groups acting on behalf of a specific nation or client intent on building a nuclear weapon, from terrorist groups, from mentally disturbed individuals, and from employees of nuclear plants or facilities who, for profit, may attempt to smuggle small amounts of nuclear material out over long periods of time. Clarence E. Larson asserts that once nuclear material is successfully stolen, "a supply-stimulated market for such illicit material is bound to develop. . . . As the market grows, the number and size of thefts can be expected to grow with it, and I fear such growth would be extremely rapid once it begins."[29]

THEFT OF FISSIONABLE MATERIAL

If no blackmarket in fissionable material currently exists or is likely to develop in the next decade, terrorists will be forced to obtain fissionable material through their own devices. In this connection, almost all commercial light water power reactors are fueled by approximately 3 percent enriched uranium-235, insufficient for the purpose of manufacturing nuclear explosives. A minimum enrichment of at least 30 percent is necessary for uranium from fresh fuel assemblies to have any utility to terrorists intent on building a practicable nuclear weapon; and, as noted earlier, enrichment is a technically demanding task well beyond the capability of any conventional terrorist group today. Thus, while stolen uranium fuel assemblies could be utilized in the commission of other kinds of antisocial acts, it is clear that the U^{235} used in the commercial fuel cycle is of insufficient enrichment to be of real value to bombmakers. And, "if the fuel for today's reactors is far too dilute for weapons use when it goes into the reactor," it is "far too radioactive to handle when it comes out."[30]

The spent fuel assemblies, which contain fissionable plutonium[239] as a byproduct, are extremely radioactive and represent a grave danger, in terms of fast neutron and gamma radiation, to anyone attempting to divert them for illegal purposes. Even if terrorists were successful in diverting spent assemblies, which is highly remote, their work would just be beginning. In the nuclear fuel cycle, plutonium is never in metallic form, and, therefore, it must be converted to metallic form before it is of use to the bombmaker. Moreover, reactor-grade plutonium is only 60 percent pure, and it contains 40 percent other isotopes of plutonium, which contaminate the Pu^{239}.[31] The plutonium contained in the discharged spent fuel is "highly diluted and intimately mixed with fission products whose intense radioactivity makes the spent fuel essentially inaccessible for at least a century."[32] To be useful to a bombmaker, therefore, the plutonium must be separated from the spent fuel rods in a process known as reprocessing. Although the U.S. government has detonated an experimental low-yield nuclear device using low-grade impure plutonium with a high content of the 240-isotope produced by light water commercial reactors,[33] terrorists would most assuredly have to reprocess the fuel from a stolen assembly, a feat requiring great technical skill and elaborate facilities. Thus, "as long as the plutonium in spent reactor fuel has not been reprocessed to separate it from the highly penetrating radiation in the reactor waste products, it is relatively immune from theft."[34]

Until recently, reprocessing was the exclusive domain of a few Western nations and the Soviet Union, constituting a virtually insurmountable obstacle to the use of plutonium contained in spent reactor fuel in the manufacture of nuclear weapons. But in recent years, several European countries have indicated a willingness to provide reprocessing services and technology on a contract basis to other nations. Moreover, reprocessing techniques currently being developed promise to make the technology available to almost any reasonably sophisticated nation, and, perhaps in the not too distant future, even to nonnational groups with sufficient money and expertise.

L. Douglas DeNike asserts, "It is widely conceded that the private manufacture of nuclear explosives is 'within the capability of many groups once those groups are in possession of the requisite 11 pounds of plutonium-239.'"[35] Nevertheless, while the design and fabrication of a crude but functional nuclear device are hurdles that could, with enough time, money, and resourcefulness, be surmounted, the chief obstacle to the creation of an illegal fission weapon is, and will remain, the availability of adequate fissionable material.

In the event that terrorists were somehow able not only to obtain the necessary plutonium, technology, and other resources required to manufacture a crude nuclear device, there is little assurance that all of the elements would come together in such a way that the device would work. "Any do-it-yourself bomb would stand an excellent chance of producing either a predetonation fizzle or a dud," Thomas Johnson concludes.[36]

THEFT OF A NUCLEAR WEAPON

Granting that there is currently little likelihood that terrorists or other nonnational actors could design and manufacture a nuclear weapon, one turns to the remote — but nonetheless more credible — scenario in which an effort is made to seize or steal an existing nuclear weapon stockpiled for military purposes. According to retired Brig. Gen. Joseph J. Cappucci, a former top Defense Department security expert and consultant to the Nuclear Regulatory Commission, "If I were a terrorist I would not waste my time trying to get nuclear material from a power reactor, but would focus instead on seizing a nuclear weapon in U.S. arsenals in Europe."[37] The United States, the Soviet Union, France, Great Britain, and China have significant military stockpiles of nuclear weapons, more than 40,000 of the United States alone, and such countries as Israel, India, and South Africa, and perhaps Pakistan in the near future, possess the technology and materials to produce nuclear weapons and may already, in fact, be members of the nuclear club. Estimates vary, but it appears that there are more than 100,000 nuclear weapons in the world today, providing terrorists with a wide range of potential targets.

For the United States, the approximately 7,000 nuclear weapons deployed overseas, principally in Europe, represent the greatest problem. North Atlantic Treaty Organization (NATO) security standards are badly in need of upgrading, and NATO members have shown a reluctance to provide the necessary funds to underwrite major improvements. Moreover, a significant number of these weapons are moved to and from production plants for routine servicing and maintenance every year, and they are most vulnerable during the transportation phase.

The U.S. government has repeatedly ruled out the possible theft of a nuclear weapon from its stockpiles, stating that the risk of that happening is negligible. "I think we have to bring this possibility of your being incinerated by a diverted or stolen nuclear bomb down to a level of risk comparable to . . . being struck by lightning," John O'Leary, former director of Licensing of the Atomic Energy Commission, offered.[38] O'Leary's comment is less than reassuring when one considers how many people are struck by lightning every year.

"No self-respecting nation that wants to beat the safeguards system and steal a (nuclear) weapon will be thwarted,"[39] George Murphy, former staff director of the Joint Committee on Atomic Energy of the U.S. Congress, maintains. When queried whether terrorists could do likewise, Murphy noted that, if well enough trained and equipped, a band of terrorists could force its way into a U.S. military installation in Europe and probably take physical control of a nuclear weapon.[40] So called "black hat" teams from the U.S. Army Special Services routinely conduct exercises in which they attempt to gain access to nuclear-weapons stores, and they have succeeded on a number of occasions. If they can do it, so can terrorists.[41]

It would not be possible to remove the weapon surreptitiously, but it could be held hostage by the terrorists, who most likely would threaten to detonate it if their demands were not met. Although detonation itself is not an easy task, the very fact that terrorists had in their possession a nuclear weapon would likely put enormous pressure on the affected government to comply with their demands. Intricate electronic locks are built into every strategic nuclear weapon, which would require terrorists, without the proper codes, to virtually take the weapon apart and put it back together in order to detonate it. Nevertheless, tactical theater weapons are not as sophisticated, and several sources posit that it would be possible to set off a tactical weapon by both electronic and physical methods.

In response to growing world terrorism, the Nuclear Regulatory Commission has stepped up security at all federal nuclear research centers and at test and weapons fabrication facilities during the past three years. At the 328-acre Rocky Flats facility near Denver, a key nuclear weapons plant, the annual security budget is $3.3 million. The 130-person security force includes a SWAT team, bomb squad, and fire and paramedic unit. The security force is outfitted with automatic weapons and has two V100 armored vehicles mounted with .30 caliber machine guns. The facility is surrounded by three separate eight-foot-high, chain-link fences and a virtual minefield of intrusion detectors and alarms. High-resolution, closed-circuit television cameras with night-vision capabilities also sweep the entire perimeter and all key access points within the complex.

Guards at the Nevada nuclear test site have been given orders to "shoot to kill" in the event of attempts to either sabotage or steal nuclear weapons or material. This is reflective of a "shoot first and ask questions later" policy at all U.S. military installations at which nuclear weapons are stored or deployed. According to Calder, "Near the bombers that stand fully loaded with nuclear weapons on American airfields, ready to take off at a few minutes' notice, a red line is painted on the taxiway; the visitor is warned that, should he cross the line, he will be shot by the sentries."[42] If hostages were used as a means of gaining access to an area where there are nuclear weapons, the Defense Department has directed that the welfare of the hostage not be considered in devising actions to meet the situation.[43] In other words, the sole consideration must be the protection of the weapon so that it cannot be used in any antisocial way.

TRANSPORTATION OF RADIOACTIVE MATERIAL

It is widely recognized that the transportation mode is the weakest link in the field of nuclear safeguards. "If a terrorist is going to make an attempt, that's where he'll make it,"[44] Ed Gillen of the Atomic Energy Commission observed. Over the years, mock attempts to hijack radioactive cargos have succeeded, most often during the transport of nuclear material by truck.

Procedures for safeguarding fissionable material in transport have been upgraded significantly in recent years. When a nuclear weapon is moved by rail, it is transported in a specially designed gray metal car with a two-ton top secured by massive bolts. Land vehicles transporting all special nuclear material are designed, in the event of an attack or diversion attempt, to become immovable fortresses until help can arrive. In one test, it took a crack team of experts posing as hostiles nearly 16 hours to penetrate the vehicle. Like an armored car used in transporting money, the cab can be sealed off to prevent access. The cab and trailer are superhardened, with bullet-resistant glass, armor plating capable of withstanding every projectile up to a bazooka shell, and locking brakes that immobilize the truck so that it cannot be towed away. The safe security trailer (SST) contains various active deterrents to entry. In addition, the main vehicle is accompanied by special tactical escort vehicles, and members of the escort team have a wide variety of heavy weaponry at their disposal. Since 1972, each vehicle has been linked to a nationwide communications system, capable of handling as many as 100 shipments simultaneously, which allows continuous monitoring of the progress of each shipment in the continental United States. A van, constructed along the same lines, has been developed to transport smaller shipments.

Despite the progress that has been made in safeguarding highway shipments of fissionable materials, a confidential internal Nuclear Regulatory Commission study rated truck transport as less secure than moving radioactive materials by air. Air transport was deemed the most satisfactory method, followed by highway, rail, and water transport. Ship and barge transport was assessed to be the most vulnerable mode since such vessels are relatively slow-moving, are easily boarded, are often out of contact for long periods of time, and, on occasion, are far from a friendly port. It was the conclusion of NRC experts that the most optimal transportation system involved the movement of radioactive shipments from one secure installation directly to another secure installation, thus eliminating the risk of diversion between the areas of controlled access and maximum security. The only plausible security problem associated with air transportation would be the possible compromising of the flight crew. The flights would avoid all heavily populated areas, and the nuclear material would be transported in heavily shielded casks to reduce the chance of an accidental release of radioactivity in the event of an air crash. Supporters of the air transport mode note that the Soviet Union reportedly moves all of its radioactive material by air, using both fixed-wing aircraft and helicopters.

Some NRC officials, nevertheless, maintain that surface transport is a satisfactory mode of shipment, demonstrated by the fact that the United States has successfully prevented any hijackings since the advent of the nuclear age. While it is correct that no highway shipments have ever been lost, it should also be noted that — with the exception of simulated hijackings — no attempts have ever been made to hijack or divert a highway shipment. According to one former top Pentagon security expert," If no one has ever attempted to divert a shipment, how do we know that the system is any good?

After all, you could move the material on a bicycle if no attempts are made on it."[45]

Operating on the premise that the SST and cab could delay forcible entry long enough for help to arrive, NRC planners and other observers contend that the safeguards built into the vehicle "could be easily circumvented merely by hijacking the entire truck."[46] Accordingly, the NRC undertook a variety of internal studies aimed at developing credible scenarios for "hijacking" the SST and whisking it away to a safe location where the vault could be penetrated, including one in which a mammoth construction crane lifted the SST off the pavement and rumbled away with it at five miles an hour. The futility of such scenarios, however, should be evident. A giant crane with an SST in its grasp would hardly be inconspicuous, and, at its snail-like pace, it could hardly spirit the vehicle and its radioactive cargo away before the authorities were able to mount a recovery action. The possibility of the malefactors employing a heavy-duty helicopter has also been explored, and, while this gives authorities more cause for apprehension, it is also regarded as an extremely unlikely scenario for a variety of technical and other reasons.

The most credible threat, according to knowledgeable experts, involves stopping the truck on the highway and hijacking the radioactive cargo on the spot by speedily overriding the deterrents both inside and outside the vault. The truck could be halted using a variety of methods, including ruses, barricades, and externally induced mechanical problems. The crew could be forced to surrender by attaching a magnetized magnesium bomb to the cab of the truck. As it burned through the metal, the heat generated by the bomb would compel the occupants of the cab — if they valued their lives — to surrender in less than a minute. Once access to the cab were achieved, the brake locking system and other external deterrents could be deactivated, permitting the SST to be detached from the cab and coupled to another power plant and driven away. Similarly, properly placed magnesium bombs could be used to penetrate the hull of the SST, although it would still be necessary to override certain internal safeguards. If the terrorist goal were simply mayhem, magnesium bombs could be used to breach the hull of the SST and the casks or containers of radioactive material, releasing radioactivity into the atmosphere.

One recent development complicating the land transport of nuclear material has been the proliferation of local ordinances prohibiting the transportation of such material through various cities and local jurisdictions. For example, most nuclear material must be carried by barge around New York City, one of the localities that recently imposed a ban on nuclear shipments. As a result of such restrictions, trucks transporting nuclear material are often relegated to back roads and forced to take indirect routes, making them more vulnerable to diversion attempts and accidents than they would be on high-speed, well-traveled freeways.

Although fairly elaborate precautions have been implemented in the United States to prevent the diversion of nuclear material in such an attack, the EURATOM (European Atom Energy Community) nations lag far behind the United States in developing adequate physical security systems for the transport of nuclear material, a particularly alarming situation in view of the serious growth of terrorism in western Europe in recent years.

LOW-LEVEL RADIOACTIVE INCIDENTS

One of the most serious incidents to date involving radioactive terrorism took place in Austria in the 1970s when terrorists poisoned a railroad car with radioactive iodine. This incident and others like it underscore perhaps the chief threat posed by terrorists today with respect to the malevolent use of nuclear material. In this connection, the possibility of terrorists constructing a nuclear bomb or stealing a nuclear weapon is, for the time being, very remote. Both are extremely complex undertakings that involve extraordinary risks for the malefactors. Moreover, because of the anticipated massive response on the part of the threatened state or polity, the likelihood that the terrorists would succeed is also quite remote. Thus, instead of incidents of catastrophic potential, according to Brian Jenkins,

During the next few years, we will probably witness a growing number of low-level nuclear incidents: nuclear hoaxes, low-level sabotage of nuclear facilities, seizures of hostages at nuclear facilities, contamination of symbolic targets with non-lethal radioactive material, perhaps a few fake devices.[47]

The maximum radioactive threat that can be credibly advanced today would be for terrorists to steal radioactive material and threaten to poison a city with it. This would not require the knowledge, elaborate infrastructure, and money that it would take to build a bomb, nor would it involve the risk inherent in stealing one; it would require only the nuclear material. And, whereas only bomb-grade uranium or plutonium could be employed in the fabrication of a nuclear device, virtually any radioactive material would suffice for the purpose of contaminating a specific target. Of course, for sheer toxicity, plutonium would be most effective; the effects from most other types of radioactive material might take months, even years, to show up.

Nevertheless, plutonium is far from being one of the most toxic substances known, as some writers have inferred. E. B. Giller notes that botulism toxin, belladonna, hemlock, oleander extract, various bacteria and viruses, and certain insecticides are all more lethal.[48] The deadliest of all synthetic substances, TCDD (2,3,7,8-tetrachlorodibenzoparadioxin), known as Dioxin, a byproduct of the manufacture of 2,4,5-T and Silvex herbicides, is far more toxic. The toxicity of plutonium is attributable not to any chemical properties, but rather to its various radioactive elements that emit ionizing radiation.[49] Thus, plutonium is highly carcinogenic. While it may produce skin tumors with concentrated exposure, it is inside the human body, whether by absorption or inhalation, that it is most dangerous. Since plutonium is an alpha emitter, it has very little penetration power, as Karl Morgan of the Georgia Institute of Technology has pointed out, and thus, "There is no danger in getting plutonium on the surface of your body, no immediate danger."[50] Once inside the body, however, plutonium seeks out certain body tissues and, once deposited in these tissues, irradiates them for the rest of the individual's life. According to Willrich and Taylor, "The total weight of plutonium-239 which, if inhaled, would be very likely to cause death by lung cancer is not well known, but it is probably between ten and 100 micrograms (millionths of a gram). Even lower internal doses, perhaps below one microgram, might cause a significant shortening of a person's life."[51] In addition, plutonium is capable of producing certain hereditary injuries.

Terrorists could expose a target population to plutonium or to other radioactive material in a variety of ways: by "dusting" the city by air with plutonium dust,[52] by coupling the plutonium with small explosive charges planted at strategic locations that would disperse the material throughout a particular area when the charges were detonated, or by mailing the material to selected targets. Plutonium could also be dispersed through the air conditioning or ventillation systems of large office buildings. Jenkins notes the possibility of contaminating such selective targets of high symbolic value as the New York Stock Exchange.

In what was surely one of the most novel murder plots in history, an employee of a nuclear facility attempted to slowly kill another man by placing highly radioactively contaminated metal rods under the seat of his car. The plot was fortunately discovered in time and the perpetrator arrested, but the potential for radioactive mischief of this kind is almost unlimited. In November 1979, the NRC reported, for example, that thousands of items contaminated by radiation – ranging from a cement mixer to small gauges – had been stolen from a nuclear waste dump near Beatty, Nevada. Many of the missing items could harm those who might unknowingly use them.

SAFEGUARDS MEASURES

Former German provincial minister Friedhalm Farthmann observed, "Any country that possesses atomic power plants is no longer really defensible."[54] Flood notes that in the event of open warfare between countries possessing nuclear facilities, those facilities would become, for all intents and purposes, indefensible "Trojan Horses," easy targets for sabotage, bombardment, or air strikes, and hence a serious threat to the country within whose boundaries they are located.[55] If nuclear facilities are vulnerable in time of war, they are also vulnerable to the designs of terrorists.

The greatest potential for danger involves nuclear facilities in the developing world; it is there that security is the weakest, that internal strife is most common, and that conventional wars are most likely to erupt. Although India, South Vietnam, and Israel possess nuclear facilities and have been involved in recent major conflicts, their facilities were never attacked. However, in 1980, during the Iran-Iraq conflict, air strikes by F-4 Phantom jets with Iranian markings heavily damaged a $500-million, French-built nuclear facility near Baghdad. Fortunately, the Iraqi reactor was not operational and contained no fuel.[56] The only such previous incident

involving a nuclear facility occurred in 1973 when Argentine guerrillas seized a nuclear station in that country and held it for a short
time.[57] The possibility that terrorists may one day seize a nuclear
power plant or nuclear material and use that facility or material to
win concessions from an embattled government, or perhaps even
power itself, can no longer be dismissed. In another potential
scenario, Willrich and Taylor suggest the possibility that units of the
armed forces of a country in turmoil might be persuaded to seize
nuclear material from a domestic plant and use it to support a
particular faction vying for power.[58]

The international ramifications of a serious incident or "event"
involving a nuclear power reactor in an unstable nation must be a
matter of grave concern to all nuclear exporting nations. Nuclear
material stolen in one country could be used against a target almost
anywhere. What would be the impact on German-American relations,
not to mention on the NATO alliance, for example, if nuclear
material and technology transferred from Germany to Brazil disappeared and were later used to fabricate a bomb detonated in the
United States?

In years past, the nature of terrorist targets was limited only by
the resources available to terrorists. Today, if a band of terrorist
malefactors were able to gain possession of a threshold amount of
fissile material and use it to construct a viable nuclear device, there
would be few restraints to prevent the terrorists from carrying out
their designs. In this regard, actions to ensure against radioactive malevolence, such as safeguards designed to prevent threats to nuclear
facilities, to guard against the attempted diversion of nuclear material, and to protect nuclear secrets from espionage, are far more
meaningful than countermeasures taken after the fact to head off
a nuclear catastrophe.

There are essentially four methods of preventing the diversion
or misuse of nuclear materials and of ensuring the security of nuclear
plants and weapons against the designs of violent nonstate actors:
safeguards measures, taking preemptive action against terrorists and
other potential threats, defusing the issues that give rise to terrorism,
and limiting the proliferation of nuclear weapons and technology,
thereby reducing the targets of opportunity. Because of the obvious
difficulties and limitations connected with the last three methods,
all of which involve political questions, authorities in this country
and abroad have opted for the implementation of stringent safeguards

systems – or, in other words, technical solutions – designed to protect nuclear materials and facilities and to reduce their vulnerability to threats, generally by denying would-be aggressors access to the target. In this connection, "safeguards" has been defined as "an intergrated [*sic*] system of audits, controls, and protection that combine to provide a timely warning of diversion and dissappearance [*sic*] of nuclear materials, particularly those that could readily and quickly be made into bombs"[59] and can be broken down into three categories: physical "hardening" of facilities and transport modes, materials measurement and accountability, and facility design. Traditionally, the greatest emphasis has been placed on the physical hardening of nuclear sites by means of personnel screening programs, armed guards, intrusion detection systems and alarms, secure communications links, fences, reinforced vaults, and well-trained and equipped emergency response forces. Only recently have real efforts been made to upgrade facilities design and to improve materials accountability. During the 1970s, up-to-date threat intelligence was recognized as an indispensable element in any comprehensive safeguards system. It should be emphasized that, to be truly effective, any safeguards system must have the capacity not only to grow with the industry but also to adapt quickly to the changing threat environment.

EMERGENCY RESPONSE CAPABILITY

Following several incidents – including one in Boston in which extortionists vowed to detonate nuclear devices if ransoms were not paid – that underscored the federal government's unreadiness to meet nuclear crises, the Nuclear Emergency Search Team (NEST) was created in 1974. Composed of several hundred experts, many of them on call from various federal agencies, NEST has developed detailed crisis management procedures for dealing with nuclear incidents. Its major function to date, however, has been to investigate nuclear threats to ascertain their veracity (all have been hoaxes), and, in this connection, more than $100 million has been spent on special planes, helicopters, ground vehicles, and radiation detection equipment designed to identify the radioactive signature of unauthorized or clandestine bombs and to pinpoint their location.

In addition, a number of other special units, modeled along the SWAT concept and trained in the protection of nuclear facilities and shipments and in the recovery of diverted nuclear material, have been formed to respond to serious threats involving radioactive materials by terrorists and criminals. The Department of Defense has established similar units to deal with accidents and threats to nuclear weapons. To be effective, such units must be able to mobilize rapidly with sufficient resources and personnel to repel or otherwise deter the threat. Generally, their strategy is to throw a ring around the threat or would-be divertor so as to prevent any possibility of escape and, once escape has been foreclosed, to address the threat in the appropriate manner.

Since most counterthreat programs are predicated on a thorough knowledge of actual vulnerabilities, the special knowledge possessed by response units is a source of some concern to authorities, who point out that a disgruntled former member of such a unit would stand a good chance of organizing a successful diversion attempt or orchestrating a believable nuclear extortion hoax. In recognition of this possibility, all members of response units should undergo intensive screening and constant behavior monitoring. Moreover, every effort should be made to provide excellent salaries, benefits, and working conditions to members so as to ensure that selectivity and high recruiting standards can be maintained and to discourage personnel turnover.

PHYSICAL SECURITY AT NUCLEAR PLANTS

Although the security at U.S. nuclear power plants and at processing and enrichment facilities is perhaps the best in the world, incidents have occurred that indicate that safegurads, no matter how good, will never be perfect. In February 1979, FBI agents arrested a temporary worker of a General Electric (GE) subcontractor who had stolen 150 pounds of low-grade uranium from a GE plant and had threatened to disperse the material through one or more major U.S. cities to produce a general panic if he were not given $100,000. Although the missing uranium was far from bomb grade and constituted a minimal health hazard, the threat, if publicized, could well have terrorized an entire city had the FBI not been successful in capturing its perpetrator. In another incident, two employees of a nuclear plant in Bradwell, England, were able to steal fuel rods from the plant and drop them over the perimeter fence, where they apparently intended to retrieve them later.

A 1977 report to Congress by the U.S. Comptroller General called physical security at nuclear power plants, at best, inadequate. Security systems were far from uniform and provided vastly different degrees of protection, the report stated. Whereas one plant surveyed had many of the latest perimeter defenses, including magnetic gate alarms, and infrared periphery detection system, closed-circuit television, a computerized key-card system, a hardened guard house, and a fulltime professional security chief, the primary security device at another plant was a perimeter fence topped with barbed wire. The plant lacked any kind of gate or perimeter alarms or detection systems and employed only a part-time security officer.[60] This confirmed previous findings by the NRC, which indicated that there were probably security deficiencies at all nuclear power plants in the United States. A 1975 NRC study concluded that guard forces at commercial nuclear facilities were deplorable and were characterized by little training, inferior equipment, a high turnover rate, little background screening, and inadequate supervision, to cite but a few of the more serious charges.

Nuclear power plants are characterized by numerous special vulnerabilities. Since the reactor fuel in a nuclear power plant is, for all intents and purposes, too "hot" for terrorists to handle, it is the possibility of sabotage that most concerns authorities. L. Manning Muntzing, former director of Regulation of the AEC, conceded to a reporter that a band of technologically competent terrorists could take over a nuclear power plant and sabotage it in such a way as "to kill thousands – perhaps even millions – of people."[61] According to Speth, "Sabotaging a reactor is necessarily a minor technological task compared to building one."[62] If they were able to take control of a reactor, terrorists could produce a core meltdown, most likely by inducing a failure of the cooling system and causing the reactor to overheat. Nevertheless, it should be noted that it would be far from a simple matter to produce the sequence of events necessary to override all of the redundancies built into the system, including automatic shutdown devices, and would require individuals highly familiar with the operations of the facility.

DeNike also raises the specter that power plants could be sabotaged from the outside.

> Saboteurs could drop improvised time-delayed depth charges onto the cooling intake pipes from an innocuous-appearing boat. With scuba

equipment, underwater demolition activities could be carried out unobserved from the surface. These might reach the sophistication of introducing heat-sensitive explosives into cooling pipes after removal or breach of the fish screens. Such explosives could travel on the intake current to the pump or condenser, there to explode with maximum effect.[63]

If they were able to get inside, terrorists could attempt to blow up the reactor containment building, releasing a cloud of deadly radioactivity. But such a scenario would require a very large number of well-placed explosive charges, both to strip the reactor core of its protective shielding and to rupture the three-foot-thick walls of the containment building. The containment structure alone is so massive that it would take a five-ton guided bomb just to breach the concrete containment shell. Despite the heavily reinforced nature of the containment building, there was considerable concern on the part of authorities in 1972 when two hijackers buzzed the Oak Ridge nuclear plant in a pirated light aircraft, threatening to crash the plane into the structure if their demands were not met. Without a significant number of explosives on board, such a kamikaze attack would have probably produced only superficial damage, but the threat itself resulted in such panic that the residents of Oak Ridge jammed the roads leading from the city. A plane loaded with explosives is a highly effective projectile and represents a most serious threat to nuclear power facilities.

While the seizure of a nuclear reactor by terrorists and the threat to deliberately sabotage it and to release the radioactivity within could be expected to inspire public panic, as it did at Oak Ridge, it is clear that the ability of terrorists to actually carry out their threat is relatively limited without special preparations and expertise. On the assumption that terrorists generally seek targets at which a great deal of damage can be produced with minimal effort or risk, former AEC chairman Dixy Lee Ray concluded, "A nuclear plant, therefore, is likely to rank quite low on a saboteur's list of priorities."[64] There are many other potential technotargets less well-protected and hardened that could produce equal or greater catastrophes with less terrorist effort or sophistication, including the sabotage of a major dam or liquefied natural gas storage facility or transport vessel.[65]

STRENGTHENING SAFEGUARDS

The social, political, legal, and moral implications of a nuclear society are profound and far-reaching, and they are only beginning to be fully understood. Perhaps Alvin Weinberg best puts the issues into perspective:

> We nuclear people have made a Faustian bargain with society. On the one hand, we offer — in the catalytic nuclear burner — an inexhaustable source of energy. Even in the short range, when we use ordinary reactors, we offer energy that is cheaper than energy from fossil fuel. Moreover, this course of energy, when properly handled, is almost nonpolluting. Whereas fossil fuel burners must emit oxides of carbon and nitrogen, and probably will always emit some sulfur dioxide, there is no intrinsic reason why nuclear systems must emit any pollutant — except heat and traces of radioactivity.
>
> But the price we demand of society for this magical energy source is both a vigilance and a longevity of our social institutions that we are quite unaccustomed to.[66]

The safe and prudent operation of nuclear power plants, the stewardship of radioactive wastes, and the control of nuclear weapons require political stability together with the development of permanent institutions capable of ensuring safe and responsible supervision of nuclear materials and facilities for centuries, even millenniums. Pioneering work on the transmutation of nuclear material to reduce its radioactive decay half-life and render it more inert, perhaps shortening the period of necessary stewardship from 500,000 years (20 times the radioactive decay half-life of plutonium) to a few hundred years, is proceeding, but this work is a long way from producing significant results.

Some observers believe that the growth of nuclear power will put unprecedented strains on modern civilization, resulting in diminished personal freedoms and a decline of civil liberties. A British study predicts that Great Britain could, by the end of the century, undermine its civil liberties to protect its fissionable material. The study foresees widespread mail-opening, surveillance, and wiretapping, armies of armed private guards, and other measures designed to protect nuclear materials from theft or diversion. A recent Office of Technology Assessment study maintains:

Potential terrorist threats to obtain and use nuclear, chemical, or biological weapons pose especially knotty problems of civil liberties policy. . . . Yet safeguard measures which would sweep so widely as to curtail basic liberties for substantial numbers of people or for broad sectors of public life could move our society toward the kind of garrison-state environment that political terrorists hope to force upon democratic nations to undermine the vitality of their social orders.[67]

While there is little proof that an effective safeguards system will have to routinely include elements incompatible with a free and open society, nuclear emergencies are another matter. There is little question that a government confronted with nuclear blackmail or some other serious radioactive threat would have to move with dispatch and perhaps even ruthless, single-minded efficiency, at least for the duration of the crisis, to protect its citizens and counter the threat. Secret U.S. contingency plans reportedly provide for the assumption of extraordinary emergency powers by the federal government in the event of such an emergency. In this connection, it is not unreasonable to postulate that the institution of martial law would be necessary under some circumstances and that the state would have to be granted unprecedented police powers, including search and seizure without warrant, detention of suspects without warrant, imposition of press censorship, and the interrogation of suspects without benefit of legal counsel.

Since the growth of the nuclear power industry presents many new possibilities for the diversion and antisocial use of radioactive material by terrorists and other nonstate actors, the need for a complete and effective "defense in-depth" safeguards system to minimize the risks associated with the custodianship of nuclear material and to ensure that such material does not fall into irresponsible or malevolent hands is obvious. While critics rightly argue that no safeguards system can be 100 percent effective and, therefore, that nuclear power should be abandoned as a means of power generation, such a view is highly unrealistic considering the billions of dollars that electric utilities have already invested in the technology and the critical need for new energy sources if our way of life is to be preserved and our economy is to continue to grow. Moreover, even if the United States unilaterally decided to forgo nuclear power development, this would hardly solve the problem since much of the rest of the world is irrevocably committed to the nuclear path, and, consequently, the threat of nuclear theft or diversion would still exist. Finally, inasmuch as the national defense of the United States and the Western alliance is based on a nuclear deterrent, processing and enrichment facilities, weapons fabrication plants, radioactive wastes, and large arsenals of nuclear weapons will require an ongoing and comprehensive safeguards program irrespective of decisions relating to the development of commercial nuclear power.

In this connection, opponents of the development of the Liquid Metal Fast Breeder Reactor maintain that, by not moving to a plutonium-based national energy economy, the safeguards problem will be rendered substantially more manageable. According to critics of the breeder technology, a decision to put commercial breeder reactors on line would result in the existence of vastly increased quantitites of plutonium and would perhaps remove the final obstacle to terrorists and other nonstate actors in their efforts to obtain enough fissile material to manufacture a bomb. Speth also suggests that the introduction of the experimental High Temperature Gas Cooled Reactor, which is fueled by weapons-grade uranium, together with the development of new and less expensive enrichment technologies, would also introduce unacceptable new hazards that would be impossible to control.[68] While not commenting directly on either technology, there is little question that safeguards procedures will have to undergo constant revision to keep pace with the new demands imposed by continued expansion of the nuclear power industry and with any decision to proceed with the Breeder or High Temperature Reactor. In this regard, a review of some of the alternatives that have been raised for strengthening nuclear safeguards is in order.

Corrupting Nuclear Material

Efforts are currently underway to develop methods to "corrupt" or despoil special nuclear material so that during transit it would pose new hazards to divertors and would be unsuitable for manufacturing nuclear weapons. For example, plutonium can be "spiked" with highly penetrating levels of radiation to substantially increase the risks to terrorists or other unauthorized personnel handling it without proper facilities. Similarly, highly enriched uranium can be despoiled by isotopic dilution with natural uranium, rendering it virtually useless to terrorists; the material could be reconstructed only at a facility such as a gaseous diffusion plant, with isotopic separation facilities.

Federal Nuclear Security Force

One of the chief weaknesses with respect to current safeguards programs is that physical security at nuclear plants is primarily a commercial function, involving private security guards earning minimal salaries. The NRC has been lobbied so heavily by private security companies that it has, against the recommendations of its own experts, permitted this situation to continue for far too long. Indeed, the question must be asked: What low paid, undertrained, and poorly motivated security guard is going to lay down his or her life to protect a nuclear facility or to prevent the theft of special nuclear material? Moreover, such guards are often neither prepared nor equipped to thwart a ruthless and heavily armed band of terrorists bent on stealing nuclear material. What is needed instead is a federal Nuclear Security Force (NSF) with good salaries and commensurate benefits, rigorous training, the latest weapons and equipment, and military discipline. Not only would it provide protection to all nuclear plants, facilities, and shipments of special nuclear material, but it would also have an elite corps that would constitute a nuclear response force in the event of an attempted diversion of special nuclear material or an effort to sabotage a nuclear power plant. Since both the nature of the potential threat and the general safeguards environment are characterized by constant change, the nuclear security force should be subject to periodic review and ongoing efforts to improve and update its skills. The NSF should maintain close and continuous liaison with the FBI and CIA so as to be appraised of all potential threats and intelligence relating to those threats.

National Command and Communications Center

Consideration should be given to establishing a national command and communications center to ensure an immediate and systematic response to terrorist threats against nuclear facilities and those involving special nuclear material.[69] In addition, a satellite communications system has been proposed to "eliminate blind spots which exist with the current system for communication with transport vehicles."[70]

Nuclear Parks

Considerable attention has been devoted in recent years to the siting of nuclear power plants and other related facilities. Many observers, accordingly, have embraced the view that the potential risk of diversion could be significantly reduced by the creation of so-called nuclear parks, or integrated regional energy centers, that would concentrate nuclear reactors and most of the elements of the fuel cycle at the same location. Indeed, a large site would probably consist of from 10 to 30 reactors, fuel fabrication plants, chemical reprocessing facilities, and even a waste management operation.[71] Moreover, Laurence Moss recommends, "The fuel cycle could be intentionally kept 'hot,' that is the separation of fuel from fission products in the reprocessing plant could be to a lesser degree than normal, in order to compound the difficulties of anyone attempting to remove any of the fuel."[72] The entire site would be ringed with sanitary cordons and protected by a large guard force armed with heavy weapons and the latest intrusion-detection systems. Ground-to-air missiles would even be located at the site so as to prevent attacks from the air. Since transportation operations would be virtually eliminated, the weakest link in the safeguards system would also be eliminated. No shipments of special nuclear material in a form adaptable to the fabrication of weapons would be necessary.

The disadvantages of the nuclear park concept are

a potential lack of sufficient water, problems with heat dissipation and radiation control, the potential for a domino effect in the event of a serious nuclear accident, problems with raising sufficient capital, and the institutional problem that would be posed by the presence of utilities owned by both private investors and the public on the same site.[73]

In addition, nuclear parks would be more susceptible to wars and natural disasters and would blight the landscape with transmission lines and towers. They could also be expected to encounter a great deal of local opposition inasmuch as the prime beneficiaries of the power generation would likely live hundreds, perhaps even thousands, of miles from the actual site of the nuclear park.

Among the other suggestions to strengthen safeguards is the introduction of a mandatory death penalty for any attempted or successful diversion of nuclear material, sabotage of a nuclear power plant, or antisocial use of radioactive material. Moreover, it has been recommended that the FBI and CIA be given greater authority to infiltrate terrorist groups and to develop timely intelligence regarding threats against nuclear power plants, facilities, and special nuclear material. Since accounting and measurement techniques form the backbone of the present safeguards system, greater time, effort, and money need to be allocated to developing more accurate and sophisticated equipment to detect diversions and to trace and measure nuclear material in the fuel cycle. Finally, since fusion reactors produce no neutrons and therefore leave no explosive by-products,[74] the development of this new technology, which offers a potentially inexhaustible source of energy without many of the disadvantages associated with conventional nuclear power, should be encouraged and supported to the maximum degree possible.

CONCLUSION

Like the .45 Colt revolver of the Old West, nuclear explosives have become the great "equalizers" of the twentieth century. The possession of only one weapon ensures the possessor a place on the "first team." Indeed, the day could come when there will be a handful of states that possess nuclear weapons plus one terrorist group. The possession of a nuclear weapon by a terrorist group would dramatically alter the international balance of power, not to mention the internal balance of any particular nation, and could put the terrorists beyond the reach of authorities. Confronted with the threat of a nuclear catastrophe, even a major power would have to seriously consider capitulating to the demands of the terrorist group.

In view of such sobering realities, Speth has argued, "We can no longer assume that each new innovation accompanied by financial backing should be permitted to proceed, even with regulation. Some should simply be halted for the reason that their advantages bear no reasonable relationship to the possibility of tremendous social harm they present."[75] Such pronouncements are more easily made, however, than implemented. For reasons already noted, nuclear fission power is a reality and one that will not disappear, despite serious moral implications and safety risks. Thus, exhaustive efforts must be made to minimize the hazards associated with nuclear power, especially with respect to protecting nuclear material, weapons, power plants, and other nuclear facilities from terrorists. Although the problem is admittedly global in scope and would be better addressed on a multilateral basis, meaningful multilateral actions are unlikely to be forthcoming. Therefore, it is up to the advanced industrial nations of the West, together with the Soviet Union, to take the lead in strengthening nuclear safeguards in an effort to ward off what some regard as the inevitable.

NOTES

1. Amory B. Lovins, L. Hunter Lovins, and Leonard Ross, "Nuclear Power and Nuclear Bombs," *Foreign Affairs* vol. 58, no. 5 (Summer 1980): 1138.

2. James D. Watson, quoted in the Committee on Inquiry, *The Plutonium Economy: A Statement of Concern* (New York: National Council of Churches of Christ, USA, 1975), p. 146.

3. New York *Times*, editorial, January 31, 1973.

4. Nuclear Energy Policy Study Group, *Nuclear Power Issues and Choices* (Cambridge: Ballinger, 1977), p. 147.

5. Bernard T. Feld, "The Menace of a Fission Power Economy," *Bulletin of the Atomic Scientists* (April, 1974): 32.

6. Stockholm International Peace Research Institute, *World Armaments and Disarmament: SIPRI Yearbook 1977* (Cambridge: Massachusetts Institute of Technology, 1977), p. 39.

7. Thomas C. Schelling, "Nuclear Energy and National Security," paper prepared for Washington, D.C.: Committee for Economic Development, December 10, 1975, p. 12.

8. "Growth of Plutonium Supply Forecast," Washington *Post*, February 25, 1980.

9. *Treaty on the Non-Proliferation of Nuclear Weapons*, article 4, para. 1. See Department of State *Bulletin* (1968) pp. 9-11.

10. Sen. Howard H. Baker, Jr., statement before the Commonwealth Club of California, San Francisco, June 6, 1975, p. 7.

11. *Treaty on the Non-Proliferation of Nuclear Weapons*, article 3, para. 2.

12. Mason Willrich and Theodore B. Taylor, "Nuclear Theft," *Survival* vol. 16 (1974): 186.

13. Nigel Calder, *Nuclear Nightmares* (New York: Viking Press, 1979), pp. 63-64.

14. Theodore B. Taylor, statement before the Joint Committee on Atomic Energy, U.S. Congress, June 18, 1975, p. 2 (mimeo).

15. See Sen. Abraham Ribicoff, "The Plutonium Connection," *Congressional Record*, March 11, 1975, p. S3617.

16. Mason Willrich and Theodore B. Taylor, *Nuclear Theft: Risks and Safeguards* (Cambridge: Ballinger, 1974), p. 5.

17. Schelling, "Nuclear Energy," pp. 20-21.

18. "Mushrooms for Dinner," New York *Times*, May 5, 1975.

19. The essential explosive in a fusion bomb (H-bomb) is "a chemical compound containing lithium-6, a light form of the element lithium, combined with deuterium, a heavy constituent of ordinary hydrogen." See Calder, *Nuclear Nightmare*, p. 63.

20. Willrich and Taylor, "Nuclear Theft," p. 189.

21. Lovins, Lovins, and Ross, "Nuclear Power," p. 1143.

22. Ibid.

23. "Plutonium Held Unaccounted for at S.C. A-Plant," Washington *Post*, January 1, 1980.

24. R. B. Leachman, "Preventive Criminology Applied to Fissionable Materials," unpublished research paper sponsored by a grant from the Research Applied to National Needs Office of the National Science Foundation, no date, p. 6.

25. Ralph E. Lapp, "The Ultimate Blackmail," New York *Times Magazine*, February 4, 1973, p. 12.

26. Brian Jenkins, "International Terrorism: Trends and Potentialities," mimeo, March 1976, p. 3.

27. David M. Rosenbaum, John N. Googin, Robert M. Jefferson, Daniel Kleitman, and William C. Sullivan, "Special Safeguards Study," Atomic Energy Commission, Washington, D.C., April 29, 1974, p. 3 (mimeo).

28. Che Guevara, quoted by Francis M. Watson, *Political Terrorism: The Threat and the Response* (New York: Robert B. Luce, 1976), p. 188.

29. Clarence E. Larson, "Nuclear Materials Safeguards: A Joint Industry-Government Mission," *Proceedings of AEC Symposium on Safeguards Research and Development, Oct. 27-29, 1969*, (Washington, D.C.: Atomic Energy Commission, 1969), p. Wash-1147.

30. Thomas O. Johnson, "Nuclear Energy: Key Issues," Babock & Wilcox energy brief, July 1975, p. 3.

31. It would take approximately from 28 to 30 kilograms of this material to make a bomb, almost from 10 to 15 percent of the annual output of Pu^{239} by a conventional power reactor.

32. Lovins, Lovins, and Ross, "Nuclear Power," p. 1139.

33. "U.S. Test Shows Nuclear Bombs Can Be Made From Low-Grade Plutonium," Washington *Post*, September 14, 1977.

34. J. G. Speth, statement of the National Resources Defense Council before the Joint Committee on Atomic Energy, Washington, D.C., June 19, 1975, p. 8 (mimeo).

35. L. Douglas DeNike, "Radioactive Malevolence," reprinted in *Nuclear Reactor Safety*, U.S. Congress, Joint Committee on Atomic Energy, 93rd Congress, part 2, vol. 2 (January 1974), p. 1201.

36. Johnson, *Nuclear Energy*, p. 3.

37. Gen. Joseph J. Cappucci, interview in Washington, D.C., on January 3, 1978.

38. "AEC Seeking to Cut Peril of Atomic Theft," Washington *Post*, May 27, 1974.

39. George Murphy, interview in Washington, D.C. on September 10, 1975.

40. Ibid.

41. Michael Flood, "Nuclear Sabotage," Washington *Post*, January 9, 1977.

42. Calder, *Nuclear Nightmares*, p. 64.

43. U.S., Department of Defense, *Security Criteria and Standards for Protecting Nuclear Weapons*, directive 5210.41, Washington, D.C., July 30, 1974.

44. "Fear of Nuclear Theft Stirs Experts, AEC," Washington *Post*, May 26, 1974.

45. Confidential interview.

46. Richard C. Clark, *Technological Terrorism* (Old Greenwich: Devin-Adair, 1980), p. 33.

47. Brian Jenkins, "Will Terrorists Go Nuclear?," in *Protection of Assets* (New York: Merritt, 1977), pp. 18-87.

48. E. B. Giller (deputy assistant administrator for National Security, U.S. Energy Research and Development Administration), testimony before the Subcommittee to Review the National Breeder Reactor Program, Joint Committee on Atomic Energy, Washington, D.C., June 19, 1975, p. 5 (mimeo).

49. Medical Research Council, *The Toxicity of Plutonium* (London: Her Majesty's Stationery Office, 1975), p. 1.

50. U.S., Congress, House of Representatives, Subcommittee on Energy and Environment of the Committee on Small Business, Testimony of Dr. Karl Z. Morgan, *Problems in the Accounting for and Safeguarding of Special Nuclear Materials*, 94th Congress, 2nd sess. (Washington, D.C.: Government Printing Office, 1977), p. 10.

51. Willrich and Taylor, *Nuclear Theft: Risks and Safeguards*, pp. 24-25.

52. Clark, *Technological Terrorism*, p. 57.

53. Jenkins, "Will Terrorists Go Nuclear?," pp. 18-83.

54. Friedhalm Farthmann, quoted in *Der Spiegal* 43 (October 17, 1977): 32.

55. Flood, "Nuclear Sabotage."

56. Rumors have circulated in some Western capitals that the air strikes against the Iraqi reactor facility were actually carried out by the Israelis, using F-4 Phantom jets with Iranian markings. Sources in Jerusalem state that the Israeli government acted because it was convinced that the facility is part of a long-range plan by the Baghdad government to obtain nuclear weapons. If such reports were true, it would not be the first time Israel sought to retard Iraq's nuclear program. In April 1979, as part of a clandestine operation known as "Big Lift," agents of Israel's crack intelligence organization, the Mossad, were dispatched to the French port of La Seyne-sur-Mer, where they sabotaged nearly $25 million worth of components destined for shipment to the Tamuz I and II reactors in Iraq.

57. Though not in developing nations, Scottish nationalists have threatened on several occasions to sabotage an English nuclear power generating plant, and French nuclear power plants under construction have been the repeated victims of bombings by terrorists.

58. Willrich and Taylor, "Nuclear Theft," p. 190.

59. U.S., Congress, House of Representatives, Subcommittee on Energy Research and Production of the Committee on Science and Technology, *Nuclear Safeguards: An Updated Analysis of the Concept of Safeguards as a National and International Institution*, 96th Congress, 2nd sess., serial VV (Washington, D.C.: Government Printing Office, 1980), p. 1.

60. U.S., Comptroller General, report to the Congress, "Security at Nuclear Powerplants – At Best, Inadequate," EMD-77-32, Washington, D.C., April 7, 1977, p. 4.

61. L. Manning Muntzing, quoted in Los Angeles *Times*, December 17, 1973.

62. Speth, statement before the Joint Committee on Atomic Energy, p. 3.

63. DeNike, "Radioactive Malevolence," p. 1199.

64. Dixie Lee Ray, letter to Sen. Robert C. Byrd, dated October 17, 1973.

65. Such scenarios, especially the possibility of an externally induced core meltdown, are challenged by the so-called "Rasmussen Report," commissioned by the Atomic Energy Commission (AEC). The Rasmussen Report concluded, after a two-year study, that the possibility of a core meltdown, whatever the cause, was statistically inconsequential: "The most likely core melt accident having a likelihood of one in 17,000 per plant per year, would result in little or no contamination. The probability of an accident that requires temporary evacuation of 20 square miles is one in 170,000 per reactor year. Ninety per cent of all core melt accidents would be expected to be less severe than this." See U.S., Atomic Energy Commission, "Reactor Safety Study: An Assessment of Accident Risks in U.S. Commercial Nuclear Power Plants," summary report, Washington, D.C., August 1974, p. 23. While observing that, "It is conceivable that a group of people might threaten to or carry out sabotage of a nuclear power plant in such a way as to cause great damage and loss of life," the report to the American Physical Society by the Study Group on Light Water Reactor Safety, released less than a year after the Rasmussen Report, challenged the conclusions of the AEC study and argued that there is no way to estimate the probability of such acts. See H. W. Lewis et al., "Report to the American Physical Society by the Study Group on Light-Water Reactor Safety," April 28, 1975, pp. iv-25. In recent years, many of the statistical conclusions of the Rasmussen Report have been disputed, and the report is generally held to contain basic flaws related to methodology and the assumptions on which the conclusions are predicated.

66. Alvin M. Weinberg, "Social Institutions and Nuclear Energy," *Science* vol. 177 (July 7, 1972): 33.

67. U.S., Congress, Office of Technology Assessment, *Nuclear Proliferation and Safeguards* (Washington, D.C.: Government Printing Office, 1977), p. 128.

68. Speth, statement before the Joint Committee on Atomic Energy, p. 8.

69. Theodore Taylor, "Nuclear Theft and Terrorism," *Sixteenth Strategy for Peace Conference Report* (Muscatine, Iowa: Stanley Foundation, 1975), p. 38.

70. U.S., Atomic Energy Commission, *Generic Environmental Statement Mixed Oxide Fuel* vol. 4, WASH-1327 (Washington, D.C.: Atomic Energy Commission, 1974), pp. V-40 (draft).

71. Dean E. Abrahamson, "Nuclear Theft and Nuclear Parks," *Environment* (July/August 1974): 5.

72. Laurence I. Moss, "Environmental, Safety, and Public Acceptance Aspects of LMFBRs," letter report prepared for the National Science Foundation, submitted for discussion to the Fission Energy working group of the Energy R&D Advisory Council, dated September 9, 1974, p. 37.

73. James G. Phillips, "Energy Reports/Safeguards, Recycling Broaden Nuclear Power Debate," *National Journal Reports* (March 3, 1975): 423.

74. Willrich and Taylor, *Nuclear Theft: Risks and Safeguards*, p. 76.

75. Speth, statement before the Joint Committee on Atomic Energy, p. 19.

8
The Middle East and Energy: Sources of Threat

M. C. Peck

This chapter concerns some sources of threat to energy supplies in the Middle East. It deals broadly with actual and potential instances of instability. The question of how to respond to threats and what the U.S. role has been and could be is addressed.

SOURCES OF THREAT TO OIL FROM THE GULF

At first appearance, the most obvious areas of vulnerability are the "chokepoints" along the tanker routes. Among these, the most important, because all Gulf oil exports pass through it, is the Strait of Hormuz. Conventional naval threats are more relevant in this regard than is terrorist activity. This matter is raised because it has been suggested that a small band of guerrillas with portable weaponry could block the strait. Since a large number of tankers would have to be sunk in a rather precise fashion to accomplish that purpose, terrorists could at most carry out harassing activities.

A much greater terrorist threat would be one directly against onshore oil installations. Several instances of interruptions of oil flow, whether deliberate or accidental, have suggested the vulnerability of these installations. Virtually all of Saudi Arabia's oil for export is gathered for refining or shipping at Ras Tanura, where a considerable number of the workers (variously estimated at from one-third to two-thirds of the total) are from the disaffected Shia minority, which has been stirred to violent agitation by Khomeini's calls from across the Gulf. A redress of long-standing Shia grievances would answer the threat, but this may not be an immediate prospect.[1]

The Iran-Iraq war has confirmed the primacy of indigenous physical threat to the production and transportation of oil in the region. If further evidence of the vulnerability of gathering and refining facilities were needed, this conflict has provided it. At the same time, it has shown, unexpectedly, that major oil exporters in confrontation are not necessarily constrained by mutual vulnerability from launching attacks against these targets. It has demonstrated limits of another kind by the failure of the Arabic-speakers of Khuzistan (the area of ground combat) and other ethnic minorities in Iran to rise in any significant numbers against the Teheran government in support of the Iraqis.

Palestinians in a wide range of private and governmental positions in the Gulf countries are often cited as threats to their host countries' political stability and to the flow of oil to the West. In the event of a major regional conflict, such a threat could materialize. However, the great majority of Palestinians have, over many years, assumed a low profile and have studiously avoided offending their hosts because they are acutely aware of their stateless vulnerability. What is important is their influence through communication of liberal political ideas to politically conservative societies. While this process has had at least a partly beneficent effect in pointing the way to desirable reforms, it has also introduced ideas and sentiments conducive to more direct and radical action.

The terrorist attack on the Grand Mosque in Mecca, in November 1979, suggested the degree of danger from an unanticipated direction. It indicated the strength of a hitherto largely discounted threat from religious conservatives, who, despite the sanction of the *ulema* (the religious establishment) enjoyed by the House of Saud, are deeply unsettled by the pace of Saudi Arabia's social transformation. It also revealed the degree to which discontent of that nature could coalesce with other forms of opposition to the government, indigenous and nonindigenous in origin.

At the same time, some have exaggerated the danger from the right, while the main source of threat undoubtedly lies more nearly at the other end of the political spectrum. While tightening the lax security that permitted the attack and making astute political gestures (taking both religious and economic forms), the Saudis themselves have not abandoned the basic developmental policies to which the more extreme religious fundamentalists object. The continuing rapprochement with Iraq may serve as partial proof against some subversive threats. This reflects not only Baghdad's shift from a policy of promoting radical causes aimed at toppling the conservative Arab regimes of the Gulf and Peninsula, but also the active cooperation that has now developed between the two countries on internal security issues.[2] It is significant also that in responding immediately to the attack on the Grand Mosque, the Saudis called not upon U.S. security advisors but upon a special team from France.

In the long term, both in Saudi Arabia and in the other oil-rich Arab states, the principal source of violent internal disruption will be the strains created by the profoundly disruptive process of modernization. The Mecca episode is but one dramatic symptom of the deep stresses inevitably produced by rapid transition from an impoverished society firmly based on conservative Islamic values to one of great wealth, committed to rapid economic development, yet endeavoring to preserve its spiritual essence — a society whose ultimate shape cannot be discerned. It will be increasingly vulnerable to various infections, especially that of radical Arab nationalism, and the rapid development of a modern military force may increase the level of threat prompted against the government. In Saudi Arabia and the smaller wealthy Arab states, continued heavy reliance on nonindigenous brawn and brains will exacerbate this source of danger. While the management of their reliance on imported labor has been skillful and successful, no short-term strategy to solve the problem is at hand. Ameliorization of destabilizing regional issues, most especially the Arab-Israeli conflict, would greatly enhance Saudi security. Meanwhile, stability must, perforce, be maintained by statecraft of a very high order.

SOURCES OF THREAT ELSEWHERE

Beyond the Arab states of the Gulf and the Peninsula, other sources of threat have at least an indirect bearing on the security of Middle Eastern energy supplies and upon U.S. interests, which go beyond oil. The case of Iran, caught up in the turmoil of Khomeini's revolution and the war with Iraq, to which no immediate conclusion appears likely, is perhaps both too obvious in its current dimensions and too indecipherable in its long-term implications to be discussed usefully here. Some brief observations follow in another context.

In Egypt, both Islamic fundamentalists and leftists represent sources of challenge, possibly violent, to Sadat's government. Bloody confrontations of Copts and Muslims add a further disquieting note. Sadat's inspired exercise of political power has defied all threats thus far. However, despite recent encouraging economic improvement, the difficulty of making dramatic headway against nearly intractable economic problems may cause his vulnerability, due to post-Camp David isolation, to reach a critical point. Continuing, massive U.S. economic support will certainly be of key importance in this respect.

After a span of relative stability unprecedented in the history of independent Syria, the government of Hafez el-Asad has been hard pressed by major political problems that have generated considerable violence. Sectarian divisions underlie an uneasy and dangerous situation, which could hold important implications for the wider region. Such internal stresses in 1967 and 1973 helped to induce distracting actions by the Jadid and El-Asad governments, respectively, which played a part in precipitating the events leading up to the Arab-Israeli conflicts of those years. This is not to suggest a repetition of those scenarios (though the events of May-June 1981 appeared to some in this guise) but to note the temptation that may exist for some action to draw attention away from internal divisions. Despite an ostensibly secular political system, sectarian divisions, particularly between Alawis and Sunnis, remain of commanding importance. While the Alawi minority retains essential political and military dominance over the Sunni majority, resort to repressive forms of control will constitute the essential response to threats against the regime.

As the southwest wing of the North Atlantic Treaty Organization, Turkey in its current travail is a matter of deep concern. The economic aid package put together by the United States and Europe has helped to see it through its recent crisis. Turkey is routinely able to absorb political violence that would destroy most other systems. This and the fact that the current exercise of authority by General Evren and his colleagues is in line with the military's tradition of assuming temporary control *in extremis* may be the best available safeguard in containing threats to stability until major pending economic and political problems can be really addressed.

ISLAM AS A THREAT

Popular perceptions of the Middle East, to some extent shared by U.S. officialdom, tend to ascribe threats to Western interests to "militant" or "resurgent" Islam sweeping across the region. The United States and the West generally have tended either to underestimate seriously the importance of Islam or to exaggerate it.[3] In political and strategic terms, at least, the latter is now the case. There is danger in seeing Islam as a monolithic force. A recent study points both to the pronounced plurality of cultural legacies and visions of the future within Islam and to the fact that the important sharing of a common sentiment and idiom ought not to necessarily be seen a basis for unified action.[4]

At the same time, some events may have ramifying effects and some appeals may provoke action. The Khomeini revolution and its rhetoric have had an unsettling effect on some of the Shia on the Arab side of the Gulf — in Kuwait, Bahrain, and Saudi Arabia. However, this has been an appeal principally to small communities of Shia, and it has had an impact because of their political and economic sense of grievance. At the same time, Khomeini has been able to invoke a unified Muslim sentiment against non-Muslim external threat. Thus U.S. action or contemplation of action against Iran during the hostage crisis brought into play powerful Islamic fear and hostility, charged with fresh historical memories of Western domination of Islamic lands. This compels a degree of formal alignment with Khomeini by Muslim leaders who fear and despise him, though the outbreak of armed conflict between Iran and Iraq ranged Arab leadership generally with the latter. The Saudis are alarmed at the success with which Khomeini has set traps in this way for the U.S.

Islam has always been a vital source of identity and meaning, not simply as a religion in the generally restricted sense connoted by that term in secular Western societies. With the profound dislocations flowing from rapid change in Muslim countries, attempts to reassert Islamic values tend to acquire a new urgency and can provoke violent actions. But in each Muslim country, with its distinctive cultural legacy and tradition of political rule, a different pattern is evident. It might be suggested that religious identity of every kind has acquired new importance in the Middle East as a result of the impact of traumatic events on societies in recent years. The role of sectarianism in Lebanon is obvious. In Egypt, the defeat of 1967 gave rise to a resurgence both of Muslim and Christian sentiment, which has continued. The forward policies of the present Coptic Pope help to fan passions on both sides, while the Jami'a al-Islamiyya and the Takfir w' al-Hijra spearhead Islamic opposition to the Sadat government. Indeed, in Israeli Judaism one sees a similar phenomenon. The Gush Emunim movement received a fillip from the shock to which the October 1973 war subjected Israelis.[5] Settlement activities on the West Bank have produced local tensions and violence. The regional and international implications of its actions in presenting a key obstacle to a comprehensive Arab-Israeli settlement have been thoroughly aired. Equally obvious as a manifestation of conservative religious strength in Israel and its capacity to affect the politics of the state was the coalition agreement that Prime Minister Begin worked out with the religious parties early in August 1981.

Finally, a note on Islam and the Palestinian national movement may be in order. Several non-Arab Islamic countries have been outspoken in their sympathy and support for the Palestine Liberation Organization.

This said, however, Palestinians are probably more secularized than any other Arabs, and a principle of Palestinian nationalism is its powerful localized focus on the soil of Palestine. Islam does not add any extra dimension of intensity. Palestinian political terrorism is the product of a number of factors: tactical calculations by one or another of the Palestinian guerrilla groups, Israeli actions, and, ultimately, regional or international political events and the conflict of Israeli and Palestinian claims to the same territory.

THE U.S. ROLE IN RESPONDING TO THREATS

Recent events have shown that direct U.S. intervention is unlikely to be efficacious in dealing with political terrorism in the Middle East and that it is, indeed, more apt to have an exacerbating effect. There are, however, other meaningful kinds of action to be considered, perhaps most significantly those that support positive trends in the context of indigenous origin. One of the most important of these is the developing rapprochement at Iraqi initiative between that country, Saudi Arabia, and the other Arab states of the Gulf littoral (Oman excepted), a move to cooperation that has specifically embraced issues related to local security. While the

United States and Iraq are still divided by basic political differences and are without official diplomatic ties, relations on several levels are fairly good and, perhaps, are improving so that discreet U.S. support could be given to Iraq's new policy. As of late summer 1981, it is not possible to say whether U.S.-Iraqi diplomatic cooperation in negotiating U.N. Security Council condemnation of Israel's bombing of Iraq's nuclear reactor on June 7, 1981, will lead to significantly improved political relations.[6]

The recent establishment of the Gulf Cooperation Council, including all the Arab states of the Gulf except Iraq, is a further instance of indigenous efforts to promote greater economic, social, political, and military integration.[7] While the council's role in relation to major political and security issues is apt to be modest, it may help to advance significant pragmatic steps toward cooperation.

Among the wealthy, conservative, Arab oil-producing states, there is a need for quiet, sensitive, and creative diplomacy to encourage deliberate and orderly progress toward inclusion of more of their impatient educated young people in the decision-making process, something these countries have already begun to do. Similarly, well-considered U.S. initiatives prompting greater awareness in these countries of the need to ameliorate the situation of second-class, expatriate workers (who constitute a majority in most work forces) are important as are any appropriate U.S. actions to help promote accelerated development of indigenous human resources and of the kinds of attitudinal changes needed to use them most effectively, thereby reducing dependence on foreigners. These kinds of modest activities can be of significant potential in reducing sources of threat to these regimes and to U.S. energy and other interests there.

Especially important is the restoration of a perception that U.S. policies are consistent and effective, that the United States is reliable as a friend and supporter. Without belaboring the obvious, there has been a major failure in this regard, which urgently requires a remedy. Equally important is the need for U.S. policy, throughout the area but especially in the moderate Arab states of the Gulf, that promotes more than patronizing, one-sided relationships. The Saudis and others perceive that the United States is prepared to make considerable exertions to protect its own closely defined interests in their part of the world, the "Carter Doctrine" and the Reagan "strategic consensus" serving as the latest proofs of this. At the same time, despite U.S. rhetoric that has proclaimed Saudi Arabia as its friend and ally that enjoys a special relationship with the United States, the Saudis are painfully aware that U.S. policy makers discount basic Saudi concerns and interests. For example, not only did the Carter White House disregard advance Saudi warnings that they saw the Camp David approach to an Arab-Israeli peace settlement as both unlikely to succeed and predictably unsettling and dangerous to their own position in the Arab world, but subsequently the United States castigated its "friend and ally" for not backing the Egyptian-Israeli peace treaty.

This and other specific instances of U.S. policy have caused the Saudis and their neighbors to doubt both the sincerity of U.S. declarations and the basic fairness of U.S. policy toward the Middle East. As the example cited suggests, the U.S. stance toward the Arab-Israeli conflict and toward the issue of Palestinian self-determination at its core provides the litmus test of U.S. intentions. Ultimately, resolution of this issue would remove or greatly diminish whatever threat of radical political action is posed by diaspora Palestinians in the Arab states of the Gulf and would remove the principal source of destabilization in the Arab world, which has made its impact felt much more powerfully in the Gulf following Camp David and the fall of the shah. In the meantime, U.S. initiatives that demonstrate a determination to produce real movement toward settlement will be critically important in establishing credibility for U.S. policy in general.

If there are also genuine efforts made to deal with these countries in a way that addresses their range of concerns seriously and sensitively – in short, that treats them as subjects, not objects, of U.S. interest – relationships will develop or be re-established in which the United States can act cooperatively with them to deal with sources of threat to energy and other common, vital matters of interest. The Reagan Administration projection of a more self-confident U.S. posture internationally will undoubtedly offer reassurance to friends whose security depends importantly on U.S. ability and willingness to act. If shared security concerns are approached with due regard for those local and regional realities with which they interact, one may view the future with cautious optimism.

NOTES

1. Peter A. Iseman, "Iran's War of Words Against Saudi Arabia," *The Nation*, April 19, 1980, pp. 464-65.

2. "In the Race for Gulf Security: New Roles for Old Drivers," *The Middle East* (April 1980): 19.

3. See the Honorable Robert G. Neumann's foreword to the excellent study by Martin Kramer, *Political Islam*, Washington Papers, vol. 8, no. 73 (Beverly Hills and London: Sage, 1980).

4. Ibid., pp. 39 and 83. See also Fouad Ajami's review article, "Islamic Ideas," New York *Times Book Review*, March 2, 1980, which discusses these and related themes.

5. See Milton Viorst, "Judaic Extremism Is Matching Islam's," Washington *Post*, March 30, 1980.

6. See Edward Cody, "Iraqi Leader Endorses Better Ties with U.S., " Washington *Post*, June 29, 1981.

7. See Judith Perera, "Caution: Building in Progress," *The Middle East* (April 1981).

9
Antinuclear Terrorism in the Advanced Industrial West

J. F. Pilat

The ecological movement that emerged in the advanced industrial West in the early 1970s, like the youth movements of the 1960s from which it emanated, has been issue-oriented. A multitude of issues, revolving around the protection of the environment and the enhancement of the quality of life, originally concerned the ecological activities. However, the nuclear issue, which is socially, politically, and economically potent, gradually eclipsed these other issues. By the mid-1970s, the ecological movement had been essentially transformed into an antinuclear movement.

Though the antinuclear cause is extremely complex, its advocates have usually directed their activity against the visible edifice of the nuclear industry and have demanded the termination of nuclear development in a certain region or country, or over the globe.

The movement's majority has been moderate and has attempted to attain its objectives by litigation, lobbying, forming parties, staging peaceful demonstrations, and engaging in civil disobedience. Nevertheless, radicals have become involved in the movement, violence has erupted at demonstrations, and even terrorism has been utilized.

Since the mid-1960s, scores of believable hoaxes and threats of sabotage or terrorism directed against nuclear installations have been documented in the United States and the United Kingdom.[1] The occurrence of acts of vandalism and sabotage of nuclear objects

191

has been documented since the late-1960s in these two countries.[2] Further, as early as May 4, 1969, a nuclear facility was definitely the target of a terrorist attack. On that date, a pipe bomb was discovered at the Illinois Institute of Technology reactor.

All of this activity directed against nuclear installations since the 1960s could be construed as antinuclear terror.[3] Yet, acts occurring before the mid-1970s are unlikely to have had a specific and conscious antinuclear motivation.

Antinuclear activists are thus not alone in directing terrorism against nuclear objectives, which are prestigious, vulnerable, and symbolic targets.[4] Consequently, the destiny of terrorism motivated by antinuclear sentiments, which can be expected to target nuclear objectives (even if these are only ephemerally related to the nuclear establishment), is bound to that of terrorism directed against nuclear objectives but committed for other motives. On the one hand, acts committed by antinuclear activists will augment the credibility of terrorists threatening nuclear terrorism, or they may dissuade the latter from acting, if they were unsuccessful or resulted in an unacceptably adverse reaction from broad strata of the population. On the other, terrorists targetting nuclear objectives might further the antinuclear movement or, perhaps, discredit it by their deeds.

The convergence of these two transnational tendencies of terrorism, neither of which is likely to diminish in the near future, has conjured up a specter. Haunting the advanced industrial West, it is the specter of a terrorist act resulting in the release of radioactivity into the atmosphere; the specter of terrorists possessing nuclear weaponry or radioactive materials. The deadly dream has not become a reality. However, as terrorists become increasingly aware of nuclear objectives (such an awakening has already developed under the influence of the antinuclear movement and will continue), and as antinuclear activists become more and more embittered and disillusioned and adopt terrorist tactics on a wider scale, a tragedy involving antinuclear terrorism is virtually inevitable. Enhancing the probability of this prospect is the emergence of the "plutonium economy."

Despite the phenomenological relations of these two types of antinuclear terrorism, only terrorism with nuclear targets, irrespective of motivation, has been the subject of a significant, technical literature.[5] Terrorism with antinuclear motivation has been virtually ignored, especially in Anglo-Saxon scholarship. This chapter focuses on the latter, although both types of antinuclear terrorism are deeply and profoundly interrelated[6] and cannot be fully isolated.

UNALLOYED ANTINUCLEAR TERRORISM

Acts of terrorism inspired solely by antinuclear sentiment, in so far as they can be ascertained, are rare and have only occurred relatively recently. This is not surprising. With the birth of the antinuclear movement in the mid-1970s, individuals, groups, and organizations committed to terrorism perceived the publicity and popularity that might be generated by associating their causes with the antinuclear movement and by engaging in antinuclear terrorism. Only later, as the movement matured, would it attract people with a propensity for political violence. Further, only later would members of the movement come to believe, whether from bitterness or frustration, that only terrorism could effect their objectives. A parallel development occurred a decade earlier – the antiwar movement of the late-1960s and early-1970s had to be radicalized before it could germinate such terrorist organizations as the Red Army Faction and the Japanese Red Army.

The earliest act of unalloyed antinuclear terrorism apparently occurred on May 31, 1978. On that day, the municipal building and the German Church in the city center of Göteborg, Sweden, were damaged by a bomb apparently placed by an antinuclear group. It was declared by the group, but did not come to pass, that until the Swedish nuclear industry ceased to exist, "We will explode one charge a day in Göteborg City center."[7]

Apparently in conjunction with a referendum on the nuclear question in Switzerland,[8] the information center of the Kaiseraugst nuclear power plant, in the vicinity of Basel, was severely damaged by an explosion on February 19, 1979. Within a week, an explosion occurred at the construction site of a nuclear power plant at Liebstadt, Switzerland. A storage facility near the site suffered minor damage, but there were no injuries. The only apparent motivation for these Swiss incidents was antinuclear.

On April 8, 1979, a pylon supporting the high-tension powerlines originating at the Esensham nuclear power plant at Bremenshaven, in the Federal Republic, was damaged by two homemade explosive devices. The damage was not extensive, and the line was not severed. The inexperience exhibited in the strike as well as its objective suggest that only antinuclear motivation was involved.

An explosion occurring outside the 920-megawatt Goesgen nuclear power plant in Switzerland, early in November of 1979, brought down its weather control tower. The Goesgen facility, the object of other antinuclear demonstrations, was not damaged although the reactor nearly ceased functioning. The deed resulted in blackouts and damage to the station onto which the control tower dropped.

The Swiss Sarelli nuclear power plant was bombed on Christmas Day in 1979. Considerable damage was done to the transformer station and to the transformer beam, and some villages lost electrical power. While no group claimed responsibility and one antinuclear group disassociated itself from the act, an antinuclear motivation is suggested by closeness in time to the Goesgen bombing and by the absence of other known motivations.

On December 4, 1980, an explosion in the Cologne office of a governmental nuclear energy research group resulted in considerable damage. No group claimed responsibility, but the choice of the target does not suggest motivations other than antinuclear.

NATIONAL-SEPARATISM AND ANTINUCLEAR TERRORISM

As early as August 15, 1975, when the Monts d'Arée reactor was damaged by explosions, a terrorist act directed against a nuclear objective was apparently perpetrated by a national-separatist organization.

The Monts d'Arée nuclear reactor at Brennelis, already in operation, had to be closed as a consequence of damage to its water cooling tank and to its radiotelephone room by two bombs. The bombs were believed to have been placed by the Breton Liberation Front, a national-separatist organization, following an anonymous call stating that the act was a protest against the construction of nuclear installations in Brittany.

The question arises whether antinuclear sentiments played a significant role in this incident, for the nationistic motive must be accorded primacy. The early date of the deed might appear to suggest minimal significance. The importance of the antinuclear movement was only clearly established later, in the autumn of 1976. However, a momentous demonstration at Wyhl had occurred before the date of the explosions;[9] during early and middle August, Brittany itself was an arena of antinuclear protest; and acts of antinuclear terrorism had been perpetrated in France, the United States, and Argentina.

The Breton organization can be understood to have been inspired by these earlier events to direct an attack on a nuclear power plant. However, at that stage of the antinuclear movement, it could not fully expect, or receive, higher degrees of publicity and popularity due to the nature of the target. Terrorist acts, it should be recollected, often mimic earlier terrorism.

The Breton separatists might, too, have perceived the facility as a symbol of the control of the province by the centralized authority of the French government. If a nuclear installation were believed to be a tenacle of Paris' ubiquitous bureaucracy, whose intervention in Brittany was believed intolerable, concerns (already in pre-Harrisburg France, the subject of a growing public debate and an awakening general recognition) over the presence of a nuclear power plant in the region could only be exacerbated.

Breton separatists may have been involved in other acts of antinuclear terrorism, both before and after the government in Paris essentially resolved the problem of Breton aspirations for autonomy. The explosions at the Saint-Malo and Dinan offices of Electricité de France, in July 1977, appear to have been perpetrated by Breton separatists. And, early in 1980, a bomb exploded near the site of the proposed Plogoff nuclear power plant, during a period of intense antinuclear activity by the local populace. Nevertheless, the Bretons did not direct a systematic assault against nuclear objectives in Brittany.

Freedom for the Basque Homeland (ETA), since December 1977, has directed a campaign of terror against the nuclear power plant under construction at Lemóniz, near Bilbao, and against Iberduero, the utility that is building it. Among the acts of antinuclear terrorism perpetrated by the Basque terrorist organization, which have resulted in four deaths and more than $20 million in damages, are the following.

In December 1977, four ETA separatists, masked and armed with grenades and machine guns, assaulted the guardpost at the Lemóniz construction site. The guards repulsed them, killing one separatist.

Incendiary bombs were utilized to destroy properties of Iberduero and its affiliates on March 1, 1978.

On March 17, 1978, an explosion in the nuclear installation being constructed at Lemóniz resulted in the deaths of two workers and injuries to 14 others. The damage to the facility was extensive.

Early in April 1978, explosions destroyed four electricity pylons of a firm contracted to construct the controversial nuclear facility, and electrical equipment near the Lemóniz construction site was damaged by explosives.

Early in June 1979, the killing of two Civil Guards in Madrid by terrorists wielding automatic weapons may have been effected by the Basques in retaliation for the death of a Basque antinuclear demonstrator. This is suggested by the occurrence of the act during days of Basque reaction to the death.

Later that month, one worker died in an explosion at the nuclear power station. Three armed terrorists breached the plant's security, subdued three workers, and placed an explosive device near a turbine in the plant. ETA claimed responsibility for the deed.

Two explosions severely damaged the Equipos Nucleares factory in Maliaño, Spain, one night in mid-November 1979. The terrorists entered the installation, subdued 10 guards, placed the explosives, and kidnapped the employees, who were later released at the border of the provinces of Santander and Vizcaya. ETA's military wing claimed responsibility for the act.

Early February 1980, terrorists forcefully entered a factory in Vitoria and used explosive charges to destroy electrical equipment for the Lemóniz plant.

The offices of Iberduero in Eibar, Spain, were breached in early August 1980 by terrorists who burned company documents. Later in the month, Iberduero offices were again the object of arson.

ETA used an explosive device to destroy the control room of an Iberduero switching station located near San Sebastian in December 1980. And, in January 1981, the Basque terrorist organization bombed the Spanish utility's power stations in Guipuzcoa province and its business office in San Sebastian.

On February 6, 1981, Jose Maria Ryan, Iberduero's chief engineer for the Lemóniz project, was assassinated by ETA, having been kidnapped more than a week earlier. ETA had demanded that the Lemóniz installation be dismantled or Ryan would die, and it followed through on its threat.

Following the assassination, 33 other Iberduero technicians were threatened. According to ETA, Ryan's death "was not an isolated act, but rather the opening of a new front which will affect all specialized personnel".[10] Furthermore, power pylons were destroyed by explosives in April 1981, causing a blackout in certain sectors of Bilbao, and, in May, switching stations in Guipuzcoa province were destroyed, with resultant blackouts in Oyarzun and Vergara.

It has been suggested that ETA terrorizes nuclear objectives because it desires the approval of the populace.[11] This suggestion once seemed quite plausible. The earliest incident, in December 1977, occurred after the antinuclear movement had manifested a broad appeal in 1976-77, and, more significantly, after 200,000 citizens had demonstrated against the Lemóniz nuclear power plant earlier in 1977. And, in the following years, it appeared that in the Basque region of Spain, the vulnerable and apparently symbolic target was the object of terrorism that paralleled popular, and frequently violent, demonstrations. What was plausible in the 1970s no longer seems valid, especially following the February 3, 1981, murder of Ryan. On February 9, in Bilboa, popular revulsion to the act brought out from 100,000 to 150,000 demonstrators against ETA terrorism. And, since the assassination, support for the power plant project has been growing in the Basque region, most notably among local officials and trade unions.

Other national-separatists have apparently recognized the potential of antinuclear activity. The Armed Forces of National Liberation (FALN), the Puerto Rican separatist organization, was believed, in the autumn of 1979, to be organizing a bombing of the Indian Point nuclear installation in Peekskill, New York. More recently, antinuclear terrorism has been utilized by separatists in Cataluna, Spain. A separatist-ecologist group claimed responsibility for the June 1981 bombing of the offices of Fesca, the utility constructing the Asco nuclear power plant near Tarragona.

Antinuclear terror not only offers national-separatists an opportunity to enhance their publicity and popularity by a spectacular event; antinuclear terror is a symbolic event with ideological significance.

ANTICAPITALISM AND ANTINUCLEAR TERRORISM

Anticapitalism is a significant undercurrent in the antinuclear movement. Even though those who oppose nuclear energy are not often ideologically conscious, if ideology is professed it involves elements of anticapitalism. These may be expressed innocuously, as in criticisms of consumer society, or more radically, by certain extremist organizations operating under the antinuclear umbrella and by certain antinuclear terrorists.

A moderate act of antinuclear terrorism was perpetrated by Sam Lovejoy. Lovejoy, as a student at Amherst in the 1960s, protested U.S. involvement in Vietnam. He is now an organic farmer living on a commune in Montague, Massachusetts, an ecological activist, and an advocate of "ecotage." He destroyed a nuclear survey tower in Montague by unbolting its stays on February 22, 1974. The anticapitalism manifest in Lovejoy's countercultural life and in his earlier activity was probably an undercurrent of this act.

Usually, an anticapitalist impulse expressing itself in antinuclear terrorism is generated by more radical elements (and is thus usually more severe in its consequences).

Though not known for their antinuclear activism, members of the Manson cult were involved in a conspiracy to perpetrate assassinations. Emerging into light in the autumn of 1975, its rhetoric and targets suggest a relationship between anticapitalist and antinuclear motivations.

Sandra Good and Lynette "Squeaky" Fromme, the latter indicted for the attempted assassination of President Gerald Ford, stated:

> PG & E, the people who are building nuclear power plants, the people that are polluting the air, the people that are poisoning the water, the people who are killing the wild life, the people who are falsely advertising to the public — all of them will be butchered in their bedrooms because they are living off the blood of the little people.[12]

Good, in an interview, declared that the International People's Court of Retribution — "several thousand people throughout the world who love the Earth, the children and their lives"[13] — had condemned business executives, placing them on an assassination list. Floyd Lewis, the president of Middle South Utilities, engaged in the nuclear industry, was included. Good later revealed 72 other executives on the list, including those of Westinghouse, Bechtel, Pacific Gas and Electric, General Electric, and Exxon.

The appearance of antinuclear terrorism in Europe in 1975 involved anticapitalist and antinuclear motives. On May 3, 1975, the casing of the nuclear reactor at the Fessenheim facility near Strasbourg, France — the construction of which was nearly completed — was extensively damaged by two explosions. Responsibility was claimed by the "Puig Antich-Ulrike Meinhof Commando," probably composed of Germans, whose title, suggestive of a neo-anarchist ideology, was derived from Ulrike Meinhof, the German anarchist and terrorist who was discovered hanged in her prison cell in 1976, and Puig Antich, a Catalan anarchist and nationalist executed under Franco's regime in 1974.

The explosions at Fessenheim were obviously antinuclear. The "Commando" expressed "solidarity with Wyhl" in a communiqué. Yet it voiced the negation not only of the nuclear industry, but of all industry. It decried the capitalism of the multinationals, whose "blind pursuit of productivity" was believed to be symbolized by nuclear energy, as unnecessary as "day-long working to produce goods." The act at Fessenheim was "an expression of life's primordial protest against Capital." For "Antich-Meinhof," as the communiqué stated, nuclear energy was "radical genocide," the successor of earlier, more primitive capitalist genocide.[14]

Other terrorist acts have probably involved elements of anticapitalism, as one may surmise from public pronouncements made by the terrorists or from titles they have assumed.[15]

Framatone, a French subsidiary of Westinghouse engaged in the nuclear industry, was the object of a terrorist explosion on June 6, 1975. Extensive damage to the input terminals of Framatone's main computer resulted from a simultaneous explosion at Courbevoie. The "Garmendia-Angela Luther Commando" claimed responsibility.

On October 10, 1977, the "New World Liberation Front Environmental Assault Team" detonated an explosive device outside the gates of the Trojan nuclear power plant in Rainier, Oregon. The windows of a visitors' center were shattered by the explosion.[16]

During the night of November 19, 1977, terrorists armed with automatic weapons and explosives struck a series of ostensibly nuclear objectives in France. Seven facilities connected to the state electricity company or to recipients of contracts from the Defense Ministry were affected.

Explosions at five of the facilities resulted in damage of varying degrees, but no injuries occurred. An explosion brought down a pylon supporting a 400,000-volt powerline near Lyons. Explosions occurred at the enterprise's main office in Paris, as well as at its Narbonne office and one of its garages, at the nuclear physics laboratory at Toulouse University, and at a factory producing paint for the French nuclear industry.

Devices that had not exploded were discovered at the Carcassonne office of the power company and at a nuclear power station near Metz.

On November 21, responsibility for these concerted actions was claimed by the "Carlos Committee," which declared its objective to be the termination of nuclear energy development in France. According to a letter received by *Le Monde*:

The fight against nuclear energy cannot be confined to the legalistic opposition of the parties and unions. It is essential to intensify the acts of sabotage which directly affect the authority's economic interests and delay or halt the construction of generators, mines and factories linked to nuclear power.[17]

Other motivational mutations have appeared. An unusual incident, fusing antinuclear sentiments to antimilitarism and a concern for children, occurred in September, 1979. A Lufthansa 727 was hijacked on route from Frankfurt to Bonn. Before surrendering to authorities, the hijacker pronounced a communiqué to government officials over the radio.

The hijacker, expressing concerns about the development of nuclear energy, indigent children, and militarism, demanded, in negotiations with Schmidt's chief aide, Hans-Juergen Wischenewski, a referendum on nuclear energy in the Federal Republic, the enhancement of the quality of children's lives, and the abolition of the military. All of these demands were apparently unified in his mind. He proclaimed, "All I want is a more humane world in which it is worthwhile to live."[18]

INFILTRATION AND SURROGATE WARFARE

As has been noted, terrorism directed against nuclear facilities may be motivated by antinuclear sentiments alone or in alloys with national-separatism, anticapitalism, or other sociopolitical beliefs. But what if such motivation is not present? What if antinuclear sentiments are absent or insignificant; what about cases in which antinuclear terrorism is perpetrated by infiltrators or used for surrogate warfare (which may or may not involve infiltration)?

Antinuclear groups and organizations have been, or are likely to be, infiltrated. Extremist sects and societies — whether political or religious, whether of the right or of the left — may infiltrate the movement for motives as diverse as these groups are legion.

Anarchists, Maoists, and Trotskyists could use terrorism to radicalize the movement, repel its moderate majority, and gather its reins. Religious cultists might utilize antinuclear terror for manipulative or punitive purposes. Radical rightists might wish to capitalize on the movement's broad popular appeal. Or, alternately, they might believe that terrorism will discredit the movement.

But antinuclear terrorism used for pronuclear purposes would be self-defeating: the material costs of the action could be debilitating to the nuclear industry, and the action might augment antinuclear feelings in the general public. Further, all of the moderates in the antinuclear movement could not be expected to abandon it if it became violent, even if many would. Nevertheless, the rhetoric of the right suggests this irrational strategy might be implemented. For the reasons that should dissuade the pronuclear radical right from engaging in antinuclear terrorism, the governments of the Western democracies should be inhibited from engaging in "secret agent" scenarios.

What is the significance of the use of terrorism by infiltrators of the antinuclear movement? If infiltrators are able to exert only limited influence on antinuclear parties and demonstrations, in the subterranean realm of terrorism they are able to act with impunity, if not also with extraordinary purpose.

Discussion of the infiltration of the antinuclear movement by the Soviet Union or its satellites, by other countries, or by mercenaries enters the realm of surrogate warfare, which can be waged by infiltrating the antinuclear movement or by using it as a cover.

The Israelis, in April 1979, may have utilized antinuclear terrorism in their struggles with the radical Arab states and, thereafter, may have attempted to use the antinuclear movement to cover their deed.

On April 6, 1979, explosions in a nuclear manufacturing plant at La Seyne-sur-Mer, France, produced millions of dollars in damages. Most significantly, certain components of a reactor being built for Iraq were damaged. The Iraqi reactor was the apparent objective of the bombing, and French officials believed foreign agents, probably Israeli, rather than ecological terrorists, were responsible for the deed. The object of the explosion and the expertise shown in its implementation suggest this. *Le Monde*, however, received an anonymous telephone call stating that the explosions were detonated by the "Group of French Ecologists." According to the caller, the act would "neutralize machines dangerous to human life."[19] The caller further stated:

> The Harrisburg catastrophe proved to us once again the dangers of the atomic industry. We have turned to action, and we will do what is necessary to safeguard the French people and the human race from nuclear horrors.[20]

Other countries can be expected to utilize antinuclear terrorism in a similar manner, whether their own agents perpetrate the act under the shroud of the antinuclear movement, they hire mercenaries, or they hire, support, or infiltrate terrorist groups, especially those of antinuclear terrorists whose objectives would parallel their own.

Qadhafi might become involved in antinuclear terrorism for a variety of reasons – political, ideological, or economic. The Soviet Union and its satellites might also become involved, in the hope of furthering the decline of the nuclear industry in the West[21] and, thus, the decline of the West itself, both economically and strategically.

THE OBJECTIVES OF ANTINUCLEAR TERRORISM AND ITS DANGERS

Obviously, serious damage due to terrorism may result in an operating installation being shut down or in a delay in the opening of an unoperational one. In both cases, the costs of nuclear energy would be increased, not only by the damage but also by the delay. Even the destruction of materials and components at a plant, or of those destined for a plant, would serve this purpose (as would, to a lesser degree, damage done to powerlines running from an operating station).

Terrorists could conceivably prejudice nuclear energy by increasing its costs, but it is unlikely that their sporadic acts could result in sufficient damage to do so.

If terrorists desire seriously, if not irrevocably, to wound the West's nuclear programs, they would have to do one of two things: divert radioactive materials, allowing them to build an atomic weapon or to disseminate radioactivity; or incapacitate a reactor or its electronic systems, by explosives or other means, so as to cause a catastrophe, releasing radioactivity into the atmosphere.

The consequences of the former possibility are obvious. Concerning the latter, the accident at Harrisburg suggests that the immediate impact of any nuclear catastrophe will be antinuclear sentiment, nationally and internationally. Yet, from another perspective, Harrisburg – along with all of the previous acts directed against power plants, none of which resulted in the release of radioactivity of any magnitude whatsoever – shows that if a nuclear incident is to be debilitating to the nuclear industry, it must be truly catastrophic. Otherwise, its memory will be dimmed before it can be effectual.

It might be believed that an incident that definitively proves the possibility of a catastrophe would have a similar effect. As earlier terrorist incidents suggest, such is not the case. Two cases demonstrate this point.

The first case is that of Andre Schmidt, an antinuclear activist who obtained access to the cooling water building of the installation at Dodewaard, in the Netherlands, one summer night in 1976. His deed, which was filmed and broadcast on television, affected only the community of Dodewaard, and that only temporarily.

A more serious incident, occurring in Virginia on April 27, 1978, appears also to have had primarily a local effect. In that case, the Virginia Electric and Power Company (VEPCO) Surry installation was sabotaged. Damage to 62 fuel elements, amounting to more than $800,000, was discovered on May 8. William E. Kuykendall and James A. Merrill, Jr., employees at the plant, admitted to the sabotage, stating that it was done as a consequence of VEPCO's inadequate security procedures and safety conditions. They asserted that a catastrophe could occur and believed that their deed proved the possibility. Nevertheless, the impact of the act and the trial was not great, save perhaps in the vicinity of the plant.

A third case, the case of Klaus Traube, an eminent German physicist who directed research on fast breeder reactors for Interatom, a subsidiary of Kraftwerk Union, may be considered. Traube's case further illuminates the grave dangers of terrorism directed against the nuclear industry (as well as the serious social consequences of combatting such terrorism, or even its suspicion, in the industrial democracies of the West).

Though he was formally absolved by authorities in mid-March 1977, during January and February of 1976 his residence had been broken into, he was the object of electronic surveillance, and he was dismissed from his position at Interatom.

Why was Traube subjected to this?

Traube, it was alleged by Interior Minister Werner Maihofer, was an acquaintance of Hans-Joachim Klein during a period of several months in 1975-76. Klein, a terrorist, had been one of the organizers of the kidnapping of OPEC officials in Vienna on December 21, 1975. Other direct and indirect contacts with terrorists were alleged. Traube's position, according to Maihofer, allowed him "access to all blueprints for nuclear power plants in operation in West Germany. He could have given instructions for attacks from the outside as well as for penetration by terrorists, and unleashed the potential dangers of nuclear energy against the public."[22]

While Traube's guilt was not established, the dangerous ramifications of his case are significant and should not be dismissed. On the one hand, whether or not Traube was believed to have been motivated by antinuclear sentiment, do antinuclear activists have access to information necessary to sabotage or destroy nuclear facilities? Would antinuclear activists cooperate with terrorists (who might have other motives) in acts directed against nuclear objectives? On the other hand, without questioning the propriety of the West German action in Traube's case, does the specter of a Baader-Meinhof with a nuclear arsenal, or disseminating radioactive materials into the atmosphere, or in control of a nuclear facility justify encroachments on civil liberties? To what degree? Are the anti-democratic consequences of nuclear security a sufficient reason to terminate nuclear development?[23]

ANTINUCLEAR TERRORISM IN THE 1980S

What are the prospects for antinuclear terrorism in the 1980s?

Though antinuclear terrorism has occurred in France, the Federal Republic, Spain, Switzerland, Sweden, and the United States, it has occurred randomly and sporadically. It could occur anywhere in the West, like other manifestations of terrorism. Patterns are virtually impossible to discern. One need not be mute, however.

Whether or not a catastrophe occurs as its consequence, antinuclear terrorism is not likely to diminish in the immediate future. It is rather more likely to increase. The expected continuation, if not growth, of the antinuclear movement in the 1980s will be a magnet to terrorists of all persuasions. Further, the democratic resolutions of national nuclear questions can be expected in the industrial democracies of the West over the next decade. Pronuclear decisions will placate the moderate majority of the antinuclear movement. If they then abandon the movement, it will become the preserve of radical groups, as well as of those who became isolated, radicalized, and disillusioned by democracy in the wake of decisions affirming nuclear energy. The probability of terrorism, in these circumstances, would rise. Thus, antinuclear terrorism may be expected to correlate with both the rise and decline of the antinuclear movement.

Basque antinuclear terrorism, in conjunction with the ETA campaign of terror in Spain, can be expected to be a recurrent phenomenon, and a campaign of Catalan terrorism is conceivable. Though Breton separatists have largely been appeased by limited autonomy, acts of antinuclear terrorism might occasionally occur in the region. Other national-separatist groups and organizations, which plague European politics, might undertake acts against nuclear targets, especially in conjunction with an antinuclear movement manifesting a "nationalistic" face.

The national-separatist utilization of terrorism against nuclear facilities, as has been intimated, will be only one among many manifestations of antinuclear terrorism in the future. As anticapitalism engulfs the "capitalist" countries, it will appear in amalgamations that inspire antinuclear terrorism.

Such countries as France, the Federal Republic, Spain, and Italy are more likely than others to show increases in incidents of antinuclear terrorism. Of these countries, Italy is the most likely locus of antinuclear terrorism. As its national nuclear program develops, so too will a viable, and probably violent, antinuclear movement. Should this occur, terrorism is probable in that unstable country plagued by political violence.

NOTES

1. Michael Flood, "Nuclear Sabotage," *Bulletin of the Atomic Scientists* vol. 32 (October 1976): 32.

2. Ibid., p. 33.

3. In this chapter, apolitical acts of vandalism and sabotage, as well as acts perpetrated by criminals or lunatics — that is to say, acts motivated by personal or other nonpolitical reasons — are not considered. Acts considered here are political, to the extent that this can be ascertained. Further, this chapter does not consider threats and hoaxes; an act must be attempted or accomplished, not merely threatened or contrived, despite the political potential of the latter behavior.

4. Nuclear facilities are, thus, potentially appealing to terrorists bearing any banner. Let us systematically explore the reasons for this appeal.

The profusion of potential nuclear objectives is an element of their appeal. Nuclear power plants are the most obvious nuclear target and, expectedly, have most frequently been targetted. Nevertheless, facilities for enriching uranium and fabricating fuel, as well as for reprocessing and storing spent fuel, are potential targets. Indeed, the entire infrastructure of the nuclear industry, including suppliers, subsidiaries, and even powerlines, could be the object of antinuclear terror.

Nuclear objectives are also appealing because their security is generally inadequate in relation to the strength terrorists can command, especially at certain types of installations. The prestige of these facilities is also significant, as is the power that terrorists might gain by destroying, occupying, or even robbing one (which suggests nuclear terror may be qualitatively different from non-nuclear terror). Further, since the antinuclear movement arose, the popularity and publicity terrorists might expect from antinuclear acts has greatly increased. Finally, nuclear installations may mean many things to many people – they may symbolize unlimited capitalism, national oppression, or other objects of hatred and resistance.

5. Brian Michael Jenkins is the dean of studies on nuclear terrorism. From 1975 through 1979, he has published "High Technology Terrorism and Surrogate War: The Impact of New Technology in Low Level Violence," Rand Corporation (Santa Monica, Ca.) paper series, P-5339, 1975; "Will Terrorists Go Nuclear," Rand paper series, P-5541, 1976; "Terrorism and the Nuclear Safeguards Issue," Rand paper series, P-5611, 1976; "The Potential for Nuclear Terrorism," Rand paper series, P-5876, 1977; "Attributes of Potential Criminal Adversaries of U.S. Nuclear Programs," Rand report series, R-2225-SL, 1978; and "The Consequences of Nuclear Terrorism," Rand paper series, P-6373, 1979. Among other studies of nuclear terrorism are Mason Willrich and Theodore B. Taylor, *Nuclear Theft: Risks and Safeguards* (Cambridge: Ballinger, 1974); David Krieger, "Nuclear Power: A Trojan Horse for Terrorists," in *Nuclear Proliferation* (Stockholm: Stockholm International Peace Research Institute, 1974), pp. 187-198; L. Douglas DeNike, "Radioactive Malevolence," *Bulletin of the Atomic Scientists* vol. 2 (February 1974), pp. 16-20; Michael Flood, "Nuclear Sabotage"; Martin H. Greenberg and Augustus R. Norton, eds., *Studies in Nuclear Terrorism* (Boston: J. K. Hall, 1979); and Louis René Beres, *Apocalypse; Nuclear Catastrophe in World Politics* (Chicago and London: University of Chicago Press, 1980).

6. Consider the problems of delineating these two types of antinuclear terrorism.

Do we, on the one hand, limit antinuclear terror to those acts of violence committed for political objectives and directed against nuclear installations? How, then, does one categorize those acts directed against the prestigious targets of the nuclear establishment that could bring terrorists extraordinary publicity and power?

On the other hand, do we limit antinuclear terror to those terrorists acts for which antinuclear motivation is established? If so, what of those acts for which no motive is known? Moreover, how do we classify those terrorists, opposed to the development of nuclear energy, whose deeds are directed to other institutions and installations, perhaps only indirectly connected with the nuclear establishment, when we can, however, expect some connection? Perhaps more significantly, how do we conceive of those acts that manifest an antinuclear inspiration conjoined with another motive such as nationalism?

7. Quoted in Bayard Stockton and Peter Janke, "Nuclear Power: Protest and Violence," *Conflict Studies* no. 102 (December 1978): 2.

8. Originating in an initiative of May 1976, the organization of which was inspired by the antinuclear activists who occupied Kaiseraugst in 1975, a Swiss referendum on nuclear energy was held in mid-February, 1979. The referendum, which would have imposed more rigid requirements for licensing nuclear installations and granted authority for their approval to parliament, contingent upon the approval of the electorates of all communities in a 30 kilometer radius, was opposed by 51.2 percent of the voters.

9. On February 18, 1975, the site of a prospective nuclear power plant at Wyhl, in the Federal Republic of Germany, was occupied, inaugurating a transatlantic wave of antinuclear demonstrations, often involving occupations of nuclear sites, that has continued to the present.

While the 150 people who originally occupied the Wyhl site were removed by police using water cannons, the site was reoccupied by approximately 8,000 people and was held for eight months.

10. *Nucleonics Week*, March 26, 1981, p. 3.

11. By Stockton and Janke, "Nuclear Power," p. 2.

12. *Nuclear News* (October 1975): 38.

13. Ibid.

14. Derived from a communiqué issued by the "Commando," partially reproduced in Stockton and Janke; "Nuclear Power," p. 12.

15. It does not seem appropriate to consider the targets of the terrorists as indicative of an anticapitalist motivation. With the exception of government installations, virtually all nuclear facilities that might be targetted are owned and operated by "capitalist" enterprises.

16. By December 1978, approximately 30 explosions had occurred at Pacific Gas and Electric Company facilities, perpetrated by the New World Liberation Front, according to Stockton and Janke, "Nuclear Power," p. 7.

17. London *Times*, November 22, 1977, p. 8.

18. Washington *Post*, September 13, 1979, p. 29.

19. New York *Times*, April 7, 1979, p. 3.

20. *Facts on File*, 1979, p. 276.

21. Sweden, Austria, the Federal Republic, and the United States are among the countries experiencing an effective, if not formal, moratorium on nuclear power plant construction. Throughout the West, the nuclear industry is depressed. The ambitious nuclear programs proclaimed in the wake of the Arab Oil Embargo have been drastically reduced in scale in virtually every industrialized state in the Western world.

22. New York *Times*, March 1, 1977, p. 6.

23. The prospect of an antidemocratic society as a consequence of the regulations necessary to assure the security of nuclear fuel cycles has been explored by a number of authors. See David Krieger, "Nuclear Power: A Trojan Horse for Terrorists"; Michael Flood and Robin Grove-White, *Nuclear Prospects: A Comment on the Individual, the State and Nuclear Power* (London: Friends of

the Earth in Association with the Council for the Protection of Rural England and the National Council for Civil Liberties, 1976); and Robert Jungk, *Der Atomstaat* (Munich: Kindler, 1977).

10
Corporate Vulnerability — and How To Assess It

Brooks McClure

With the onset of the 1980s, the international business community could look back upon a decade of turbulent history and contemplate an uncertain legacy for the balance of the century. Trade imbalances and dislocation, currency fluctuation, inflation, rising operating costs, and growing concerns about pollution, overpopulation, hunger, and revolutionary disruption in the Third World had all matured as problems over the past ten years, and none with a glimmer of hope for easy solution.

And then, in the midst of it all, is the perplexing phenomenon of political terrorism. This type of low-level conflict flowered in the 1970s and seeks to become an instrument of world revolution in the 1980s. It has little chance of achieving this goal, based on its record so far, but it may be capable of causing costly damage and disarray in both the political and economic lives of a number of countries. It has links with most of the basic problems of the times, being able both to capitalize on and to promote social distress of all kinds.

A record total of 2,773 terrorist incidents occurred worldwide in 1980, according to Risks International, a firm that surveys political violence in depth. Nearly one-third of these cases involved a business target. But certain kinds of attack concentrated even more heavily on the commercial community: 46 percent of the 124 kidnappings involved businessmen victims, for example, and nearly 49 percent of the bombings were targetted against business properties. Only

100 of the 859 business-related incidents involved foreign firms, but nearly half of these, 42, were American.

This, then, is the general nature of the threat that confronts international business. There is little comfort in the recent slack in the targetting of foreigners while, overall, terrorism continues unabated. The threat remains, and the techniques and tactics of terrorist groups are being refined. Given this state of the art, how can corporations evaluate their vulnerability to attack?

Evaluation of corporate vulnerability to terrorist attack is anything but an exact science. It does not lend itself to quantification, and one must be wary of mathematical models and comparisons because the variables are too numerous. But there are certain considerations that, when examined each in its own context and then in combination, can give a valid overall picture of a company's exposure to attack. At the same time, such an evaluation sometimes suggests where specific improvements in defense can be made.

Following are five general factors in corporate vulnerability that can be systematically analyzed for any facility that might be targetted. The components under each major heading are necessarily limited by space considerations here, but they indicate areas that should be examined in detail. When the whole exercise is completed, the potential exposure of the facility to targetting will be evident.

COMPANY VISIBILITY

The first factor to consider in assessing a company's vulnerability to terrorist attack is its general visibility. Since political terrorists rank propaganda and other psychological effects high among their objectives, any conspicuous symbol of capitalistic enterprise offers an attractive target. Among the questions one should ask are the following:

Is the Facility Obviously U.S.?

If the facility is obviously U.S., it may well have a better-than-average chance of being hit. This is not because organized terrorists need a sign to point out U.S. interests; they have rather sophisticated intelligence methods to help in their targetting. The low-profile U.S. company abroad, with a local name and perhaps local management, is not invisible to political terrorists, but it is not likely to be a prime target because of its relative obscurity.

When a U.S. subsidiary "flies the flag," however, it risks providing a propaganda incentive for attack because terrorists can make the point of striking at "U.S. imperialism." Depending upon popular attitudes in the host country, this type of target may be selected to reinforce a growing xenophobia or to otherwise stimulate anti-"capitalistic" sentiments. The target can thus provide a rallying point for radical agitation. The fact that two of every five international terrorist incidents in the past decade have involved U.S. property or citizens as targets testifies to the symbolic appeal of anything conspicuously U.S.

Certain company names are synonymous with an obviously U.S. product (Coca-Cola), suggest superior U.S. technical achievement (IBM), or otherwise project a distinctly U.S. image. Firms of this kind tend to be choice targets of terrorist groups seeking to demonstrate opposition to U.S. political power or to foreign influence in general. Despite spectacular inroads into world markets by Germany (which also has been targetted by terrorists abroad) and Japan – and the traditional commercial role of such countries as Great Britain, France, and the Netherlands – the United States remains the pre-eminent symbol of "capitalism" and "imperialism" to Marxist-oriented extremists.

Is the Company Regarded as a Multinational?

Although all companies with operations in several countries are by definition "multinational," some are clearly more so than others for political propaganda purposes. Firms engaged in extractive operations (oil production, mining), for example, are singled out by radicals as being particularly exploitative. So are companies involved in defense-related production or in the computer-electronics field.

The symbolic multinational corporation in recent years has been criticized in liberal, non-Communist circles in industrial countries because of its ability to "shop around" for favorable production or marketing conditions in developing countries and for its ability to operate largely beyond control of national governments. To capitalize on this negative sentiment and to suggest common cause with moderate socialist and social-democratic groups, terrorists have found the multinational corporation an especially attractive target.

Beyond this consideration, however, the international corporation is seen universally by Marxists as a key element of capitalism and as a source of economic power to the developed Western nations. The degree to which any company can be portrayed as a "typical multinational" therefore has a bearing on its vulnerability to targetting by left-wing terrorists.

Is the Product Symbolic?

Certain products, as already noted, have developed a negative social connotation among political critics, who often use and enjoy the very same products. Thus one hears of the "Coca-cola (or Pepsi) civilization," denoting an all-pervasive, materialistic, Philistine U.S. culture being exported around the world. Radical propagandists are quick to exploit any such symbolic linkage, trying to reduce complex attitudes toward the United States to simple slogans.

Other product associations singled out for attention by radicals — and hence by terrorists as well — center on military production of any kind. Thus a chemical company that produced napalm during the Vietnam war is constantly identified with that product, although its product line includes hundreds of items with a vast range of utility.

Does the Company Have Local Management?

Local management is no guarantee that the plant will not be hit or its manager targetted, but the locally run subsidiary is generally a less inviting target than a branch run by expatriots, when the aim is to emphasize the "foreign" enemy. Much depends on how the local population perceives the enterprise and identifies with it. (Of course, any native company can be hit by terrorists in its own right, as the statistics show.)

IMAGE FACTORS

Another set of criteria for measuring corporate vulnerability is what might simply be called image factors: how the company is regarded by the community around it. These are broken down into four categories for analysis.

Labor Relations

Are there any current union difficulties, or have there been any significant strikes in the past that have left emotional scars? What about layoffs? Have these been accomplished with minimum worker bitterness? What sort of cushion exists to tide over those temporarily out of work? Answers to these questions may reveal possible seeds of trouble.

Political agitators are quick to exploit any festering dissatisfaction among workers, and the company should ask itself how well it is prepared to detect early signs of such agitation and what it can do to blunt the effect. In this regard, the level of plant vandalism and sabotage should be watched carefully. Even if the damage is relatively small, a growing incidence of such activity can indicate the beginning of an orchestrated campaign by political terrorists, which can spell serious trouble ahead.

Health, Safety, and Environmental Impact

This is an area of particular importance because it involves the entire social panorama around the company plant or facility. What about past accidents in which there may have been loss of life or community property damage? Have the social and emotional effects been outlived? Is the company still blamed for some past incident, such as a mine cave-in? Are there embittered individuals who feel they have a score to settle with the company, no matter how unreasonable this attitude may be? Here may lie fertile grounds for agitation and propaganda exploitation and a chance for a terrorist group to penetrate the plant with spies or saboteurs.

On another plane is the question of continuing occupational hazards. Has the company taken steps to minimize the sometimes inevitable consequences of dealing with toxic or other harmful substances? What is the general employee view of the company's measures to protect workers and to take care of them if they develop occupational disorders?

Environmental concerns affect not only the "company family" but the surrounding community as well. Does the plant generate water, soil, or air pollution? Is this pollution within tolerable limits, or is the condition likely to get worse? To what degree is there local political or academic-professional opposition, and how much publicity is being given to the problem? Since 1977, there has been a discernible growth of political violence in Europe around environmental issues, centering on antinuclear sentiment but extending to other pollution and contamination charges. Terrorist organizations have also shown tendencies to exploit these broader-based protest movements.

Community Relations

The role and general relationship of the company to the community around it is of utmost importance in determining potential terrorist threat. Again, there are no simple answers. A company with fine community relations may be targetted in order to intimidate the population as a whole or to cause the townspeople, out of fear, to avoid contact with the company. (The political counterpart to this tactic is to attack municipal officials, suggesting in the process that any ordinary citizen who has contact with them may also become a target.)

In general, however, strong community relations will only help any company. In societies that have not reached a point at which terrorist activity is so massive and pervasive that it can exercise a countergovernment authority, communal social pressure can minimize the terrorist threat to respected institutions and industrial facilities in the neighborhood.

Usually terrorist groups seek to exploit existing grievances and identify with a popular cause, thus earning the grudging support of those otherwise repelled by their violent methods and, perhaps, also winning recruits from among disgruntled youth. If one plant does not offer much opportunity for such exploitation, there is always another that will.

Some touchstones for evaluating community relations with the plant: company tax contributions — does the populace consider these to be reasonable and fair? social services — is the company seen as contributing to them or drawing excessively from them? role as an institution — is the firm socially integrated with the community or does it stand physically and institutionally apart?

To raise all these questions is not necessarily to imply a remedy. The optimum role of a company in any society depends upon cultural, sociological, psychological, and even historical circumstances. Overparticipation in community activities in some cases can arouse popular concern about company domination or dictation. Excessive support for certain projects — such as building a community center — can lead paradoxically to resentment and rejection of the company's self-assigned role. This is the lesson learned on a larger scale, incidentally, by foreign aid programs of large countries in the developing world. Institutional largesse must be handled with great care to avoid creating an intolerable psychological obligation on the part of the recipient, which can be a whole community.

As a rule, however, reciprocal benefits between company and community can operate effectively within the economic sphere. When the population at large regards the company's contribution to the community as commensurate with the benefits the company receives (in labor availability, public services, and so on), a firm basis for good relations is established. If there are further offsetting factors, such as plant-generated pollution or the inhibition of other commercial development because of the nature of the company's operations, still other compensation from the company may be in order. Beyond this point, there are perhaps other modest company contributions that can enrich community life without appearing overly paternalistic or intrusive. As long as the relationship is a partnership between the community as a whole and the company, with each making its proper contribution to a mutually profitable endeavor, the danger of psychological rejection is avoided.

While popularity of a company within its community is no assurance that the company will be spared by either terrorists or radical agitators, the likelihood of trouble is certainly significantly reduced.

Political Symbolism to the Left

Akin to the direct product symbolism already mentioned is the political propaganda image of certain companies, which is nurtured by international left-wing movements. Thus the International Telephone and Telegraph Corporation has been targetted by both radical groups and terrorists in various countries because of its reported financial support of opponents of Salvador Allende in Chile, in cooperation with the CIA. The attempt here has been to exploit whatever moderate socialist dissatisfaction exists against ITT while perpetuating and reinforcing the company's negative political image. This tactic extends as well to firms which provided munitions and other materiel during the Vietnam war, or which operate plants today in South Africa. Such targetting is appealing to extremists who stress what they call the worldwide "fraternity" of liberation movements.

NATURE OF THE THREAT

External threats to a company come in many forms and vary in nature from place to place. It is therefore vital that the general security climate be correctly evaluated for each separate facility. Only on the basis of sound assessment of the local threat can cost-effective and workable defense measures be developed.

Political violence tends to follow predictable patterns, although there can always be surprises. In general, radical activists start with relatively mild, nonviolent actions (demonstrations, leaflet distributions) and move on to more intimidating measures (blockades, sit-ins), feeling their way and measuring the reaction at each step. When the political terrorism stage is reached, the activists tend to start with less sophisticated operations, gradually escalating as experience and opportunity warrant.

In terms of organizational skill and technical competence involved, terrorist actions rank roughly in this order: petty vandalism; small-group picketing and distribution of radical literature; mass demonstrations (which usually enlist the participation of basically nonviolent, liberal but nonrevolutionary students); firebombing; sabotage in easy-access areas; explosive bombing; felonious assault of targetted individuals; professional sabotage of key functions; assassination and kidnapping.

Seldom does the violence escalate abruptly from the lower range of operations, such as mass demonstrations or small-group picketing, to the upper level of sophistication, such as kidnapping or assassination. This is due in part to the group's lack of readiness; it must train itself to take more complex and dramatic measures in turn. But perhaps even more important is the need to prepare the public at large to accept a high level of violence as a political rather than criminal act.

The abrupt assassination of a company official by a political group, without having first passed through lesser stages of violence accompanied by political propaganda, might cause a strong shock reaction from the public, which could result in concerted public action along with the authorities to crush the revolutionary movement. But a long period of slowly accelerating political violence can condition the public to accept such measures as a fact of life.

As this graduated process develops, the public loses confidence in the police who are unable to end the trouble, it gradually feels more vulnerable to the threat itself (although wise terrorists carefully avoid harming "innocent" people at the outset and try to isolate the targetted institution), and it is "educated" by the terrorists' propaganda to recognize their actions as political rather than criminal. By the time the kidnapping-assassination phase comes, the public feels both helpless and intimidated. It is no longer prepared to respond wholeheartedly and spontaneously against even cold-blooded murder.

The corporate security analyst can be guided by the principles outlined here in determining the level of threat directed at any plant or facility around the world. It is important to first determine the general condition of stability and control in the society at large and what the record has been for political (and, indeed, for organized criminal) violence. A simple checklist for evaluating the level of threat might include the following factors.

Groups Operating in the Area

What are the political motivation, the modes of operation, the weapons-and-tactics sophistication, and the size of groups operating in the area? Also, what is the nature of their support mechanisms? Aside from members of the group itself who provide safehouses and specialized technical and professional services, there is frequently a sympathizer element within the general population that gives invaluable moral and material support. The extent and influence of this support element — often found in professional, artistic, and academic circles — may determine how far the terrorists are likely to go.

Nature of the Violence

Where along the spectrum of possible violent acts has the terrorist group arrived? If it is at the mass-demonstration stage, which might be predominantly of a nonviolent radical nature rather than incipient terrorism, the threat may be contained at that level. If there is bombing, does it seek to take casualties or is it confined to causing property damage at night? In the context of prevailing public attitudes, would the group be encouraged to escalate to a more lethal form of violence?

The kind of current terrorist activity indicates, of course, what immediate defensive measures are needed. In addition, some precautions should be taken against the next likely level of violence, and contingency plans should exist for meeting any conceivable escalation of the threat. But it is important to avoid excessive defenses, for the cost can become prohibitive and a siege mentality can be created, which will reduce the operating efficiency of the plant. The art is to meet the current level of threat, to have some excess capacity to meet a sudden rise in the threat level, and to be ready to cope with more serious dangers in the future — all without making a gross overinvestment in security.

How Have Others Coped?

No opportunity should be lost to profit from the experience of other companies in the area, of foreign or domestic ownership, that have suffered terrorist threat or attack. Learn in detail what tactics were used by the terrorists, what countermeasures were taken by the company, and what the response of the authorities was. In some respects, a company's basic circumstances may differ from those of the targetted company, requiring modifications in the lessons learned. But the information gained will be valuable both for ascertaining the probable nature of a threat as well as in determining what measures may be effective against it.

Available Outside Assistance

If the plant were attacked, how quickly and effectively would the police respond? Would there be military or other reserves upon whom to call? Terrorists always evaluate the effectiveness of the authorities in making their plans, and the possible victim should do likewise. Deficiencies in police protection or in the ability of the police to respond to an emergency might have to be compensated for by the company itself. Any evidence that the plant has compensated for inadequate police support, which would become evident to the terrorists through surveillance when they planned their attack, would tend to discourage an attempt.

The quality of firefighting services should also be assessed. In most places, the company is wise to have a considerable capability of its own to cope with arson or firebomb attack. Even the quickest response of the community fire department may be too slow to deal with an incendiary assault.

In the case of either police or fire services, it is well to remember that well-organized terrorists frequently turn in false alarms to divert emergency services to a distant place just before they attack, thus assuring that help will not be readily available.

PHYSICAL SECURITY PROFILE

Surveys of building security are routine for every large corporation, and many of the precautions taken against criminal acts or industrial sabotage apply equally well against possible terrorist attack. But the terrorist poses a threat beyond the limits of either conventional criminals or vengeful individuals trying to cause damage to the company.

Criminals normally seek personal gain; they are trying to get something of value. The amount of damage they do is therefore usually circumscribed by this objective although they might cause an explosion or start a fire as a diversion. The terrorist group, on the other hand, is not seeking what is normally thought of as "selfish gain"; rather, the aim is to cause damage, attract attention, create an illusion of strength, and generate fear. This is an easier mission to accomplish than that of the criminal, and the consequent destruction or loss can be many times greater.

Furthermore, terrorists generally have greater resources at their command than do criminals or the individual saboteur. The terrorists often have excellent intelligence from spies within the plant; they can draw on a variety of technical skills from among their members and sympathizers; they are usually well financed; and they frequently have access to particularly effective weapons and technology.

When considering defense measures against terrorism, therefore, one must look far beyond established security precautions. A physical security profile for any facility or installation under potential terrorist threat must take into account the following factors.

Relation of the Plant to Other Possible Targets

In politically motivated mass disturbances, a facility may come under attack as an alternate or incidental target. The primary target may be nearby and less accessible or might draw an attack that results in the damage of other property in the neighborhood.

Distance of the Plant from the Street

Space between the company building and the nearest point of public access (normally a street screened off by a fence) constitutes both warning time and a territorial buffer in an emergency. Often it is not until the fence has been breached and the company's "territory" invaded that a serious threat is recognized, so, generally, the greater the distance from the building to the front fence, the better the possibility of defense.

In mob actions, it is possible to perceive a threat and use both the time and space afforded by the distance from the street to take defensive measures. Obviously, the danger from this kind of threat is greater when there is no buffer zone or when the public has casual access to the facility itself. Retail establishments and automobile showrooms are afforded much less natural protection, and special precautions must then be taken for them in high-risk areas.

Situation of the Facility on the Grounds

Certain features of the plant layout can be important to security. If the building is less than 35 yards from the nearest public-access area, for example, it might be hit by a hand-thrown Molotov cocktail. Within that range, then, certian other circumstances must be considered: Are there large front windows (which might be wire-screened or inexpensively reinforced with Mylar or some other invisible sheet-plastic coating)? Is it advisable to move workers from the immediate window area to prevent possible injury? Is there volatile or inflammable material in the front of the building that could be moved elsewhere?

In any case, it is wise to consider how the building might be evacuated during a bomb threat or if an explosion were to occur. Is there space and are there suitable exits to the rear of the building? Since about three-quarters of all actual bomb plants have been either in the public-access areas of the target building or immediately outside it, one must always consider the danger of evacuating people directly into the explosion. Rear areas are generally less accessible to strangers than are front areas, and they should be kept clear of receptacles where a bomb might be hidden. Escape to the rear, preferably out of view from the street in front of the building, might be necessary if a mob threatens to attack from the front. Existing fire-evacuation plans, which bring the employees out all exits, have to be modified for bomb-threat and mob-threat evacuation to avoid exposed areas.

Other points of vulnerability for a facility involve the elevation of the building and the general character of the surrounding terrain. Blind approaches, ground undulation, location and character of the shrubbery, the positioning of fences, gates, and other possible obstacles, the layout of parking areas and access walks or roads should all be examined in the light of any possible hostile approach or infiltration.

Structural Characteristics

Particularly if fire or explosive bombing is a danger, the facility should be analyzed for fireproofing and blast-resistance. Such factors as the thickness and composition of exterior walls, the size and design of windows, materials used for nonstructural partitions, and the load-bearing capacity of floors determine what contingency plans might be developed for various kinds of threats. The division of work areas is particularly important for limiting possible damage.

Location of Key Elements of the Facility

Certain functions constitute the very organic substance of a plant and are particularly vulnerable to attack.

Fuel Storage

Many factory complexes have fuel tanks on the periphery of the industrial estate, where they can readily be resupplied and pose no danger to the rest of the compound. Since terrorists frequently target fuel depots, should such tanks be relocated deeper within the fence? From a production standpoint, is there a standby reserve that could be drawn upon if the main tanks were attacked?

Power Source

Is the power source also located near the fence, relatively accessible to the outside? Is there a reserve transformer if the main one were to go out? If the facility uses community power, is there an emergency backup system that would permit at least partial operation if the transmission lines were cut?

Communications

Is there a radio or other backup system that could maintain external contact if the telephones went out? (Even a CB radio in a vehicle parked on the grounds would be a help in an emergency.) Is there at least one direct line that does not run through the switchboard? Is the switchboard room kept locked to all but authorized persons? (And, incidentally, are the phone operators properly instructed on how to handle bomb warnings and other threats?)

Sensitive Records

Is the computer in a safe area and kept under proper security control? Are duplicates of important automatic data processing (ADP) tapes available off the premises? Are key papers kept secure with access limited to designated people? Penetration of sensitive files, both in industry and government, has been accomplished by terrorist groups in virtually every country.

Volatile Materials

Are volatile materials kept in specially shielded areas, with quantities in the plant limited to the amount necessary for current production? Are reserve supplies also kept in a reasonably well-protected place? Are critical spare parts likewise secure? It must be assumed that any terrorist group contemplating sabotage will know the potential squeeze points and bottlenecks of the plant and its process.

Basic Security Precautions

Most of the measures to safeguard against theft and sabotage generally apply to the terrorist threat. The danger of political violence, however, calls for a new dimension to conventional security doctrine, enlisting the help of the personnel and public affairs departments. Terrorism is largely a psychological weapon directed at people. Effective countermeasures must therefore involve everyone who can be reached by terrorist propaganda.

Personnel Security

The staffing of key functions must be re-evaluated. Is all sensitive information handled on a need-to-know basis? Is there limited access to executive files? Are secretaries and other clerical personnel properly vetted for security? (At the height of terrorist violence in Argentina, one U.S. company hired only married women older than 30 for key secretarial positions, since nearly all terrorists and their sympathizers were young and single.) In some countries, the investigation of staff members is resented, and in Italy it is forbidden by law. But most companies could scrutinize their key staff more carefully than they have.

Rationalization of Functions

Restructuring of administrative procedures and the division of labor in the executive suite might be advisable if leaks of information were suspected or to avoid the concentration of sensitive data in the hands of certain clerical personnel.

Briefing of Employees

Probably a variety of orientation classes on the terrorist threat is required for such personnel as secretaries of executives, phone operators, security personnel, safety officers, and so on. One must avoid engendering undue fear, but key staff members in high-risk areas must be informed of their role if emergency contingency plans are to work. It is helpful as well for everyone in what might be called a pivotal role, including the receptionist at the front desk, to be sensitized to danger signs. This provides an early-warning system to detect impending terrorist actions. Not the least of those needing training are executives – potential kidnap victims – who should be advised on how to detect terrorist surveillance, how to evade seizure, and, if need be, how to survive as a hostage.

Intraplant Access and Security

Since sabotage is often most easily accomplished by someone from outside a critical area but who has casual access to it (the principle of "neighborly sabotage"), it might be well to declare such areas closed to routine visits. Color coding identification cards and screening movement from one part of the plant to another – at least for the most vulnerable areas – could facilitate this control.

Executive Movement

Nearly every company can improve its measures for protecting top executives, although some of the executives themselves resist changes in their routine or work habits that would improve their security. In light of the oft-demonstrated ability of terrorists to penetrate corporate headquarters, it is wise not to generally distribute the executive appointments schedule around the office. Use of the "core day" – which assures that top executives will be on hand for the same few hours every day (permitting scheduled meetings), while they vary their arrivals and departures at either end of the day in irregular fashion – is another measure that greatly reduces their exposure to possible ambush without totally disrupting the daily routine. Random choice of routes to work or to other predictable stopping places also adds materially to their safety. Such "soft-security" measures are indispensable to any company's protection system.

CRISIS MANAGEMENT CAPABILITY

The ability to determine and to correct weaknesses in the company's defense against terrorist attack is the greatest possible insurance that there will be no attack at all. This is not a foolproof precaution, however. While studies of political terrorism show that attackers usually pick the least protected among desirable targets, well-organized groups can bring to bear the resources necessary to hit a truly prime target almost regardless of defense. When a particular target is sufficiently important for psychological or symbolic reasons, it must be assumed that terrorists can, and very well may, overwhelm the defenses to accomplish their mission.

What remains, then, is the ability to deal with an incident when it occurs, despite all reasonable precautions to prevent it. This requires additional contingency planning, backed by a top-level company command unit to handle such emergencies. It should be stressed that the requirement here goes beyond the need for a crisis-management system to deal with natural disasters or major accidents, which are nonpremeditated, impersonal events. A terrorist incident is a planned hostile act that has anticipated probable reactions by the company and by law enforcement agencies; there are plans for further psychological exploitation of the incident, and any countermeasure will encounter a further (and usually well-planned) terrorist response. The situation frequently constitutes a series of engagements — a dynamic, evolving campaign — built around the original attack.

How does a corporation prepare for such a problem? First, it must recognize that its normal management machinery is not able to cope. The typical business enterprise is not equipped to conduct hour-by-hour operations against a cunning and violent adversary or to "negotiate" for the return of a kidnapped executive. But with proper foresight and realistic planning, it can develop the necessary capacity.

Steps to establish this kind of capability are outlined here.

Determine the Extent of the Problem

Based on the history of terrorism worldwide, what would realistically be the worst possible case in each category of terrorist attack with which to contend? How might these threats be applied against the company's assets, either at home or abroad? Any one of several consulting firms could staff out this background.

Develop Basic Policies for Each Contingency

What should be the general response to threat/extortion? Will the company pay ransom for kidnapped executives, and, if so, what should be the limit? What is the policy for handling the family of a kidnap victim? Should a kidnapped executive automatically be replaced, or should his job be kept open until he is returned? Should the company "negotiate" with terrorists without involving the police? (Separate judgments must be made, depending on the conditions in each place of operation.)

These are among the matters that should be settled before a crisis develops, in an atmosphere free from tension and anxiety. It is exceedingly difficult to make sound decisions during an actual emergency, particularly if someone's life is at stake, and it is even more difficult to command the necessary consensus of board members or other top management officials when no basic principles have been agreed upon in advance.

Inform Managers in the Field of the Policy

Advise key executives of general company plans for handling a kidnapping: whether ransom will be paid, whether the family will be removed from the scene (usually a good idea), whether the victim will be automatically replaced. By knowing the general tactics of the company, victims are less susceptible to psychological pressure by the kidnappers, who usually try to destroy their confidence in the company and convince them that they have been abandoned.

Delegate Necessary Authority to the Field

Branch managers should be instructed on how to respond to a sudden terrorist action and should be given authority to act immediately when necessary, particularly in a kidnapping. Such crises cannot be managed from the outset by corporate headquarters. The very first steps taken by management at the scene in response to a kidnapping might well affect its outcome.

Establish a Corporate Crisis-Response Unit

A crisis-response unit can be built upon whatever apparatus already exists for dealing with emergencies, but everyone must be aware that terrorist acts are not "normal" crises. At a minimum, the group should include the senior representatives of security, personnel, finance, legal affairs, and public affairs. It should be headed by an executive vice president or comparable official with a clear mandate from the chief executive officer.

Proper organization and training of a crisis-response unit (CRU) is a complex matter. Effectiveness depends upon the soundness of the corporation's basic policy for dealing with terrorism, the degree of mutual confidence and respect between the unit and the corporate leadership, the extent to which the unit melds with the organizational structure and management style of the company, and the experience it has gained (through crisis-simulation exercises, among other things) in working together under stress. Ideally, the unit should have two basic functions: to staff out the problem and provide options for decisions by top management and to supervise the execution of the decisions reached.

Political terrorism is a fact of life in the world today, and, after a decade of development and demonstration, it shows no sign of going away. Companies with international operations must contend with this phenomenon as one more problem to be solved or mastered — and at additional inconvenience and expense that must be chalked up to the cost of doing business. Nothing has happened so far — despite spectacular terrorist events in the Middle East — to indicate that this mode of violent disruption will materially affect the flow of international trade. But the individual corporation wishing to continue to operate abroad (and, to some extent, at home as well) must adjust to the terroristic component of the world's lifestyle, which is certain to continue into the 1980s and perhaps beyond.

11
Toward a More Effective U.S. Policy on Terrorism

Ernest Evans

The fundamental problem with the current U.S. policy on terrorism is not so much what is being done as what is not being done. Specifically, the various steps that have been taken in response to terrorism in recent years, such as the strengthening of physical security at airports, embassies, and nuclear power plants and the establishment of special counter-terrorism offices in a number of government departments, have been valuable contributions to the struggle against terrorism. However, despite the value of the antiterrorist measures that the U.S. government has already taken, U.S. counter-terrorism policy is incomplete in a fundamental sense. There are a number of issues that U.S. counter-terrorism policy has not yet effectively addressed; only parts of the whole cloth are in place, the rest are waiting to be woven in. This chapter recommends steps in five areas (civil liberties versus national security, military technology, international law, crisis management, and government personnel) that would increase the effectiveness of the U.S. policy response to terrorism by making this response more complete.

CIVIL LIBERTIES VERSUS NATIONAL SECURITY

The first step has to do with the problem of civil liberties and terrorism. It is time for the United States to face up to the hard choices that must be made concerning the legal responsibilities and the legal limitations that should be placed on its domestic and international security and intelligence services. There has been a great deal of debate in the United States in the past few years on such responsibilities and limitations, but the necessary choices have yet to be made.

Any democratic society is faced with a series of acute dilemmas whenever it has to deal with social groups such as terrorist movements that refuse to accept democratic norms. Such basic democratic rights as the rights to privacy, due process, free association, and freedom of conscience are inevitably brought into question by steps taken against terrorist movements. In all of the democratic societies that have been faced in recent years with serious challenges from terrorist organizations, there have been charges that basic liberties were being eroded in the struggle against terrorism. In West Germany, there have been claims that certain of the steps taken in response to terrorism constitute a West German variant of "McCarthyism."[1] In Northern Ireland, there have been repeated accusations against the British army and the Royal Ulster Constabulary to the effect that these security forces were mistreating and torturing suspected and actual terrorists. (These charges were reviewed and substantially confirmed by an Amnesty International mission that went to Northern Ireland in November and December of 1977.)[2] In Italy, it has been revealed that the head of the intelligence organization exceeded his authority by gathering personal information of no relevance to legitimate national security requirements on various public figures and private citizens. (Much of this material was used by the intelligence head for the purposes of blackmail.)[3]

For the United States, the problem of the tradeoff between civil liberties and national security in the context of counter-terrorism measures is made particularly difficult by past activities of the intelligence agencies. The Senate Select Committee on Intelligence, chaired by Senator Frank Church, found that, in the post-World War II decades, there have been systematic and widespread violations of the civil liberties of U.S. citizens by the CIA and the FBI.[4] This past history of civil liberties violations has created a sustained controversy in the United States over the whole question of civil liberties and national security; discussions of this question with reference to the special problems raised by terrorism frequently refer to these earlier violations of civil liberties.[5]

While there are lessons to be learned from past violations of civil liberties, the traumatic memories caused by these violations should not bar the resolution of several of the outstanding issues between national security and civil liberties. Specifically, action is urgently needed in the following two areas: the boundaries to be observed by intelligence and security agencies in their surveillance activities directed toward U.S. citizens and the regulation of the use of informants by these agencies.

Before moving on to these two issues, it should be noted that this chapter accepts as valid the idea that there should be a distinction made between the proper limits of the intelligence agencies as they operate vis-à-vis U.S. domestic society and their proper limits overseas. Given the lack of democratic norms and political freedoms in the great majority of countries of the world, U.S. intelligence agencies operating overseas must necessarily resort to the sort of clandestine and covert intelligence-gathering techniques that are inappropriate to the domestic politics of a democratic society. For example, there is general agreement in U.S. society that it was wrong for certain elements in the Nixon Administration to try to wiretap the Democratic National Committee. Such surveillance techniques, however, are essential in gathering vitally needed intelligence about totalitarian countries such as the Soviet Union. Given the closed nature of Soviet society, without such surveillance techniques little worthwhile data could be gathered on such important subjects as Soviet compliance with arms control agreements. The following discussion is restricted to establishing the proper limits of the intelligence agencies with respect to U.S. citizens living within the domestic confines of the United States; it is explicitly accepted that the sort of strict limits that should be placed on the domestic operations of the intelligence agencies cannot be placed on their international operations.

The problem of the proper boundaries for the surveillance activities of the intelligence and security agencies basically comes down to the following question: In what sort of actions must a group in domestic U.S. society engage before it is put under surveillance? The current guidelines for surveillance, established by former Attorney General Edward Levy, state that there must be a likelihood that the activities of the individuals or groups in question involve or will involve the use of force or violence in violation of federal law.[6] Levi stated that security investigations would be restricted to the following sorts of activities:

> . . . overthrowing the Government of the United States or of a State; interfering with the activities within the United States of foreign governments or their representatives; influencing Government policies by interfering by force or violence with Government functions or interstate commerce; depriving individuals of their civil rights; and creating domestic violence or rioting when such violence or rioting would necessitate as a countermeasure the use of Federal armed forces. There is also a provision for limited investigation when there is a clear and immediate threat of domestic violence which is likely to result in a request by a State for Federal armed assistance.[7]

There is a twofold problem with the Levy guidelines, stemming from the fact that these guidelines are in the form of an executive order rather than in the form of statute. Since these guidelines can be revoked on little or no notice by administrative fiat, they are inadequate both for giving guidance to the intelligence agencies and for protecting the civil liberties of U.S. citizens. The intelligence agencies are aware that the limits of their responsibilities are not based in law, and hence they are confronted with the fact that investigations that they are currently pursuing (and that they believe to be legal) may later be held by the courts to have been illegal.[8] The result of such an inadequate foundation for legitimizing investigations may well be a marked reluctance by the intelligence agencies to undertake investigations even when such investigations are necessary for national security. While the Levy guidelines hamper the legitimate operations of the intelligence agencies, they also fail to adequately protect the civil liberties of U.S. citizens: because these guidelines are only an executive order, they can be revoked by any administration that wishes (as did the Nixon Administration) to harass and persecute individuals who are opponents of its policies but who are not in any sense threats to national security.

In order to resolve this problem of the proper limits of surveillance and investigation in U.S. society to the intelligence agencies, two steps should be taken. First, any charter for the intelligence agencies passing through Congress should clearly spell out the guidelines to be observed by these agencies in undertaking investigations in domestic U.S. society. Such a charter would be federal law, avoiding the problems of executive orders. Second, in order to make sure that the intelligence agencies are obeying charter guidelines, this charter should require that those agencies responsible for terrorism-related investigations and surveillance within the domestic United States keep comprehensive lists of all individuals and groups being investigated. These lists should be submitted to the intelligence committees of the Congress for review.

A second important issue is the question of the use of informants. The potential dangers to a free society posed by the misuse of informants have long been recognized. In the mid-nineteenth century, British historian Sir Thomas May wrote:

> Men may be without restraints upon their liberty; they may pass to and fro at pleasure: but if their steps are tracked by spies and informers, their words noted down for crimination, their associates watched as conspirators — who shall say that they are free?[9]

The Church committee documented two specific patterns of abuse by informants. The first is the "agent provocateur" syndrome. This syndrome arises from the following dilemma. An informant seeking to maintain his or her cover in an environment in which people are constantly on the watch for infiltrators will often be tempted to try to appear to be the most militant member of a political group. The result of these efforts at militancy will be that the informer ends up inciting acts of violence that otherwise might not have occurred. The Church committee report noted several instances of this agent provocateur syndrome;[10] including one in which an FBI informant in the Ku Klux Klan got up before a crowd of thousands and stated, "We are going to have peace and order in America if we have to kill every Negro."[11]

A second civil liberties problem with informants is that they may pass on to their superiors personal information about the people they are keeping under surveillance that may be well beyond the legitimate knowledge requirements of the security and intelligence agencies; hence such surveillance may result in an unnecessary invasion of privacy. The Church committee documented a number of cases in which informants passed on to their superiors very personal details about the private lives of individuals active in a number of peace, antiwar, and radical groups.[12] An FBI informant in the Vietnam Veterans Against the War gave the following account of the scope of her reporting:

> . . . I was to go to meetings, write up reports . . . on what happened, who was there . . . to try to totally identify the background of every person there, what their relationships were, who they were living with, who they were sleeping with, to try to get some sense of the local structure and the local relationships among the people in the organization.[13]

The use of informants must be regulated if civil liberties are to be preserved and protected. Clarence Kelly, former director of the FBI, acknowledged in his testimony before the Church committee that informants could indeed commit abuses, but he maintained that the proper way to prevent such abuses was to allow the Inspection Division of the FBI to oversee the use of informants.[14] The problem with allowing the control of informants to be handled by such internal procedures is that these procedures have failed to prevent serious civil liberties abuses in the past.

Another proposed method of regulating the use of informants is to require that intelligence agencies obtain judicial warrants when they want to infiltrate a given group. The rationale behind this proposal is that the requirement would lessen the likelihood of harassment of groups that pose no danger to national security. However, such a proposal is also unsatisfactory because the judiciary is already overburdened with responsibilities, and it lacks the expertise necessary to decide which groups are threats to national security.

The best solution to the difficult issue of the regulation of the use of informants is to establish an independent panel in the federal government to hear complaints concerning abuses by informants.[15] Unlike internal controls by the intelligence agencies, it would not have the problem of covering up abuses to protect others in one's own agency; and a specialized panel with an adequate staff would not encounter the problems of lack of expertise and of an already excessive workload that would plague judicial control of informants.

MILITARY TECHNOLOGY

The control of military-related technology so as to prevent terrorists from exploiting such technology is a second problem area concerning which the United States must take action if it is to have an effective policy against terrorism. Past decisions made by the policy makers of the United States and of other nations with reference to military-related technology have resulted in an increase in the destructive potential of terrorist groups. Three examples follow.

In the 1950s, a great deal of information concerning nuclear energy was declassified by the U.S. government. This declassification was motivated by the desire to facilitate the growth of the peaceful nuclear industry. In testimony before the Senate Committee on Governmental Affairs in 1978, the Department of Energy (DOE) indicated that it regretted that the process of declassification had gone as far as it had because much of the declassified material could be useful to terrorists in manufacturing nuclear weapons. The DOE noted that once such information was declassified and widely distributed, there would be little benefit in reclassifying it. The officials testifying went on to state that future declassification decisions concerning nuclear energy would take into account the possibility that terrorists might find the declassified information useful.[16]

In the 1960s, U.S. tactical nuclear weapons in Europe were widely dispersed so as to minimize the chances of the Warsaw Pact forces being able to destroy these weapons in a single pre-emptive strike. However, this process of dispersion went to the point at which the weapons were scattered in so many places that there was not adequate physical security for all of these weapons. In 1969, U.S. NATO officials discovered a half-forgotten cache of 16 nuclear weapons in Mannheim, West Germany. The weapons were being guarded by a small, poorly equipped civilian force.[17] (Security at U.S. nuclear weapons storage sites has been tightened considerably in the 1970s in response to the problem of terrorism, but there is still a possibility that terrorists could seize a nuclear weapon.)[18]

The decade of the 1970s has witnessed many new developments in conventional arms. The United States and other countries have developed a number of sophisticated anti-armor, anti-aircraft, and antipersonnel weapons. One such new weapon that has potential applications for terrorists is the portable anti-aircraft missile. In September 1973, the Italian police arrested a group of Palestinian terrorists at the Rome airport as the terrorists were waiting to try to shoot down an El Al airliner with two Soviet-made, portable, heat-seeking, ground-to-air missiles.[19]

While controlling military-related technology so as to prevent its being exploited by terrorist groups is an important goal of U.S. national security policy, it cannot be the only concern of U.S. policy makers with reference to military-related technology. The threat posed to U.S. national security by terrorist groups is by no means the only threat to U.S. national security. On the contrary, the United States is faced with a broad range of threats to its national security, and, consequently, it must develop military technology to meet this broad range of threats. What is needed is some mechanism whereby the "terrorist angle" can be taken into account in decisions on the development and deployment of military-related technology.

The arms control impact statements of the Arms Control and Disarmament Agency could be well used for this purpose. Currently, the Arms Control and Disarmament Act requires that any weapon program with certain characteristics be the subject of an arms control impact statement.[20] These statements assess the impact of the program in question on arms control and disarmament. This act should be amended to provide that any military-related program that could be exploited by terrorist groups should also be subject to an arms control impact statement. The statements thus issued should discuss how the danger of terrorists exploiting the weapons program in question could be minimized.

To illustrate how issuing arms control impact statements from the terrorist angle might work, consider the following hypothetical case. The U.S. Army decides to develop a new surface-to-air missile for protection of its ground forces against hostile tactical air power. Under the proposed amendment to the Arms Control and Disarmament Act, an arms control impact statement would be required on this missile, because such a weapon could definitely be misused by terrorists. Cognizant of the army's needs and requirements as well as of the potential dangers posed by terrorists, this statement could recommend two possible courses of action.

It could recommend that the new missile be made jeep- or truck-mounted rather than shoulder-fired. A mounted missile would be much less portable and easy to conceal, hence less useful to terrorists. (Sweden has apparently accepted the idea that making anti-aircraft missiles too compact and portable risks misuse by terrorists, having incorporated this idea in the design of its RBS-70 surface-to-air missile, which is a bulky, tripod mounted system that is not easily moved or concealed.[21]

If it were decided that the military requirements were such that a portable, shoulder-fired, surface-to-air missile were essential, the statement could recommend a pattern of deployment that would limit the danger of these missiles falling into the hands of terrorists.

The statement could insist that such missiles be deployed by U.S. forces only in areas with adequate facilities to ensure their physical security and that they not be sold to any foreign nations that might pass them on to terrorists.

INTERNATIONAL LAW

In response to the contemporary wave of terrorist violence, the United States has supported a number of international conventions against terrorism, including three antihijacking treaties: Tokyo (1963), The Hague (1970), and Montreal (1971). It backed the regional antiterrorism conventions of the Organization of American States (OAS), which was adopted in 1971 and came into effect in 1973, and of the Council of Europe, which was adopted in 1976 and came into effect in 1977. And the United States supported the United Nations convention against attacks on diplomatic personnel, which was adopted by the General Assembly in 1973 and came into effect in 1977.

These treaties and conventions are clearly important steps in responding to the problem of terrorism. The antihijacking treaties and the U.N. diplomats' convention address two of the major manifestations of terrorism in the 1970s: attacks on aircraft and attacks on diplomatic personnel. And the regional conventions of the OAS and the Council of Europe are important measures against terroristic violence in regions of the world that have witnessed a great deal of such violence in the past decade.[22]

While these international conventions have been worthwhile contributions to the struggle against terrorism, the question arises as to what the United States should do next in its efforts to obtain international action against terrorism. For while it is true that the current conventions are useful steps against terrorism, it is equally true that the response to terrorism by the international community has been incomplete and inadequate and that much work remains to be done in fashioning a more effective response to terrorism by this community. This chapter makes the following recommendation with respect to U.S. efforts to obtain international action against terrorism: Given the current attitude of many of the nations of the world on terrorism, there are enormous obstacles in the way of further multilateral treaties against terrorism. Therefore the United

States should concentrate its efforts on making the existing international conventions against terrorism more effective rather than on trying to get new conventions. The periodic debates on terrorism in the United Nations show that the international community is hopelessly divided on this issue. The United States and its allies have pushed for a number of measures against terrorism, but the Middle Eastern, African, Asian, and Communist bloc countries have been most reluctant to take steps against terrorism because they fear that such steps could hinder the wars of national liberation currently being waged against Israel, South Africa, and Namibia (Southwest Africa).[23] The United States should continue to support action by the United Nations against terrorism, but it should realize that it is most unlikely that there will be any effective United Nations' initiatives against terrorism in the foreseeable future.

The fact that new international treaties against terrorism are unlikely does not mean that there is no scope for further multilateral action. Specifically, much work needs to be done to make the existing international conventions adhered to more universally and to make nations that are signatories to these conventions live up to their legal obligations.

In order to illustrate the scope for further international action against terrorism, it is appropriate at this point to discuss in detail the limitations of the existing multilateral treaties. Looking first at the antihijacking treaties, there are still a significant number of countries that are not signatories to any of these three treaties (currently the Tokyo Convention has 91 parties, the Hague Convention has 101 parties, and the Montreal Convention has 95 parties).[24] There are a total of 42 states that are not signatories to any of the antihijacking conventions.[25] With nearly a third of the 152 members of the United Nations not bound by any of the treaties, it is clear that this network of treaties is a very incomplete answer to the problem of aircraft hijacking.

A second problem with antihijacking treaties as they now exist is that there are no sanctions applied to nations that refuse to live up to their obligations under these treaties. A recent study on the legal aspects of international terrorism noted that a number of states that are bound by one or more of the antihijacking treaties have evaded their responsibilities under these treaties.[26]

The U.N. convention against attacks on diplomats and the OAS regional convention against international terrorism have a common problem: at present only a small minority of the member states of these two international organizations are parties to these treaties (seven members of the OAS and 40 members of the U.N.).[27]

In short, the current treaties against terrorism are far from being an effective response to the specific manifestations of terrorism that they seek to address. The United States must take steps to get more nations to become parties to these treaties and to get nations to live up to their obligations under both the letter and the spirit of these accords.

In seeking to strengthen the existing conventions against terrorism, the United States should try to persuade nations by quiet diplomacy of the merits of these accords, but it must also be prepared to resort to sanctions against nations that refuse to become parties to international accords against terrorism or that refuse to live up to their obligations under such accords if they are already parties. Several possible courses of action against such nations follow.

One promising example of U.S.-supported sanctions against nations that refuse to cooperate against terrorism is the agreement on hijacking reached at the Bonn summit of the major industrialized powers in July 1978. The nations present at the summit (the United States, Canada, Japan, Great Britain, Italy, West Germany, and France) agreed to cut off air service by their airlines to nations that refuse to extradite or punish hijackers. They also pledged to stop all flights by any other airlines between their own countries and states that give sanctuary to aircraft hijackers. Given that these seven nations account for more than 75 percent of the world's commercial air traffic, such a sanction would represent a significant loss to a country.[28]

In addition to such multilateral cooperation against nations tolerating terrorists, the United States can also take unilateral steps to get nations to become parties to the existing conventions against terrorism and to live up to their obligations under these conventions. For example, the United States has applied certain sanctions against Libya in retaliation for Libyan support of terrorist activity. Specifically, the United States has refused Libyan requests for sales of equipment with potential military uses and of nonmilitary aircraft. The United States has also refused Libyan requests for expert help in certain areas and for licenses for third-country transfers of U.S. equipment and technology that would enhance the military capability of the third country in question.[29]

In contemplating the use of sanctions so as to make international agreements against terrorism more effective, the United States must address the issue of whether it wants to make sanctions automatic or discretionary. Legislation has been introduced in both the 95th and 96th Congresses that would impose sanctions on countries that support international terrorism, and this legislation has led to a debate as to whether the laws concerning sanctions should be written such that they must automatically be applied to any country supporting international terrorism or whether their application should be left to the discretion of the responsible officials of the executive branch.[30]

There are two very convincing arguments against making the application of sanctions automatic. First, sanctions are not always effective in forcing nations to change their behavior. For example, the imposition of sanctions against Rhodesia by the United Nations following that country's unilateral declaration of independence in 1965 was not very effective in forcing Ian Smith's government to accept majority rule; the Rhodesian whites accepted majority rule in 1980 not because of the U.N. sanctions but because it had become clear that the alternative was an endless war against the guerrillas fighting to end white domination in Rhodesia. Similarly, U.S. attempts to effect changes in the emigration policy of the Soviet Union through such measures as the Jackson-Vanik Amendment have not resulted in the Soviets allowing complete freedom to leave for those of its citizens who wish to do so.

Not only are sanctions not necessarily effective, they can even be counterproductive. Consider, for example, the case of the Hickenlooper Amendment. This amendment to the Foreign Assistance Act was passed by the Congress in 1962. The amendment required the suspension of foreign aid to any country that nationalized the property of U.S. citizens without appropriate compensation. The amendment was mandatory in nature; the president had no authority to continue foreign aid even if he believed that such a continuation in aid was in the best interests of the United States.[31] Only once was this amendment invoked, against Ceylon in 1963, and the result was that the Ceylonese government not only refused to reverse its expropriation of the installations of two U.S. oil companies but also seized additional assets of the same two companies.[32] The Hickenlooper amendment was substantially modified in 1973. The application of the amendment was made discretionary rather than mandatory; the new language stated that the amendment could be waived if the president "determines and certifies that such a waiver is important to the national interest of the United States."[33]

Given that sanctions are not necessarily effective, they should not be applied in instances in which they will not achieve the desired end. It is unwise to apply ineffective sanctions because there are always costs in invoking sanctions. Third-party states can be angered if a nation that they consider a friend is the target of sanctions, and the United States will lose prestige if it applies sanctions whose targets do not change behavior.

A second argument against making the application of sanctions automatic is that the United States has a vast array of international interests, only one of which is combatting terrorism. In certain instances, the United States may decide that while a given state is supporting international terrorism in some region of the world, overall U.S. foreign policy interests would not be served by applying sanctions against it. For example, the Soviet Union has supported such revolutionary movements as al-Fatah and the Eritrean Liberation Front, which have engaged in international terrorism. But the United States has a broad range of interests and concerns with respect to the Soviet Union, and the national security of the United States would not be well served by applying sanctions against the Soviet Union solely because of its support of certain terrorist groups.

CRISIS MANAGEMENT

The terrorist incidents of the past decade have confronted U.S. policy makers with a new manifestation of a recurrent problem in national security: the successful management of crises. A crisis can be defined as a situation that has the following characteristics: the high-priority objectives of the nation are threatened, the amount of time available to respond effectively to the threat is restricted, and the nation's policy makers are surprised by the occurrence of the situation.[34]

Terrorist incidents, especially those that involve the taking of hostages, fall within this definition. The hijacking of an airliner with U.S. citizens on board or the kidnapping of a U.S. diplomat definitely constitute a threat to the national security interests of the United States; the United States has a very real stake in seeing that its nationals can travel safely and in seeing that its diplomats can carry on normal diplomatic activities. The amount of time available to respond to terrorist hostage incidents is usually limited by a deadline set by the terrorist group. And while U.S. officials can be reasonably sure that terrorist incidents will occur with a certain amount of regularity, exactly when and where specific terrorist incidents will occur cannot be predicted with any degree of certainty.

Terrorist incidents are thus typical examples of crisis situations. In successfully managing such situations, there is a premium on rapid decision making and on the ability to successfully implement those decisions. At present, however, the U.S. government is poorly prepared to respond to crises caused by terrorist groups. The reason for this difficulty is that the U.S. government is plagued by the problem of divided authority: authority for dealing with terrorist incidents is divided at the federal level among various departments and agencies and is further divided among the federal government and state and local governments.

At the federal level, the State Department is responsible for coordinating policy on international terrorist incidents, while the Justice Department is responsible for coordinating policy on domestic terrorist incidents.[35] However, even with the designation of certain agencies as having the leading role in handling domestic and international terrorist incidents, there have been difficulties in establishing a coherent policy response to such incidents at the federal level, as Brian Jenkins of the Rand Corporation indicates:

> A recent example of these sorts of (crisis management) problems would be the hijacking of the TWA airliner by Croatian extremists in September 1976, when according to one government official who was involved in the handling of the episode, the responsibility for the action "bounced around the Government like a floating crap game." It was not certain who would maintain full jurisdiction over the episode. The FAA claimed jurisdiction. Because it was an American airliner hijacked in the United States, the FBI became involved. Once the airliner crossed the national frontiers and flew to Canada and ultimately France, there was a definite State Department involvement. There was, I understand, some difficulty in deciding at the moment who precisely was making the decisions that had to be made.[36]

Given the work done in recent decades by social scientists on bureaucratic politics, these sorts of problems are hardly surprising.

The coordination of bureaucratic structures so as to rationally and effectively respond to political problems is a perennial problem of officials in any political system. Getting an appropriate response to the sorts of crises created by terrorist incidents is simply one more manifestation of this problem.

A second instance of the problem of divided authority that confronts U.S. officials dealing with terrorism is the division of authority in the U.S. political system in federal, state, and local levels. Federal systems have on occasion had difficulties in responding effectively to outbreaks of political violence, as the following two examples illustrate.

In July 1967, the city of Detroit experienced several days of rioting. By the time order was restored, 39 people had been killed and property damage from looting and arson was estimated at more than $200 million. Governor George Romney of Michigan requested federal troops after some 22 hours of rioting, but the dispatch of such troops was delayed because of disputes between Romney and federal officials in Washington, D.C., and on the scene in Detroit. These federal officials insisted that the law required that Romney would have to declare that a state of insurrection existed before federal troops could be dispatched to Detroit. Romney was reluctant to use the term "insurrection" because he was afraid that it would void insurance policies, thus victimizing those citizens who suffered property damage in the rioting.[37]

After several consultations between Romney and U.S. Attorney General Ramsey Clark, a compromise was worked out. Romney sent a telegram to the federal authorities that requested aid in putting down the rioting but did not use the term insurrection. U.S. Army units were then flown to a base outside Detroit, but federal officials on the scene further delayed the use of these units until they were convinced that these forces were essential to restore order. The federal troops were finally ordered into Detroit approximately 21 hours after Romney had made his initial request for federal assistance.[38]

On September 5, 1972, an eight-person squad from Black September, a Palestinian terrorist group, broke into the living quarters of the Israeli team at the Munich Olympics village. Two Israeli athletes were killed, and nine were taken hostage. After a day of negotiations, the terrorists and their hostages were taken to the Munich airport. At the airport, the West Germans attempted to rescue the captured Israelis, but their attempt miscarried; all nine of the hostages, five of the eight terrorists, and a West German police officer were killed in a shootout between the police and the terrorists.[39]

In West Germany immediately following the Munich Olympics incident, there was frequent criticism of the refusal by the Munich police to accept help from either the Bavarian state police or the West German federal police in their attempted rescue of the Israeli athletes. Chancellor Willy Brandt and other West German officials apparently believed that the local police would have benefited from the assistance of these state and federal police forces.[40]

Both the Detroit rioting of 1967 and the 1972 Munich Olympics incident illustrate a problem inherent to federal systems: when there are instances of political violence at the lower levels of the federal structure, there can be major difficulties in bringing desperately needed security forces from the higher levels of the structure. What is needed in such federal systems is a clear set of mechanisms to facilitate the use of the security forces of the central government when such forces are needed to effectively respond to violence.[41]

These concerns about divided authority have been expressed by a number of individuals with expertise in the area of terrorism,[42] but the U.S. government has done little in response. This chapter proposes that two steps be taken to help alleviate the problem of divided authority.

As suggested by Brian Jenkins, a small staff should be located in the executive office of the president to help government leaders coordinate policy on terrorist incidents within the departments and agencies of the executive branch. The ultimate authority to resolve serious terrorist incidents must of course rest with the president and his top officials and advisers, but such a staff could provide very valuable assistance to these individuals when terrorist incidents occur. The basic function of the staff would be as an information center to provide government leaders with the sort of prompt access to governmental resources of intelligence and expertise that is required in a crisis.[43]

It is important that such a staff be placed at the highest possible level of government because, while serious terrorist crises are relatively rare, such crises can pose a major threat to national security. Consider, for example, the crisis in Italy over the kidnapping and subsequent execution of Aldo Moro or the crisis that would be created in the United States if terrorists had a nuclear device and threatened to destroy a city with it. In such a serious crisis, it would be essential to have a means of effectively coordinating the policy response of the national government. A staff within the executive office of the president with expertise in the area of terrorism would be a definite asset in carrying out such coordination.

And, in order to prevent the sorts of difficulties that took place in Munich and Detroit, this chapter proposes that the United States pass legislation that eases the restrictions on the use of federal military forces in cases of domestic violence.

There are, to be sure, sound arguments in favor of the ideas that the use of federal troops domestically should always be undertaken with great caution and only as a last resort and that, consequently, the laws regulating such use should not be changed lightly.[44] However, the laws currently regulating the use of federal troops in domestic situations do not adequately address the special problems raised by terrorism. Existing U.S. laws allow the use of federal troops domestically only if there is an insurrection against the government of a state, if federal laws cannot be enforced by normal judicial means, or if a state government refuses to enforce federal laws and to protect the rights of U.S. citizens under these laws.[45]

There are many conceivable terrorist incidents that would not fall within these categories, but that would constitute a very serious problem for U.S. national security. For example, suppose a group of terrorists seized members of one of the athletic teams at the 1984 Olympics in Los Angeles. The local authorities could conceivably want help from a U.S. military unit with special counter-terrorist training,[46] but, under existing law, the provision of such assistance would be problematical from a legal point of view. The holding of hostages cannot automatically be considered an insurrection, an obstruction of the laws of the United States, or a refusal by a state to enforce federal laws. Hence, a request for federal aid could run into the same kind of problems that occurred in the 1967 Detroit riot.

This chapter proposes that the U.S. code be amended so as to take into account the special problems created by terroristic violence. Such an amending process must, however, be kept within certain definite limits. The law should be written such that, in addition to the sorts of situations in which the use of federal troops is currently allowed, the president could use such troops in instances of domestic violence that pose a grave and pressing danger to the national security of the United States.

GOVERNMENT PERSONNEL

The terrorism of the 1970s has raised two major issues concerning government personnel. First, the number of persons in government assigned to combatting terrorism has grown dramatically in recent years, but there has not been much thought as to how this increase in personnel is to be managed by the government. Second, the U.S. government has had to provide ways to help government officials who have been victimized by terrorists recover from their experiences.

With respect to the issue of the management of counter-terrorism personnel, there are currently two unresolved questions. The first is the proper balance to be maintained between public and private sector employees. Specifically, how far should the federal government go in providing security forces to protect against terrorist attacks?

There is general agreement that the federal government should provide security forces to protect certain types of U.S. government targets. For example, there is little disagreement that storage sites for nuclear weapons should be protected by federal forces. Similarly, it is accepted that the president and members of his family should receive protection from the Secret Service. Preventing the unauthorized use of nuclear weapons and protecting the lives of the members of the first family are believed to be such high priority national security goals that federal forces are justified to help protect these targets.

It is also agreed that certain nongovernmental individuals, installations, and targets should be protected by federal security forces. In addition to protecting high U.S. officials and foreign diplomats, the Secret Service provides protection to presidential candidates. This protection of presidential candidates reflects the feeling that arose after the assassination in 1968 of Robert Kennedy: providing adequate protection to presidential candidates is vital to the proper functioning of the U.S. political process, and, consequently, the responsibility for such protection should be undertaken by the federal government rather than being left to individual candidates. The federal skymarshals program of the early 1970s reflected a similar feeling: the protection of commercial aviation was such a crucial national concern that it merited a federal security force.

Are there other areas in which the federal government should take direct responsibility for providing the security personnel needed to guard against terrorist attacks? This chapter argues that there is indeed one such area: commercial nuclear power plants. Specifically, the federal government should set up a special security force to provide protection for the nuclear power industry.

The nuclear power industry is currently besieged with difficulties. In the wake of the Three Mile Island incident, there is a great deal of concern about the possibility of nuclear power plants leaking radiation or melting down. There is also concern about the problem of the disposal of nuclear wastes. And there is a debate over what to do with nuclear power plants once they are no longer in commission. The upshot of these various concerns is that the nuclear power industry is being subjected to more and more governmental regulation. Such regulation may well be necessary to make nuclear power safe, but, in part because of this regulation, the costs of nuclear power have risen to the point at which its economic viability is being called into question.[47]

In other words, the nuclear power industry is confronted with the task of restoring public faith in nuclear power without so increasing its own costs that nuclear power becomes commercially unattractive. This promises to be a long and difficult task, and, consequently, the industry should not be burdened with the additional responsibility of maintaining adequate security for nuclear power plants and for fissionable materials.[48] The United States has a vital national interest in seeing that such adequate security is maintained, and, hence, the federal government should take direct responsibility for protecting the nuclear power industry against terrorists.

A second unresolved question concerning governmental counterterrorism personnel is the proper balance to be maintained between public and private funding of such personnel. Specifically, in those cases in which it is accepted that there is no requirement for a special federal force to provide security against terrorists, who should fund those nonfederal forces that are provided for security purposes?

There is no easy answer to this question because many security forces have roles in fighting terrorism, and the federal government cannot finance all of them. However, a good basic principle to establish the boundaries of federal funding could be that when there is a potential terrorist target whose protection is crucial to the national interests of the United States, and when the private sector individual or group responsible for the target in question is under such financial strain that it cannot provide adequate security for the target, the federal government should supply funding so as to make sure that the target receives sufficient protection.

To illustrate how this principle might be put into practice, consider the case of aerial hijacking. In the late 1960s and early 1970s, aircraft hijackings posed a very serious threat to the future of civil aviation. Worldwide, there were 70 instances in 1969 in which an individual or individuals succeeded in hijacking an aircraft, and there were 55 such successful hijackings in 1970. The following table records the number of successful aerial hijackings worldwide in the period 1968-77.[49]

1968	1969	1970	1971	1972	1973	1974	1975	1976	1977
29	70	55	22	23	11	8	7	7	16

However, as this table shows, the number of successful hijackings began to decline significantly in 1973. A major reason for this decline was strengthened security measures at airports, such as machines to screen passengers and luggage for weapons and explosives and the development of the so-called "hijacker profile," a set of distinguishing characteristics to enable airport personnel to spot potential hijackers.[50]

Currently, the funding for such security programs at U.S. airports is provided for by an additional charge on each passenger ticket.[51] However, there are certain potential problems with such a funding arrangement. Suppose there were a new wave of terrorist attacks against aircraft and that, as a result, there were a need for a greatly strengthened security effort. Would the U.S. commercial aviation industry, which has already had a number of financial difficulties in recent years,[52] be able to shoulder the expenses of such security measures? Such a hypothetical question cannot be answered with any certainty. However, in such a case, if there were a genuine doubt as to the ability of the private sector to provide adequate security, there would be a strong argument in favor of public financing of the required security measures. This type of case would clearly meet the criteria of when a security program should be federally funded: the safety of civil aviation is definitely a vital national interest of the United States, and, if such safety cannot be adequately provided by private sector funding, the federal government must finance the program.

In the past decade, a number of U.S. officials and their families have been victimized by terrorists. This victimization has been direct (officials are kidnapped or assaulted by terrorists) or indirect (officials and their families suffer the strain and tension of having to live and work in countries in which there is significant terrorist activity).

In recent years, U.S. society has become increasingly sensitive to the suffering of victims of violence.[53] There is a growing realization that victims of violence have frequently been poorly treated by society — for example, women who have been raped are often, in effect, put on trial themselves during the trials of their assailants, and individuals who have been robbed are told that they would not have been victimized had they been smarter.[54] This increased social concern about the plight of victims of violence has manifested itself in several ways. A number of shelters for wives who have been abused by their husbands have been set up in the past few years.[55] And legislation to compensate victims of crime has been enacted in several foreign nations and in many of the states of the United States.[56]

The insensitivity to the suffering of victims of criminal violence has also frequently characterized the treatment of U.S. government officials who have been the targets of terrorist violence. A study by the Rand Corporation noted that many individuals who had been kidnapped and held hostage by terrorists complained that, upon release, they were treated like pariahs, as if they were lepers.[57] The former hostages complained that they were regarded as being "bad for morale" and that, as a consequence, their careers suffered.[58]

In more recent years, there appears to have been a growth in government sensitivity to the suffering experienced by the victims of terrorism. Officials who have been kidnapped or assaulted by terrorists now receive extensive counseling for themselves and their families to help them recover from their traumatic experience. And the government has tried to counteract the "pariah syndrome" by reintegrating terrorist victims into the mainstream of their agency's or department's work as soon as possible.[59]

These programs to help victims of terrorism cope with their trauma are important both for humanitarian reasons and for national security reasons. Government insensitivity to victims of terrorism has been reported to have hurt morale in the Foreign Service, for example.[60] It is therefore crucial that these programs be continued, and this point must be emphasized because special programs to deal with terrorism are always in danger of being eliminated, as Brian Jenkins has noted. Jenkins argues that because spectacular terrorist incidents are not an everyday occurrence but, on the contrary, take place at irregular intervals, there are continuous budgetary pressures in favor of eliminating counter-terrorism programs during those periods when terrorists are not active. As an example of such budgetary pressures, he notes that prior to the liberation of the hostages on a hijacked Lufthansa airliner at Mogadishu by a special West German commando unit, there had been pressures to eliminate this unit because it was a waste of money.[61]

The same sort of fiscal pressures operate in the United States. For example, one means that the State Department uses to compensate officials living in countries with a high risk of terrorist violence is to give pay differentials – percentage salary increases – to these officials. Such differentials are also used to compensate officials serving in disease-ridden or otherwise unattractive countries. However, there is always a temptation to try to economize on the pay differentials. In one country, State Department officials received a 10 percent differential after the U.S. ambassador was shot. A year later, the State Department was preparing to abolish the differential; apparently the department had decided that since no U.S. official in that country had been attacked for a year, a pay differential was no longer justified. Before the State Department had a chance to terminate the differential, however, a U.S. attaché in the country in question was kidnapped; as a result, the pay differential was increased to 15 percent.[62]

In other words, on both humanitarian and national security grounds, it is important that there be ongoing programs to help U.S. officials and their families recover from the suffering caused by terrorist violence; such programs must not be dismantled every time there is a short lull in terrorist incidents.

In conclusion, it must be recognized that even if all of the steps recommended in this chapter were taken, terrorism would still remain a serious national security problem for the United States. In a world marked by ideological rivalries, ethnic clashes, and extremes of wealth and poverty, it is utopian to hope for an end to politically motivated violence. However, while it is true that implementing these proposed measures will not mean that U.S. citizens will no longer be the targets of terrorist violence, were the United States to enact these measures, it would have a more effective policy response to terrorism because such measures go a long way toward addressing many of the issues that the current U.S. counter-terrorism policy has not yet addressed.

NOTES

1. Peter Weiss, "Joe McCarthy is Alive and Well and Living in West Germany: Terrorism and Counter-Terrorism in the Federal Republic," *New York University Journal of International Law and Politics* 9 (Spring 1976): 61-88.

2. Amnesty International, *Report of an Amnesty International Mission to Northern Ireland* (London: Amnesty International Secretariat, 1978).

3. Vittorfranco S. Pisano, *Contemporary Italian Terrorism: Analysis and Countermeasures* (Washington, D.C.: Library of Congress Law Library, 1979), pp. 113-15.

4. U.S., Senate, *Intelligence Activities and the Rights of Americans*, final report of the Select Committee to Study Governmental Operations with Respect to Intelligence Activities, Senate report no. 94-755, 94th Cong., 2 sess. (Washington, D.C.: Government Printing Office, 1976), Book II.

5. See, for example, Irving Louis Horowitz, "Can Democracy Cope With Terrorism?" *Civil Liberties Review* 4 (May/June 1977): 29-32; National Advisory Committee on Criminal Justice Standards and Goals, *Report of the Task Force on Disorders and Terrorism* (Washington, D.C.: Law Enforcement Assistance Administration, 1976), pp. 90-92.

6. U.S., Senate, *Intelligence Activities, Senate Resolution 21*, hearings before the Select Committee to Study Governmental Operations with Respect to Intelligence Activities, 94th Cong., 1 sess. (Washington, D.C.: Government Printing Office, 1976), vol. 6: *Federal Bureau of Investigation*, p. 317.

7. Ibid.

8. In this connection, one might note the criminal prosecution currently underway against former high-ranking FBI officials L. Patrick Gray III, W. Mark Felt, and Edward S. Miller. These individuals are charged with violating the civil liberties of U.S. citizens in the course of their investigation of the Weather Underground; they claim that at the time they undertook the investigation they believed that their investigatory activities were completely legal.

9. U.S., Senate, *Supplementary Detailed Staff Reports on Intelligence Activities and the Rights of Americans*, Book III, p. 227.

10. Ibid., pp. 243, 252, 267-70.

11. Ibid., p. 252.

12. Ibid., pp. 235-39, 245-51.

13. Ibid., 236.

14. U.S., Senate, *Intelligence Activities, Senate Resolution 21*, vol. 6: *Federal Bureau of Investigation*, p. 293.

15. For a discussion of such an independent panel as a means of regulating the use of informants, see National Advisory Committee, *Report of the Task Force on Disorders and Terrorism*, pp. 94-96.

16. U.S., Senate, *An Act to Combat International Terrorism*, hearings before the Committee on Governmental Affairs, 95th Cong., 2 sess. (Washington, D.C.: Government Printing Office, 1978), p. 305.

17. U.S. Joint Publications Research Service, "Terrorist Programs, Internal Problems Discussed" (*Stern*, vol. 31, June 1, 1978), in *Translations on Western Europe*, JPRS L/7885, Arlington, Va., July 13, 1978, p. 38.

18. For a discussion of the security of nuclear weapons sites, see Lloyd Norman, "Our Nuclear Weapons Sites: Next Target of Terrorists?" *Army* (June 1977): 28-31.

19. Brian Jenkins and Janera Johnson, *International Terrorism: A Chronology, 1968-1974*, R-1597-DOS/ARPA (Santa Monica: Rand Corporation, 1975), p. 48.

20. The Arms Control and Disarmament Act requires an arms control impact statement on any weapons program with one or more of the following characteristics: any program of research, development, testing, engineering, construction, deployment, or modernization with respect to nuclear armaments, nuclear implements of war, military facilities, or military vehicles designed or intended primarily for the delivery of nuclear weapons; any program of research, development, testing, engineering, construction, deployment, or modernization with respect to armaments, ammunition, implements of war, or military facilities, having an estimated total program cost in excess of $250 million or an estimated annual program cost in excess of $50 million; any other program involving weapons systems or technology that such government agency or its director believes may have a significant impact on arms control and disarmament policy or negotiations.

21. Robert Kupperman, *Facing Tomorrow's Terrorist Incident Today*, U.S. Department of Justice, Law Enforcement Assistance Administration (Washington, D.C.: Government Printing Office, 1977), p. 8.

22. A CIA study on terrorism released in August 1978 estimated that some 64 percent of the incidents of international terrorism in the period 1968-77 took place in Western Europe or in Latin America. See Central Intelligence Agency, *International Terrorism in 1977* (Washington, D.C.: Central Intelligence Agency, 1978), p. 2.

23. For a discussion of the United Nations and terrorism, see Ernest Evans, *Calling a Truce to Terror: The American Response to International Terrorism* (Westport: Greenwood Press, 1979), chap. 7.

24. For lists of the nations that are parties to these antihijacking treaties, see U.S., Department of State, *Treaties in Force: A List of Treaties and Other International Agreements of the United States in Force on January 1, 1979* (Washington, D.C.: Department of State, 1979), pp. 253-55.

25. This figure of 42 states is derived by comparing a list of states not party to any of the antihijacking accords as of January 1978, provided by the State Department to the Senate Committee on Governmental Affairs, with the lists in U.S., Senate, *Treaties in Force*, pp. 253-55. For the first list, see U.S., Senate, *An Act to Combat International Terrorism*, hearings before the Committee on Governmental Affairs, 95th Cong., 2 sess. (Washington, D.C.: Government Printing Office, 1978), p. 22.

26. Alona M. Evans, "Aircraft and Aviation Facilities," in *Legal Aspects of International Terrorism*, eds. Alona Evans and John Murphy (Lexington: Lexington Books, 1978), p. 37. The nations mentioned by Evans as being derelict in fulfilling their legal responsibilities under the antihijacking treaties are Egypt, Iraq, Lebanon, Lybia, and Tunisia.

27. U.S., Senate, *Treaties in Force*, p. 342.

28. Interview with Louis Fields, expert on international law at the Department of State, November 1978.

29. U.S., Senate, *An Act to Combat International Terrorism*, p. 11.

30. For a discusison of how much discretion the executive branch should be allowed to have in deciding whether to impose sanctions, see the testimony of Ambassador Anthony Quainton before the House Committee on Public Works and Transportation. U.S., House of Representatives, *International Terrorism*, hearings before the Subcommittee on Aviation of the Committee on Public Works and Transportation, 95th Cong., 1 sess. (Washington, D.C.: Government Printing Office, 1978), pp. 41-53. Senator Abraham Ribicoff introduced legislation in the 95th Congress (S. 2236) and in the 96th Congress (S. 333) providing for sanctions against nations supporting international terrorism.

31. Richard Lillich, "Requiem for Hickenlooper," *American Journal of International Law* 69 (January 1975): 97-98. For a discussion of the background of the Hickenlooper Amendment and an evaluation of its effectiveness, see Richard Lillich, *The Protection of Foreign Investment: Six Procedural Studies* (Syracuse: Syracuse University Press, 1965), pp. 117-46.

32. Lillich, *The Protection of Foreign Investment*, pp. 143-44.

33. Lillich, "Requiem for Hickenlooper," pp. 99-100.

34. Charles F. Hermann, "Some Issues in the Study of International Crisis," in *International Crises: Insights from Behavioral Research*, ed. Charles F. Hermann (New York: Free Press, 1972), p. 13.

35. For a discussion of the division of responsibility for handling terrorist incidents among federal departments and agencies, see the testimony of Ambassador Quainton in U.S., House of Representatives, *International Terrorism*, pp. 41-53. See also Darrell M. Trent, "A National Policy to Combat Terrorism," *Policy Review* no. 9 (Summer 1979): 41-53 (Hoover Institution Reprint Series no. 22).

36. U.S., Senate, *An Act to Combat International Terrorism*, p. 108. After landing in Paris, the Croatians released the passengers and crew unharmed and surrendered to the French authorities.

37. Charles P. Stone, "The Lessons of Detroit, Summer 1967," in *Bayonets in the Street: The Use of Troops in Civil Disturbances*, ed. Robin Higham (Lawrence: University Press of Kansas, 1969), pp. 185-86.

38. Ibid., pp. 186-89. There were charges that President Lyndon Johnson was playing politics over the Detroit rioting. Some people in Detroit believed that Johnson wanted both to embarrass Romney (then a potential 1968 Republican challenger to Johnson) by forcing him to admit that he could not control the situation and to put other state and local officials on notice that he was going to be very cautious about putting his popularity and prestige on the line by sending in troops in cases of civil disorder.

39. Jenkins and Johnson, *International Terrorism: A Chronology, 1968-1974*, p. 34; David Binder, "A 23-Hour Drama," New York *Times*, September 6, 1972, p. 1.

40. "Killings Expected to Spur Debate on Police Structure," New York *Times*, September 7, 1972, p. 18; David Binder, "Brandt Says Bonn Wants 'Ruthless' Inquiry Into Olympic Killings," New York *Times*, September 9, 1972, p. 3; David Binder, "Details Provided on Munich Deaths," New York *Times*, September 10, 1972, p. 1.

41. This chapter assumes that the maintenance of the federal structure in police responsibility is, on both constitutional and normative grounds, the pattern preferred by most U.S. citizens, and, hence, it does not deal with the issue of whether having such a federal-state-local division of police responsibility is appropriate and advisable in a modern democratic society. (In the aftermath of the Munich Olympics incident, there was apparently considerable debate in West Germany about the merits of a federal police system. See "Killings Expected to Spur Debate on Police Structure," New York *Times*, September 7, 1972, p. 18.)

42. In addition to the testimony of Ambassador Quainton in U.S., House of Representatives, *International Terrorism*, pp. 41-53, and Trent, "A National Policy," see Brian Jenkins, "Upgrading the Fight Against Terrorism," Washington *Post*, March 27, 1977, pp. C1, C4; Jenkins' testimony on S. 2236 in U.S., Senate, *An Act to Combat International Terrorism*, pp. 106-28; and Robert Kupperman and Darrell M. Trent, *Terrorism: Threat, Reality, Response* (Stanford: Hoover Institution Press, 1979).

43. For a discussion of the merits of such a staff, see U.S., Senate, *An Act to Combat International Terrorism*, pp. 106-12.

44. For a background discussion of the use of federal troops in situations of domestic violence and an effective presentation of the arguments in favor of keeping tight controls on such use, see Adam Yarmolinsky, *The Military Establishment* (New York: Harper & Row, 1971), pp. 153-93.

45. The statutes governing the use of federal military forces domestically are contained in United States Code Title 10, Sections 331-336 and Title 18, Sections 1116 and 1385.

46. For a discussion of these units, see the testimony of David McGiffert, assistant secretary of Defense for International Security Affairs, in U.S., Senate, *An Act to Combat International Terrorism*, pp. 191-208.

47. For a discussion of the economic viability of nuclear power in the wake of the Three Mile Island incident, see Anthony J. Parisi, "Nuclear Power: The Bottom Line Gets Fuzzier," New York *Times*, April 8, 1979, Section 3, pp. 1, 4.

48. For a good discussion of the difficulties of (and necessity for) adequate physical security for commercial nuclear power, see Theodore Taylor and Mason Willrich, *Nuclear Theft: Risks and Safeguards* (Cambridge: Ballinger, 1974), chaps. 7-9.

49. This information is derived from a table supplied by the Federal Aviation Administration's Civil Aviation Security Service: "Worldwide Reported Hijacking Attempts — Summarization." It is available upon request from the Operations Liaison Staff of the Civil Aviation Security Service, Washington, D.C.

50. Evans, "Aircraft and Aviation Facilities," pp. 8-15. In light of attacks on the screening program as ineffective and hence an unnecessary infringement of civil liberties, one might note the following figures recorded by Evans (p. 11). In the single six-month period of January 1-June 30, 1976, approximately 2,800 weapons, explosives, and other incendiary devices were discovered by this program; the total included 1,054 handguns. In this same period, 422 people were arrested as a result of the screening process.

51. Ibid., p. 32.

52. Ibid., p. 31.

53. For an excellent discussion of the phenomenon of being victimized by crime and of what can be done to ease the suffering caused by such victimization, see Janet L. Barkas, *Victims* (New York: Scribner's, 1978).

54. Ibid., pp. 4-7, 115-21.

55. Ibid., p. 87.

56. Ibid., pp. 187-91.

57. For a discussion of how the State Department and the Foreign Service has reacted to terrorism, see Bruce Howard, "Living With Terrorism," Washington *Post*, July 18, 1976, pp. C1, C4.

58. Ibid.

59. Interview with a psychiatrist from the Department of State who is responsible for helping victims of terrorism recover from their experiences. The psychiatrist requested anonymity, and, in view of the sensitive nature of his work, the request was granted. July, 1979.

60. Howard, "Living With Terrorism."

61. U.S., Senate, *An Act to Combat International Terrorism*, pp. 120-21.

62. Howard, "Living With Terrorism."

About the Editors
and Contributors

Yonah Alexander is professor of International Studies and director of The Institute for Studies in International Terrorism, State University of New York. He is also research associate of The Center for Strategic and International Studies, Georgetown University, and fellow at both the Institute for Social and Behavioral Pathology, University of Chicago, and the Center for Strategic Studies, Tel-Aviv University.

Educated at Columbia University (Ph.D.) and the University of Chicago (M.A.) in International Affairs, Professor Alexander has taught and done research in Europe, Asia, the Middle East, and Latin America, as well as in the United States and Canada.

Editor-in-chief of *Terrorism: An International Journal* and *Political Communication and Persuasion: An International Journal*, he has authored, edited, and co-edited fifteen books. His articles and interviews have appeared in various publications, including the *Washington Quarterly*, *The New York Times*, *Wall Street Journal*, *Christian Science Monitor*, *Time*, *Newsweek*, *Chicago Tribune*, *U.S. News and World Report*, and *Middle East Review*.

Charles Ebinger joined the staff of the Center for Strategic and International Studies in September 1979, as Director, Program on Energy and National Security.

Prior to coming to CSIS, Dr. Ebinger served as vice president of the Washington-based international energy consulting firm, Conant and Associates, dealing with the political, commercial, economic, and strategic factors affecting access to energy and other raw materials.

Dr. Ebinger received his M.A., M.A.L.D., and Ph.D. degrees from the Fletcher School of Law and Diplomacy, Tufts University. He is the author of numerous articles and books on international nuclear, oil, and commodity issues and is a frequent contributor to journals specializing in African, S. Asian, and Middle Eastern political affairs.

James H. Cobbe, assistant professor of economics, Florida State University, has been a lecturer in economics at the London School of Economics and Political Science, the University of Botswana, Lesotho, and Swaziland, and the National University of Lesotho. He is author of *Governments and Mining Companies in Developing Countries*.

John M. Collins is senior specialist in National Defense at the Library of Congress. He was director of Military Strategy Studies and chief of the Strategic Research Group at National War College. Among his publications is *U.S.-Soviet Military Balance: Concepts & Capabilities, 1960-1980*.

Ernest Evans is an assistant professor in the Politics Department of Catholic University. He received his Ph.D. in 1977 from the Political Science Department of M.I.T. He has long been interested in the topic of radical and revolutionary political movements. His publications on this topic include his book *Calling A Truce to Terror: The American Response to International Terrorism* and a number of articles.

Richard J. Kessler is program director of the Energy Contingency Planning Group at the Center for Strategic and International Studies, Georgetown University. He is also deputy director of the Project on Energy and National Security at the Center. Mr. Kessler obtained his M.A. and M.A.L.D. degrees from the Fletcher School of Law and Diplomacy, Tufts University.

Neil C. Livingstone is a vice president of Gray and Company. He holds an M.A. in political science from the University of Montana. He completed his M.A., M.A.L.D., and Ph.D. at the Fletcher School of Law and Diplomacy, Tufts University. Dr. Livingstone's articles have appeared in *Conflict*, *Strategic Review*, *Army*, *The Washingtonian*, and the *International Security Review*. He is the author of *War Against Terrorism*.

Eugenie Elisabeth Maechling is deputy director of the Project on Energy and National Security at the Center for Strategic and International Studies, Georgetown University. Prior to her present position, she was an energy consultant specializing in European oil trade and U.S.-Canadian energy relations. She has studied at the Warburg Institute, University of London, and Harvard University.

Brooks McClure is director of operations for the International Management and Resources Corporation, Washington, D.C. A veteran of U.S. Foreign Service, he served with the Commerce Department's Working Group on Terrorism. A graduate of the University of Maryland and the Naval War College, Mr. McClure is the author of *The Dynamics of Terrorism* and a contributor to *International Terrorism in the Contemporary World* and *Contemporary Terrorism*.

Malcolm C. Peck has been director of research at the Middle East Institute for the last 10 years. He received an M.A. degree from Harvard University, and his M.A., M.A.L.D., and Ph.D. from the Fletcher School of Law and Diplomacy, Tufts University. Dr. Peck also taught at the University of Chattanooga.

J. F. Pilat is with the Office of Senior Specialists, Congressional Research Service, Library of Congress. He is the author of the recently published *Ecological Politics: The Rise of the Green Movement*, and his articles have appeared in *Society*, *The Washington Quarterly*, *Government and Opposition* and other scholarly journals. The views expressed in his chapter are Pilat's own, and not necessarily those of the Congressional Research Service.